Ireland and Cinema

Ireland and Cinema

Culture and Contexts

Edited by

Barry Monahan
University College Cork, Ireland

palgrave
macmillan

First published 2015 by
PALGRAVE MACMILLAN

Palgrave Macmillan in the UK is an imprint of Macmillan Publishers Limited,
registered in England, company number 785998, of Houndmills, Basingstoke,
Hampshire RG21 6XS.

Palgrave Macmillan in the US is a division of St Martin's Press LLC,
175 Fifth Avenue, New York, NY 10010.

Palgrave Macmillan is the global academic imprint of the above companies
and has companies and representatives throughout the world.

Palgrave® and Macmillan® are registered trademarks in the United States,
the United Kingdom, Europe and other countries.

ISBN 978-1-349-56410-1   ISBN 978-1-137-49636-2 (eBook)
DOI 10.1057/9781137496362

This book is printed on paper suitable for recycling and made from fully
managed and sustained forest sources. Logging, pulping and manufacturing
processes are expected to conform to the environmental regulations of the
country of origin.

A catalogue record for this book is available from the British Library.

Library of Congress Cataloging-in-Publication Data
Ireland and cinema : culture and contexts / [editor] Barry Monahan,
    University College Cork, Ireland.
        pages   cm
Includes bibliographical references and index.
Includes filmography.

    1. Motion pictures—Ireland—History and criticism.   2. Ireland—In
motion pictures.   3. Irish in motion pictures.   I. Monahan, Barry,
editor. II. Title.
PN1993.5.I85I65 2015
791.4309415—dc23   2015014919

Contents

Foreword: Irish National Cinema – What Have We Wrought? Contemporary Thoughts on a Recent History

I began my career in 1974 and spent the next 40 years teaching film and media studies until my retirement in 2014. During those years, as well as developing and teaching courses in film and television studies, I also lobbied and campaigned on behalf of a film industry in Ireland, at first in the south as Education Officer with the Irish Film Institute from 1980 to 1986 and latterly in the north during a 28-year career at the University of Ulster at Coleraine. I have also written extensively over those years on Irish film and television and wrote many policy documents for various institutions on the need to develop film and media education in tandem with the slowly developing film industry. I haven't very often written in an autobiographical mode during this time – after all, I told myself, the lobbyist, the educator and the critic should remain objective and dispassionate as much as possible. However, these current ruminations are, I fear, slightly more autobiographical than normal. Perhaps it is the valedictory mode that retirement allows; the self-indulgence that age sanctions. However, I have discovered that retirement does not just mark the end of a phase in one individual's personal narrative, it also allows – even compels – a reconsideration of the larger narrative within which that career developed. In this case, I want to consider nearly 40 years in the development of film culture in Ireland, a recent history that I lived through and played a very small part in but which has also shaped me, my career and the cultural environment in which that career has come to an end. My motivation here is, therefore, more pedagogic than self-obsessed, more political than personal. After all, the *present* has a *history*, the *now* has a *past* and it is this recent history that I want to mull over, the better to appreciate where we have arrived at in the present.

The title I have chosen for these thoughts is suggested by an article which was very influential on my generation of film scholars in the 1970s and which provides a good starting point for assessing how we have developed since then. French critic Guy Hennebelle's article

'Z-movies or What Hath Costa-Gavras Wrought?' which appeared in the American journal *Cineaste* in 1974, raises a number of key issues that continue to have relevance to national and regional filmmaking today, especially to those film industries, like Ireland's, that live within Hollywood's looming presence. Costa-Gavras is a largely forgotten filmmaker today outside of France and his native Greece (and that, in itself, is a sad reflection on contemporary film concerns). But in the 1970s and 1980s, he was synonymous with a kind of filmmaking that attempted to marry highly political subject matter with mainstream narrative forms, especially the investigative thriller. His most famous and most enduring film remains *Z* (1969), which, through the investigation into the death of a politically progressive Greek politician, explores the increasing erosion of democracy that preceded the 1967 right-wing military coup in Greece. Subsequently, Costa-Gavras tackled the Soviet invasion of Czechoslovakia in *The Confession* (1970) and the role of the CIA in Uruguay in his film about the Tupamaros guerrillas, *State of Siege* (1972). In the 1980s, he made a series of American films that explored the dirty side of US politics; *Missing* (1982), about the 1973 US-backed coup against Salvador Allende's democratic government in Chile; *Betrayed* (1988), about white supremacist neo-Nazis in America's own heartland; and *The Music Box* (1989), about Nazi war criminals in the USA. Costa-Gavras argued that his approach to filmmaking was dictated by the desire to engage with popular audiences, and therefore the need to wrap the political in generic forms that popular audiences are already familiar with: 'Cinema is about seducing an audience to have them go away and think' (http://www.theguardian.com/film/2009/apr/04/costa-gavras).

Hennebelle's objection to Costa-Gavras is that the genre forms he utilizes are not neutral and have meaning already inscribed into their generic conventions. If you want to make political films, he argues, you have to make films politically, challenging or disrupting rather than merely adopting dominant forms. Hennebelle was careful not to promote the kind of counter-cinema that Godard expounded: Godard, he felt, alienated and lost the audience and so his cinema was politically nullified. But merely to adopt conventional forms – established genres – meant that Costa-Gavras' cinema was hampered by its reliance on individual psychology and surface realism, and the politics, as a result, were rendered simplified and naïve. He coined the phrase 'Z movies' to dismiss Costa-Gavras' whole approach to political filmmaking and the debate that ensued became a key issue in the developing field of film studies during the 1970s and 1980s.

It also informed independent filmmaking at the time and this proved to be a particularly rich period for the political avant-garde. In the 1970s and early 1980s, indigenous Irish cinema was struggling into existence and many of the first independent films to emerge reflected the times and their debates. The first film to alert audiences to this emerging cinema was Bob Quinn's *Caoineadh Airt Uí Laoire* (*Lament for Art O'Leary*, 1975), a political film of such formal complexity that Hennebelle would have approved. Indeed, if you consider the films that emerged between 1975 and 1987, it is fair to say that they were concerned as much with film form as they were with the politics and society of a rapidly changing Ireland and, if they were oppositional in a political sense, they were also challenging in a formal sense. I would argue as well that the Costa-Gavras strategy of adapting a popular form for political purposes informed Frank Deasy and Joe Lee's Dublin-set *The Courier* (1987), a film that does not enjoy a very favourable reputation today but which, nonetheless, can be considered a 'Z movie' in the Hennebelle sense, and one that brings into an Irish context the debate about how genre can construct meaning and stifle political intent.

The emerging filmmakers of the time constituted an effective lobby group on behalf of state support for film (the Association of Independent Producers was formed in 1977 and saw success in 1981 when Bord Scannán na hÉireann was established). However, the lobbying and campaigning, especially among film academics and the newly reconstituted Irish Film Institute (IFI), was also directed towards developing a broad *film culture* as well as a film industry, a wider culture that included film education as well as film training, film history and aesthetics as well as film technique. To this end, in 1980, the institute set up the first comprehensive film studies summer school under the general rubric 'Film Study: The Irish Context'. During the course of an intensive week of lectures, seminars and screenings, we showed Costa-Gavras' *State of Siege* (1972) and Godard's *Vent d'Est* (1970) and discussed Hennebelle's article about political filmmaking. We also showed *The Quiet Man* (John Ford, 1952) to initiate discussion about representation of Ireland and the Irish and contrasted Ford's view of the West of Ireland with Bob Quinn's *Poitín* (1978) and Kieran Hickey's *Exposure* (1978): two of the best Irish short films of the period.

The IFI summer school was the institute's attempt at introducing wider film debates into a specifically Irish context, a two-way flow where Ireland is introduced to global issues and global issues are introduced to Irish concerns. (The only film study course in the whole island at that time was the course at the then New University of Ulster at Coleraine.)

The culmination of this project was the 'Green on the Screen' film festival, held at the Metropole Cinema in Dublin in September/October 1984 when 80 feature films and 80 shorts were shown in a celebration of 'film and Ireland'. The festival showed Irish and Irish-themed films from the silent period down to the present and juxtaposed the outsider image with the emerging new indigenous cinema. Earlier that year, two of these Irish films (Cathal Black's naturalistic look at the lives and culture of Dublin inner-city squatters, *Pigs* [1984], and Pat Murphy's feminist historical drama *Anne Devlin* [1984]) were shown out of competition at Cannes. Significantly, though, the one Irish film that was shown in competition at that year's festival, winning the best actress award for Helen Mirren, was Pat O'Connor's much more commercial and conventional narrative film *Cal* (1984), which was produced by David Puttnam and financed through a combination of British sources (Enigma and Goldcrest) and Hollywood (Warner Bros). If both kinds of film represented an emerging new cinema, there was clearly a contrast in scale, ambition and intention as well as in budget. The low-budget indigenous film tended to be more political and more formally challenging while the co-produced cinema that *Cal* represented was more conventionally commercial. As it happened, the future lay with the latter and, although it was not so obvious at the time, there were already underlying forces that would change the landscape for film culture generally and film production specifically.

Hennebelle's argument was motivated by the realization that Hollywood cinema had become the one truly global cinema and that Hollywood genres, evolving in one particular film industrial complex, were not always amenable to being adapted in other cultural environments. He set up the parameters of a debate that contrasted popular Hollywood cinema and political filmmaking, popular entertainment cinema with a kind of more robust intellectual cinema, American cinema with other national cinemas, and he foregrounded the question of genre and the construction of meaning. None of these issues has gone away in the intervening period but they have certainly lost the urgency that they once had, and Hennebelle and Costa-Gavras – and Godard – and the debates about film that they represented have become mere moments in a history that has moved on.

In the 1980s, the conservative triumvirate of Ronald Reagan in the USA, Margaret Thatcher in the UK and Helmut Kohl in Germany effected the sea change that is best described as the neoliberal turn that effectively killed off the post-war social democratic consensus. Slowly but surely, the market was promoted ahead of the social sphere

(Thatcher even famously declaring that there was no such thing as society) and a process of privatization was undertaken. The debates of the 1970s and early 1980s began to seem rather precious and increasingly irrelevant, and arguments based on the cultural, artistic and national importance of film seemed strangely unfocused as emphasis shifted to business plans, commercial potential and 'bed-night' economics. The original film board was closed down in 1987 – ostensibly as a cost-cutting exercise at a time of recession – but I have always thought that there was little enthusiasm in government for the highly political and challenging films that were emerging in the 1980s.

When it was re-launched in 1993, two factors dictated its nature. First, of course, neoliberalism had already begun to deliver to Ireland the so-called Celtic Tiger economy based on the tenets of the unfettered free market, easy access to borrowing and an unprecedented property boom. Second, Irish cinema and films about Ireland had begun to garner international attention: two Oscars for Jim Sheridan's *My Left Foot* (1989), one for Neil Jordan's *The Crying Game* (1992), both sandwiched between the critical and commercial success of Alan Parker's *The Commitments* (1990). In re-launching the film board in 1993, the then minister, Michael D. Higgins, declared that his funding package represented the integration of 'indigenous energy' with the 'commercial space that tax incentive creates'. The strategy marked an important turning point for film production in Ireland. On the one hand, although committed to diversity in the kind of films it would support, the new arrangements effectively killed off the more experimental, avant-garde (and more directly political) filmmaking that had been a feature of the earlier period in the 1970s and 1980s. On the other hand, however, it established Irish film production on a more secure basis and helped to establish a more comprehensive and more professional infrastructure than had existed previously.

According to official Irish Film Board (IFB) figures, the Irish film industry by 2013 was estimated to be worth in excess of €550 million, employing over 6,000 individuals, with over 560 small and medium enterprises (SMEs) operating in the sector. The IFB invested €7.5 million in production, which enabled Irish producers to raise a further €59.5 million, all of which was invested in Irish goods and services. In 2014, the IFB supported 15 Irish feature films, 11 creative feature co-productions, 11 short films, 4 feature documentaries, 2 TV dramas and 4 animated TV projects. In the period since 2003, the number of features supported by the IFB has nosed towards 200, many involving complex funding arrangements with American companies, European agencies and especially UK film and television companies. The year 2014 saw high levels of foreign direct investment with a large number of high-profile film and TV productions filming on location in Ireland, including the third series of the History channel's *Vikings* (Hirst, 2013–) and the BBC's *Ripper Street* (Warlow, 2012–), as well as a second series of the Showtime Network/Sky Atlantic production, *Penny Dreadful* (Logan, 2014–). There was also particular press and public excitement about the announcement in 2014 that the producers of the latest episode of the *Star Wars* franchise, *The Force Awakens*, had chosen Skellig Michael off the coast of Co. Kerry as a film location. The IFB maintains that such high-profile international productions not only bring inward investment and generate spending in the Irish economy, but also that the Irish locations featured (Michael Hirst, the creator of *Vikings* [2013–] has claimed that 70% of the first series was shot outdoors in its Irish locations, http://www.startribune.com/entertainment/tv/194379511.html) then provide a considerable post-screening boost to tourism. In 2010, for example, the IFB claims that 20% of all tourists cited film as an influencing factor on why they visited Ireland (http://www.irishfilmboard.ie/irish_film_industry/Facts_amp_Figures/35).

I think the Higgins package also had an impact on the debate in Northern Ireland, which followed a similar trajectory as in the south. The original lobbying was based on those old social democratic arguments about the artistic and cultural importance of film as an art form and the need for state subsidy of the kind enjoyed by the other arts; about the right of people in Northern Ireland to make films, to represent themselves in response to the images that flowed from the world's media covering the 'Troubles' as a running news story. However, as the main funding agency, now called Northern Ireland (NI) Screen, evolved from the 1990s on, the funding strategy was driven by a more commercial, business-oriented agenda. NI Screen is currently funded by Invest Northern Ireland (Invest NI), the regional business development agency set up by the Department of Enterprise, Trade and Investment to grow the local economy; something that explains its strong interest in attracting inward development from the international screen industry. NI Screen also administers Lottery funding for film in Northern Ireland, and although it retains a strong role in supporting film culture generally through a range of training, archive and educational initiatives, its main strategy has been to attract inward investment.

NI Screen's greatest success has undoubtedly been to persuade HBO to base the production of *Game of Thrones* (Benioff & Weiss, 2011–) in Northern Ireland, utilizing the enormous paint store at the Harland and

Wolff shipyards as its main studio space and shooting on location at many venues throughout the region. Over five seasons, the series has generated spend in Northern Ireland totalling over £85 million and provided 900 full-time and 5,700 part-time jobs. Many more studio spaces have been developed and a large pool of experienced crews and ancillary staff has been trained. The worldwide success of *Game of Thrones* (Benioff & Weiss, 2011–) has also generated a huge spin-off for the tourist industry and specialized tours of the various locations used in the series have now become a central part of the tourist experience.

There are a great many similarities, therefore, between the film industries on both sides of the border, and it would be churlish in the extreme to gainsay the real achievements of the IFB and NI Screen in building the infrastructure that can accommodate such large-scale international production. Ireland's success is the envy of many other regions in Europe. Lamenting that the Scottish film industry has been left to wither, a report in the *Guardian* noted: 'A Scottish government inquiry, expected to report within a fortnight, has heard senior industry figures describe institutional neglect, disillusionment and deep frustration as local competitors in Ireland, Northern Ireland and Wales enjoy a big- and small-screen "gold rush" ' (http://www.theguardian.com/film/2015/feb/18/scottish-film-industry-left-to-wither-holyrood).

But there are genuine worries about all of this at the same time. In 2013, NI Screen published *Opening Doors*, its strategy for the years 2014–18, phase 1 of its ambitious aim to establish Northern Ireland as 'the strongest screen industry outside of London in the UK and Ireland within 10 years' (NI Screen, 2013: 2). However, even in its ambitious strategy document, NI Screen admits that in catering for the international screen industry, it has committed less funding for local independent filmmaking than the IFB in the south (NI Screen, 2013: 19). And Terry George, the director of the Academy Award–winning short film *The Shore* (2011), has observed: 'I have to voice a note of caution as the big studios and the big productions can vanish just as fast as they appeared, so while it's wonderful to have HBO and NBC/Universal there if local productions, local film makers and local talent are not given long-term financial and structural support we'll be left with empty studio space and a lot of people having to go abroad to find work' (http://www.theguardian.com/uk/2011/dec/28/northern-ireland-game-of-thrones). Nadine O'Regan argues in relation to indigenous Irish cinema in the south: 'Irish films are often weak affairs, small of budget, limited in scope and marketed poorly. Often, they slip into the cinema like a shadow and fade away just as fast. Irish people don't go to see them' (2014: 1). There is a continuing worry that despite the success of bringing in large-scale production from outside, there has been little in the way of major international success from indigenous productions and that the only two directors to have maintained a high-profile reputation remain Neil Jordan and Jim Sheridan, who established their reputations over 25 years ago.

So, to return to the original question, 'what hath the funding regimes wrought?', it is difficult to characterize filmmaking in Ireland as a 'national' cinema, at least in any narrow, essentialist definition of the term. Not only, as we have seen, is activity funded by different national bodies across two political jurisdictions, the strategies on both sides of the border follow a similar pattern that emphasizes the importance of the international screen industries as drivers for both economic growth and trickle-down cultural development. Both the IFB in the south and NI Screen in the north seek to work with the internal national and external European support agencies, but to do so in collaboration with the international industry (especially in the UK and the USA). In this regard, then, rather than seeing the situation as a *national cinema* in itself, it is better to see the developments in Ireland, north and south, as the successful integration of Ireland into *international screen culture*; the ending of the splendid isolation of the image that characterized much of the 20th century. This does not, of course, preclude the development of local independent filmmaking, but it does mean that this independent sector is supported within this wider screen culture, living with it rather than competing against it, and therefore having to adhere to a greater extent to the aesthetic conventions of that culture. It seems impossible now to envisage any way in which the more experimental, politically engaged cinema of the 1970s and 1980s could be accommodated within this culture. In assessing Scottish film culture, Duncan Petrie likened it to 'devolved British cinema', but in truth, it is better to see all the production emanating from Britain and Ireland as a form of 'regional Hollywood'.

Again, these notes of caution are tempered by the real successes of indigenous films. The critical acclaim for the NI Screen (and IFB) supported *Good Vibrations* (Barros D'Sa & Leyburn, 2012), the Oscar win for the short film *The Shore* (George, 2011) and the BAFTA win and Oscar nomination in 2015 for the short film *Boogaloo and Graham* (Lennox, 2015) have boosted the reputation of Northern Ireland film and 2013 was a particularly strong year for IFB-funded films from the south with international and critical attention for John Michael McDonagh's *Calvary*, Lenny Abrahamson's *Frank* (Abrahamson seems the director most likely to move on to international acclaim), Ferdia Murphy's *The Stag* and, of course, the IFB also supported *Good Vibrations*.

The funding strategies for film in Ireland today highlight two other major shifts or 'turns' since the early days of state sponsorship. Writing in a book that I co-edited in 1996, exploring the relations between film and television, the then chief executive of the IFB, Rod Stoneman, noted: 'The specifics of separate traditions, of the cinema and of television, in documentary as well as fiction film, must not obscure the way in which cinema lives in, on and through television' (1996: 119). Nearly 20 years on, this is even more the case, to the extent that it might be argued that high-definition television (video) has actually replaced the cinema. The commercial success of both the IFB and NI Screen is based on attracting high-end television to Ireland (*Game of Thrones*, *Vikings*, *Penny Dreadful*) more so than major studio film production (though this remains part of the strategy). There is also an aesthetic argument to be made that the form itself, unravelling over many episodes across numerous seasons, allows for a greater complexity – in character and theme – than is possible in a two-hour feature, and the critical success of series like *The Wire* (Simon, 2002–08), *The Sopranos* (Chase, 1999–2007) and *Breaking Bad* (Gilligan, 2008–13) seems to suggest that this is now the case. The fact that Ireland has emerged as a production site for such cutting-edge narrative television is no mean achievement and one that couldn't have been envisaged in the 1980s.

A second shift in strategy for funding agencies everywhere is that film is no longer seen as a separate cultural activity but is now considered part of the 'creative industries', incorporating image-making of all kinds, across computer games, digital animation, software development and electronic publishing. NI Screen actually highlights its 'digital and interactive' funding opportunities and both major funding agencies emphasize their commitment to developing SMEs linked to this broader creative sector.

In my own field of education, especially in the academic field, I have witnessed the slow but steady influence of neoliberal economics on our university courses. This can be seen in the wider university environment. If neoliberalism shifted the definition of the individual from 'citizen' to 'consumer', then within the academy, the 'student' has become a 'customer' and the collegiality that long underpinned university structures has largely been replaced by a management structure imported from business (and one, I would contend, that is singularly inappropriate in an educational institution). Learning outcomes are now dominated by questions of 'employability' and 'skills acquisition';

'training' has replaced 'education' as the primary focus. (When I first entered the academy, I kept in mind the injunction of one celebrated broadcaster who declared, '*You* educate them, *we'll* train them.') In film and media studies courses, I feel, especially in the UK, but also increasingly in Ireland, there has been a definite 'production turn' in both student expectations and college priorities (our young people coming to university today have experienced no other culture than that of neoliberal economics with its emphasis on the market and job acquisition, and universities must be seen to respond to the needs of industry or risk funding). University courses, again especially in the UK, have also become very expensive for the student who will now run up a considerable debt for the privilege of obtaining a degree. This is an added pressure to ensure 'value for money'. In the last few years of my own teaching career, I felt that the courses I taught – on film aesthetics, film history, Irish film and representation – were merely tolerated by students anxious to get back to the studio.

The world of the neoliberal academy seems a long way away now from the social democratic institutions that pioneered film and media courses in the 1970s and 1980s, where the space was created to mull over questions about form and content and to experiment and take risks in exploring other possibilities beyond the mainstream. I do not argue that this kind of teaching has disappeared – obviously, it has not – and film and media research, its history and aesthetic concerns are still key to most good teaching in the UK and Ireland. Perhaps, as well, in recent scholarship from Ireland, there is an irritation among younger scholars with the critical concerns of the older generation who came through the original debates about national cinema. This irritation manifests itself most specifically in questions about genre and the influence especially of mainstream Hollywood on Irish filmmaking (see, for example, many of the essays in the collection edited by Claire Bracken & Emma Radley, 2013). However, it seems to me to be more challenging and more demanding to teach film theory and aesthetics today than it was when I first started my career, and I have nothing but admiration for those younger colleagues who can bring to the student experience both an informed theoretical and historical knowledge, and the necessary high levels of production skills to satisfy the expectations of 'employability'. I am well aware that age was not the only factor in my own decision to retire!

That leaves me with one final point that I'd like to make. Over the last 30 years, I have tried to gauge, through my own students' responses, what have been both the most and the least successful Irish films. The films that have left my own students unimpressed is led by the horror film *Shrooms* (Breathnach, 2007), *The Courier* (Deasy & Lee, 1986) and Michael Winterbottom's *With or Without You* (2000) (though to be honest, I have found it increasingly difficult to engage students with any of the more avant-garde films of the 1970s and 1980s). But whatever their reputation, these films can be engaged with critically, and to good effect. I have been criticized for writing about many films that are considered minor or enjoy poor critical reputations – like *The Courier* or *With or Without Me* – but I do so because they raise interesting issues that bear closer scrutiny. In the case of *Shrooms*, one of the younger scholars I have referred to, Emma Radley, has offered an interesting reading of the film, applying Lacanian, but more specifically Kristevan, approaches to its low-grade horror conventions and arguing that it does constitute a particularly interesting deconstruction of genre within an Irish context (2013: 109–23). What I am referring to here is a 'critical project' that lies at the heart of all cultural analysis – one that should be about more than validating the 'canon' and deciding which films are 'good' and which are 'bad'. This critical project, I believe, can have its own creative dynamic, pushing and suggesting, making connections and offering readings that ultimately adhere to no other agenda than the educational in its broadest sense. Even the most modest of culture, even the most critically reviled of films, can be engaged with creatively through this critical project 'to seduce the audience to have them go away and think', as Costa-Gavras would say.

As I leave the academy, I am delighted to see that this critical project is alive and well and that in Ireland, north and south, there is now a 'critical' mass of scholars whose work maintains and develops such a creative critical project. One can never for certain define what constitutes a 'national' film industry, but in Ireland we have certainly managed to develop a film culture in which that question continues to be debated.

Martin McLoone

Contributors

Laura Aguiar is a researcher at The Keynes Centre, University College Cork. She holds a BA in journalism from Fumec University, an MA in media and communication from Stockholm University and a PhD in film studies from Queen's University Belfast. Her research interests include collaborative media practice, gender representation, media and war, and interactive storytelling. She is the editor and co-director of the documentary film *We Were There* (Aguiar & McLaughlin, 2014), about the women's experience of the Maze and Long Kesh Prison during the conflict in Northern Ireland. She has also worked as a freelance journalist in Brazil, Ireland and Sweden.

Stephen Baker is Lecturer in Film and Television Studies at Ulster University. With his colleague Greg McLaughlin, he has co-authored a number of articles on the media and Northern Ireland, and two books, *The Propaganda of Peace: The Role of the Media and Culture in the Northern Ireland Peace Process* (McLaughlin & Baker, 2010) and *The British Media and Bloody Sunday* (McLaughlin & Baker, 2015).

Ciara Barrett has recently completed her PhD at Trinity College Dublin, with a research project titled *Performances of Femininity in Hollywood Musicals, 1929–40*. In April 2012, she co-organized the international conference in film studies, *Genres in Transit: Rethinking Genre in Contemporary Cinema* at Trinity College and is currently developing a book project based on this theme.

Brigitte Bastiat holds a PhD in media and communication studies from the University of Paris 8. At present, she teaches English at the University of La Rochelle, France, is collaborating with a research group on cinema based at the same university and is an associate member of the *Centre d'études irlandaises* (Research Centre in Irish Studies) of the University of Rennes 2 and of the CRHIA (Research Centre for International Atlantic History) of the University of La Rochelle. She has published on identities, gender representations, the Women's Press in Ireland and France, Irish theatre and Irish, British and American cinema. She is currently involved in a research project dealing with the contemporary Northern Irish playwright Owen McCafferty. She co-translated in French one of his plays, *Mojo Mickybo* (1998). The play was premièred in French at the University of Tours in March 2012 and has been performed in various cities in France since then. She is currently co-translating Owen McCafferty's play *Quietly* (2012).

Noélia Borges holds a PhD in Irish studies from the University of São Paulo, Brazil. She has been an assistant professor in the Institute of Letters, Department of Germanic Letters, Federal University of Bahia, Brazil, for over two decades. Together with Dr Munira Mutran and Dr Laura Izarra, she coordinated the III Symposium of Irish Studies in South America in Bahia in 2008, sponsored by the Embassy of Ireland in Brazil, the University of São Paulo and the University of Bahia. In 2010, she completed her post-doctoral research on the adaptation of Irish plays to the cinema at Leeds Metropolitan University under the supervision of Dr Lance Pettitt with a grant from CAPES – a foundation affiliated with the Ministry of Education of Brazil. She is currently writing a book, which will be titled *Film Adaptation: Irish Plays on Screen*.

Liz Carville is a final year PhD candidate at NUI Maynooth. Her research centres on representations of Irish masculinity in Hollywood cinema. Her doctoral thesis gives specific consideration to the impact of the Celtic Tiger on understandings of Irishness and masculinity in the popular culture of Ireland and America.

Ciara Chambers is Lecturer in Film Studies in the school of Media, Film and Journalism at Ulster University. She is the author of *Ireland in the Newsreels* (Irish Academic Press, 2012), and her articles have appeared in the *Journal of Film Preservation*, the *Historical Journal of Film, Radio & Television, Alphaville: Journal of Film & Screen Media*. She has contributed chapters on newsreels and amateur film to various edited collections. She has worked on archival digitization projects with UTV, NI Screen, Belfast Exposed Photography, the British Universities' Film and Video Council, the IFI Irish Film Archive and University College Cork. She was part of the academic steering group for the BBC's Chronicle project and is currently a steering group member for NI Screen's Digital Film Archive.

Silvia Dibeltulo is a researcher at Oxford Brookes University. She holds a PhD in film studies from Trinity College Dublin with a dissertation on cinematic representations of Irish-Americans and Italian-Americans in Hollywood gangster film. Her research mainly focuses on the representation of identity on screen, specifically in terms of ethnicity, nationality, gender and culture. Her work also centres on film genre theory and history, and audience studies. She is currently co-editing a book on genre filmmaking in contemporary cinema, while also working on several projects emerging from her doctoral research.

Conn Holohan is Lecturer in Film Studies at the Huston School of Film and Digital Media, NUI Galway. His publications include *Cinema on the Periphery: Contemporary Irish and Spanish Film* (2010) as well as a number of book chapters and journal articles on space and place in European cinema. His current research focuses on the domestic space in 1930s' Hollywood melodrama.

Jenny Knell is a PhD candidate at University College Dublin, where she is completing her dissertation on the representation of Dublin in contemporary Irish film. Her research has been funded through the UCD Ad Astra Scholarship and explores issues of class, space and identity. Jenny has taught on a variety of undergraduate courses relating to Irish film and culture, and her articles have appeared in international journals such as *Éire Ireland* and *Estudios Irlandeses*.

Isabelle Le Corff is Senior Lecturer in English and Film Studies at the UBO (Université de Bretagne Occidentale), France. Her research focuses on Irish cinema, film analysis and film in education. She has published *Cinemas of Ireland* (2009) and is co-editor of *Les Images en question: Cinéma, Télévision, nouvelles images: les voies de la recherche* (2011). She created and is now editor-in-chief of the peer-reviewed cinema online journal *Mise Au Point* (http://map.revues.org/).

Fergal Lenehan teaches at the Department of Intercultural Studies and Business Communications of the Friedrich Schiller University of Jena, Germany. He holds a BA and an MA from University College Dublin and a PhD in cultural studies from the University of Leipzig, Germany. He has published articles and book chapters in the areas of intellectual history, film and television studies, Internet ethics and Irish-German relations. His book *Intellectuals and Europe: Imagining a Europe of the Regions in Twentieth Century Germany, Britain and Ireland* was published in 2014.

Greg McLaughlin is Senior Lecturer in Media Studies at Ulster University. With his colleague Stephen Baker, he has co-authored a number of articles on the media and Northern Ireland, and two books, *The*

Propaganda of Peace: The Role of the Media and Culture in the Northern Ireland Peace Process (McLaughlin & Baker, 2010) and *The British Media and Bloody Sunday* (McLaughlin & Baker, 2015).

Martin McLoone is originally from Derry and was educated at St Columb's College and University College Dublin. Until his retirement in 2014, he was Professor of Media Studies (Film, Television and Photography) and Director of the Centre for Media Research at the University of Ulster. He joined the university in 1986 and was part of the media studies research culture for 28 years. He has published extensively on the media in Britain and Ireland, and is the author of four monographs and editor of six collections of essays. His recent publications include *Rock and Popular Music in Ireland: Before and After U2* (McLaughlin & McLoone, 2012) and *Film, Media and Popular Culture in Ireland: Cityscapes, Landscapes, Soundscapes* (2008).

Raita Merivirta is a researcher in the Department of European and World History at the University of Turku, Finland. She holds a PhD from La Trobe University, Melbourne. She has published articles on Indian English literature and Irish cinema and history and is the author of the book *The Gun and Irish Politics: Examining National History in Neil Jordan's Michael Collins* (2009) and a co-editor of the anthology *Frontiers of Screen History: Imagining European Borders in Cinema 1945–2010* (Merivirta, Ahonen, Mulari & Mähkä, 2013).

Barry Monahan is a lecturer and researcher in Film Studies at University College Cork. Although his monograph *Ireland's Theatre on Film: Style, Stories and the National Stage on Screen* (2009) concentrated predominantly on the period from 1930 to 1960, he has also published broadly on contemporary Irish film, with varying angles of focus, from narrative and theory to aesthetics. He contributes regularly to the online journal *Estudios Irlandeses*, and recently co-edited (with Laura Rascaroli and Gwenda Young) a collection of essays on amateur filmmaking, titled *Amateur Filmmaking: The Home Movie, the Archive, the Web* (2014). He is currently working on a book on the films of Lenny Abrahamson.

Patricia Neville is a sociologist with research interests in gender, media and cultural analysis, community research and health and well-being. She has taught at a variety of higher education institutions in Ireland, including the University of Limerick, Griffith College Cork and University College Cork. In 2011, she was a visiting scholar in the Department of Gender Studies, Queens University, Kingston, Canada. She is Lecturer in Social Sciences at the School of Oral and Dental Sciences, University of Bristol, the United Kingdom, where she teaches and conducts research on the sociology of health and oral health.

Nicholas O'Riordan is in the second year of doctoral research into representations of Irish accents on screen at University College Cork. While he is interested in elements of linguistic analysis, the thesis is cinematically focused in that it does not isolate the aural from the visual components of the medium, but reads their semiotics dialectically. He has presented his research at numerous symposia at University College Cork, and at conferences in NUI Galway and Trinity College Dublin.

Kathleen Vejvoda is Professor of English at Bridgewater State University. Her memoir 'The Death Knock' appeared in *New England Review* (as Kathleen Chaplin) and was selected as a Notable Essay of 2013 in *The Best American Essays 2014*. She has published articles on Irish cinema, Irish folklore and Victorian literature, and her current project focuses on the representation of children and childhood in Irish cinema.

Introduction

Barry Monahan

There are manifest similarities in the ways that nations and national film cultures are born and develop. Both are protean and volatile, and elude reductive teleological interpretations and categorization, and both are at the mercy of the vicissitudes of sociological, political, hegemonic, global, historical and economic events and eventualities. Even in cases where certain structural trends of film output are historically identifiable in different international contexts, specificities that are characteristic of given national and national film culture contexts can bear remarkable similarities across geographical borders. It is hardly a coincidence, for example, that the Hollywood and Bollywood mechanisms – in such cantonized, multicultural demographics – have produced cinematic cultures consistently designed around clearly recognizable generic structures (distinctly maintained film categories in the former, and imbricated and amalgamated within individual films in the latter). This diachronic peculiarity contrasts radically with the more synchronic national cinema movements that are often subsumed under a broader 'European film' epithet, but are nevertheless still identified discursively by titles such as 'German Expressionism', 'Italian NeoRealism', the 'French Nouvelle Vague', 'British Social Realism' or the 'Danish Dogme95 Project', all of which are consigned to precise temporal moments as categories of film history.

The constitutions of nation and nationality also operate in a dialectically similar way to that of a national cinema (and by this, as opposed to 'national film', I mean specifically the broader element of the cinematic apparatus). Both require an unrestricted and constantly evolving interaction between concrete manifestations, artefacts and performances, and engaged critical commentary on the same. In the light of these two frameworks for consideration – instability on the one hand and

1

the dialectical relationship between concrete components and critical discourse on the other – the case of Ireland and Irish film culture offers an interesting case study. While the burgeoning Irish nation had so tentative a birth and delivery, as has been so often noted, so, too, did an indigenous cinema – from official recognition and support, to the provision of technological hardware and studio and training facilities – have a belated and belaboured beginning, with more than one false start and recession along the way. More optimistically, and perhaps counter-intuitively in view of this prohibitive context, the development of critical commentary on Irish cinema has been consistent, strong and increasingly imaginative. On the solid foundations provided by internationally acclaimed pioneers in the field – John Hill, Luke Gibbons, Martin McLoone and Kevin Rockett – waves of second-generation academics and other cultural critics have offered wide-ranging and fruitful observations on every aspect of Irish cinema, from theoretical and political perspectives, and empirical and aesthetic analyses, to historical and practice-based interpretations. As Hill, Gibbons, McLoone and Rockett continued to produce ground-breaking research, the innovative work of other home-grown analysts was added to the critical canon: Ruth Barton, Harvey O'Brien, Lance Pettitt and Emer Rockett, to mention a few. Now, with an expanding army of academic commentators, another wave of rich and diverse analysis has come from many of my own contemporaries and the pens of Zélie Asava, Steve Baker, Ciara Chambers, Denis Condon, Maeve Connolly, Debbie Ging, Conn Holohan, Díóg O'Connell, Emma Radley, Tony Tracy and too many others to mention here.

In a number of ways, even more significant – since it has so obviously been from its inception, essentially a transnational medium – is the moment at which the national cinema finds its global purchase and there occurs a rise in overseas commentary, commensurate with the success and recognition of our indigenous films in other countries. From the earliest foray into academic considerations of Irish cinema, scholars like Elizabeth Butler Cullingford, Brian McIlroy and Anthony Slide have contributed reflections on the medium and, in time, these have been added to by highly critically recognized specialists like Michael Patrick Gillespie, Isabelle Le Corff, Diane Negra, Maria Pramaggiore and Rosa González, again to name only a few. On the global platform of increasing inter-communicational technologies, we should celebrate the ever-expanding numbers of instruments and channels of dialectical commentary that seek to progress the identity and knowledge base of our national cinema.

That the thematic range of critical perspectives has also diversified and deepened is further cause for celebration and is also testimony to an expanding canon of noteworthy films. Within the categories of historical, theoretical and aesthetic analysis, more probing accounts into fields such as genre, gender and identity studies, cinema and transnational collaboration and narration, and, more recently, aspects of intertextuality, adaptation and performance studies and eco-criticism, have all further expanded and enriched the investigative scholarly canvas. Such commentaries provide a necessary keystone in the conceptual cinematic cultural output, and offer to students in our third-level institutions inspiration and challenges to their thinking about what a 21st-century cinema should and can do. In an age – as we are repeatedly reminded – when almost everyone has some form of technological hardware for the recording of moving images (often in our pockets!), the capacity to make movies should be met all the more ardently with the requirement to have the intellectual and creative capability to make *excellent* movies. In this respect, our academic discursive input is of increasing critical importance.

This collection of essays, like so many others published in the field, hopes to bring several intellectual interventions into the cultural dialectic of the medium, by working from the potential wealth that its polyvocality and thematic variety should offer. Divided into four parts, its breadth incorporates not just commentary from analysts at home and around the globe, but also contributions from writers from several disciplines, and from both internationally established and early career scholars who have innovative interjections to relate.

The extended foreword has been written by professor of media and cultural studies, Martin McLoone, who, having only recently retired from the University of Ulster (although no less actively engaged in, and engaging with, the field), offers a magnanimous overview (across his career) from the early, hesitant days of a burgeoning Irish cinema. His account is both personally informed and analytically rigorous, as McLoone offers a historical synopsis of the fluctuations in the development of Irish and Northern Irish cinema. This outline runs parallel to an interpretation of what citizens should expect from their national cinematic culture; how it should be reflective, constitutive and transformative of the more dubious ideological forces that run the state. In this, he references an essay titled 'Z-movies or what hath Costa-Gavras wrought?', first published by French critic Guy Hennebelle in 1974, and which he says inspired him to think differently about the important position that a national cinema necessarily occupies in a healthy socio-political system. McLoone's argument moves on from Hennebelle's reflection on the activist cinema of native Greek Costa-Gavras by optimistically suggesting that mainstream cinema is capable of being politically engaged and is not inevitably caught in a politically paralysing populist hegemony. Ireland's case – although not unique – is one that must typically, constantly confront its position as marginal and peripheral to the mainstream centre, but this must not excuse it from the responsibility to challenge and inform a broader political culture. McLoone cites Bob Quinn and his contemporary Irish filmmakers working in the 1970s and '80s as activists whose films were both politically engaged and formally innovative. As his ideas unfold, McLoone comes to address the relative benefits and problems of current funding and marketing situations in both the north and south of Ireland, before he ends with an affirmative turn to reflect on some current academic writing on recent Irish cinema; a conclusion that returns to the debate about mainstream and peripheral cinematic production and the relationship between minor national cinemas and generic paradigms, where his essay began.

The main body of the collection is divided into four parts for thematic coherence and practicality for the research reader. The first of these considers the representations of space, place and the home in Irish cinema. In Chapter 1, Conn Holohan addresses the ways in which notions of home have been conceptualized and constructed in a historical dialectical relationship between cinema and other socio-cultural commentaries. Beginning his polemic with reflections on the contemporary Irish socio-economic context – a time at which earlier romanticized notions of 'the home' shifted towards the more exchange-value position occupied during the Celtic Tiger years of acquisition of 'the house' – Holohan returns to the metaphorical evocation of Ireland as homeland, using John Ford's 1952 film *The Quiet Man* as an exemplary case. From there, Holohan analyses how more recent cinematic representations problematize the earlier idealizations of homestead, proposing that the shift from the former is indicative of changing attitudes to what the home is; maintaining the displacement of both previously accepted international perspectives of Ireland as 'home' (by the considerable Irish diaspora), and national, local values of 'home' as socially cherished 'hearth'. Holohan evokes Mark Augé's notion of the postmodern, globalized non-space ultimately detached from traditional historical contexts, to problematize the formerly esteemed position of the home, having now become as significant, if not more important, in its virtual and conceptual reality as it used to be in its concrete actuality. In Chapter 2,

Jenny Knell offers an analysis of Dublin as ideologically gendered space in a number of crime films narrating or based on the life and murder stories of investigative crime journalist Veronica Guerin and criminal gang leader Martin Cahill. Knell starts by providing a broad context of cinematic representations of Dublin's gangland, notably concentrating on five films produced between 1998 and 2003, in order to establish a set of generic precedents that facilitate her analysis of how the female journalist's social and gendered position rests problematically – although, for Knell's reading, not entirely inconveniently – at odds with the masculine, working-class criminal worlds in which Guerin (or her alter ego Hamilton) circulates for investigation. The perils of mobilizing such a strong and progressive female protagonist are discernible, according to Knell, in somewhat conservative ways, as warnings and threats to her family are frequently used to mark the character's violation of territorially gendered social spaces; something that Knell argues is broadly representative of more generally pervasive social attitudes.

In the third chapter, Nicholas O'Riordan offers a new angle of reflection on contemporary representations of Dublin on screen (perhaps counter-intuitively for the visual medium, although no less innovatively as a result) by focusing on the role of accent. O'Riordan provides solid historical contextualization for invoking more contemporary concerns over certain 'inaccuracies' perceived in certain (non-Irish) actors' performances of the indigenous accent. As he questions the enduring ubiquity of the critical commentaries on such mainstream cinematic misrepresentations of the native accent, O'Riordan finds historical concerns, publically expressed over a century ago about the threat to the Irish language (by Padraig Pearse) and, latterly, to Hiberno-English (by Oliver St John Gogarty). These precedents, he suggests, may go some way to explaining the enduring – albeit latent – protectionism that might be informing contemporary critical discourses. There is ample evidence, he suggests, that in the light of developments in the Dublin accent during the Celtic Tiger years, even contemporary Irish cinema offers examples of how accent modulation and performance have become useful narrative devices – in both major and minor ways – for character exploration and the examination of changing socio-cultural and socio-economic stratification. The final chapter in this section neatly bookends with themes introduced in Conn Holohan's opening contribution. In Chapter 4, Kathleen Vejvoda echoes Holohan's problematization of the historically constituted 'cosy homestead' by concentrating on a dysfunctional set of familial relationships as depicted in Carmel Winters' film *Snap*. Vejvoda begins by calling upon stylistic traditions of gothic horror narratives – with some attention given to the role of the child character of that genre – before suggesting that those aesthetic qualities are not simply applied to, but are usefully explored by, Winters' innovative marriage of formal qualities with her manifest thematic concerns in the film. Vejvoda proposes that the multi-layered narrative movements and formal processes of subjective meaning-making in Winters' film facilitate a reading of cinematic mediation that is at one and the same time open to charges of pornographic sexualized objectification, but also, more optimistically as the film moves towards an interrogative historiographical (in-)conclusion, a possible mechanism of redemption, and release for victims of atavistic cycles of abuse.

The second section of the collection gathers fours essays around the overlapping themes of gender and stardom as globally performed on the national platform. In Chapter 5, Ciara Barrett uses two case studies of Irish female 'stardom' – the early careers of Saoirse Ronan and Ruth Negga – to explore the less obvious, and much less frequently discussed, histories of Irish female star performance in the context of mainstream cinema. Barrett begins by establishing a number of lines of interrogation, by drawing attention to the problematic discursive relegation of the construction of female stardom generally, the tentative positions held by the Irish male star within cinematic narratives historically, and then brings both of these together to question the relative paucity of dynamic and complex roles created for the recognizable – and celebrated – Irish female star. As what might at first seem to be an affirmative antidote to this dearth, Barrett examines the position of rising Irish actresses Ronan and Negga, and explores the extent of self-management of their images, as well as the construction of the same, by national and international media. What may be seen as an advance for the indigenous female actor within the category of 'stardom' more generally, Barrett implies may be matched by a commensurate dilution of the sense of a national identity within that same category. Shifting to the more established career of Jonathan Rhys Meyers (perhaps a noteworthy example, in view of Ciara Barrett's argument), in Chapter 6, Liz Carville considers how extra-textural mediation and construction of the Irish actor's image have informed both his casting and then intertextual meaning-creation as Henry VIII in Michael Hirst's television series *The Tudors*. Not without precedent – as Carville goes through a number of the on-screen roles already played by the notably 'Irish' performer – Meyers' characterization of the volatile, impetuous and problematically depicted 'masculine' English monarch is neatly drawn and maintained by references to biographical details of the actor's public persona. These are not only strategically mobilized in cultural commentary, Carville suggests, but also work from certain problematic historical essentializations of 'Irishness' within earlier colonial representations and discourses.

In the seventh chapter, Silvia Dibeltulo proposes a relationship between the ideological design of certain aspects of mainstream 'Irish' masculinity and evolving ethnicities of 'Irishness' in a way that provides appropriate continuity with the observations of the previous two chapters. In this essay, Dibeltulo invites the reader to consider the semiotics – in dialogue and visual coding – of Irishness, as constructed in mainstream American cinema. Although her focus is mostly concentrated on the Richard LaGravenese adaptation of Cecelia Ahearn's novel *P.S. I Love You*, Dibeltulo's analysis of both 'old' and 'new' ethnics and her introduction of the category of 'hyphenated identity' as informative construction both imply a much farther-reaching, and more significant, application of her theoretical framework across the breadth of mainstream visual culture. Moving towards a conclusion that increasingly concentrates on a masculine (and masculinized) Irish ethnicity, Dibeltulo frames the development in the representation of the earlier stereotype within economically motivated and hegemonically conservative and capital-based motivations. In the final chapter of this section, Patricia Neville challenges simplistic readings of Ken Wardrop's documentary *His & Hers* by confronting reductive notions of documentarian objectivity in combination with an application of the flexibility ascribed to sociological constructions of gender. As she charts an established range of cinematic and (more generally) narrative tropes that have been historically ascribed to the female character – in this case, specifically, the Irish female character – Neville goes on to measure the degrees of perceived and accepted innovation in Wardrop's film, to suggest that it may not be as revolutionary a construction of femininity as first appears. With a close reading of the film, and a provision of extra-textual information about its production, Neville contextualizes Wardrop's offering in the light of its critical reception and against its cinematic precursors in the creation of a sense of feminine identity on screen.

The third part of the book gathers together four chapters that consider themes relating to the cinema and representations of Northern Ireland. In the first of these, Chapter 9, Stephen Baker and Greg McLaughlin outline a polemic that, notwithstanding the note that films are inevitable ideological texts, representations of the Northern province have tended towards formal and, therefore, political caution.

Calling for more directly probing and engaging cinematic address to the contemporary socio-political situation of that province, Baker and McLaughlin offer analytical comparison with another innovative example of marginal filmmaking by looking at African, Abderrahmane Sissako's, *Bamako*. They hold a close analytical reading of this peripheral Malian film as a wonderful example of how even non-mainstream cinema can address global hegemonic forces, with a subversive swipe at the dominant international institutions of capital and cultural dominance. Baker and McLaughlin show how this formally challenging film simultaneously provides a critique of the moral bankruptcy of organizations like the International Monetary Fund and the World Bank, and eschews the established stylistic and structural constructing principles of mainstream generic cinema. By evoking an argument that has already been introduced in Martin McLoone's essay in this collection, they affirmatively call for a similar creative revolution in a Northern-produced cinema that, they feel, has too often fallen into the conventional and banal generic formatting of populist production. In Chapter 10, Laura Aguiar offers a personal account and assessment of her involvement in the production of the Northern Ireland documentary *We Were There*; a collaborative project constructed from interviews with former detainees in the Maze and Long Kesh prisons, and their relatives, in conjunction with the Prisons Memory Archive. As Aguiar details her roles as co-director and editor of the film, she problematizes the methodologies involved in rendering an account of various historical and personal narratives and experiences into a coherent piece of cinema that might be deemed compassionate and fair-minded by those represented directly and indirectly in the content. Referencing the highly problematic concepts of 'historical accuracy', 'objectivity' and 'impartiality', Aguiar's essay frankly addresses the desire for interested engagement with, and respect for, the personal stories behind the experiences in and around the institutions of incarceration, against the context of highly charged political and social situations offered by the documentary.

Raita Merivirta focuses on the representations of masculinity and the male body on screen by using Steve McQueen's 2008 film *Hunger* as a case study in Chapter 11. By referencing the historical context of recognizable images and iconography of the Maze Prison protest hunger strikes in the early 1980s, and their occasional cinematic representation, Merivirta analyses the development of the semiotics of Christian martyrdom – as politically mobilized and often-applied filmic shorthand – and measures McQueen's use of Michael Fassbender's naked male body in the role of Bobby Sands as one that works against established trends. She proposes, ultimately, that McQueen's approach has certain qualities that set it apart from earlier representations and draws from these a potentially refreshing alternative to mainstream depictions of the politicized naked male body on screen. This section of the book closes with Brigitte Bastiat's look at the difficulties inherent in the process of adaptation for the screen of an original theatrical text and uses Owen McCafferty's play *Mojo Mickybo* – and Terry Loane's 2004 cinematic version *Mickybo and Me* – as its main focus. Establishing the problematic nature of 'adaptation discourse' and the methodological approaches that ought necessarily to precede its theoretical application, Bastiat uses broader notions of textual (and dialogue) translation, in the form of both subtitles and dubbing script, as paradigms through which to explore the inevitable re-contextualization that occurs when an 'original' text finds purchase in a new marketplace. She attempts a reading that offers a degree of empirical consideration (as much as space will allow) of the linguistic mutations that can occur within and against any primary text that is being reworked for a new medium or audience.

Although discreetly set from the last chapter, the fourth part of the book moves to consider a number of overseas perspectives on Irish cinema and leads on quite logically from it. In the first essay of this section – Chapter 13 – Fergal Lenehan considers a particular example of generic representation of Ireland on screen by mobilizing Rick Altman's semantic and syntactic approach to understanding the configurations of mainstream cinema. In this, Lenehan finds a rich example of an Irish musical within the German *Schlager* cycle and reads … *nur der Wind (Only the Wind)* as an interesting case in its obedience to the semantic conventions of the typical Hollywood-produced Irish-themed musical, as he compares it with a large number of its contemporaries (it was made in 1961) and its precursors. More importantly, according to his analysis, Lenehan proposes how aspects of that film's syntactic elements reveal an altogether more nuanced interpretation of Irishness, as produced for, and perceived by, its contemporary German-language audiences. In Chapter 14, Isabelle Le Corff begins her study of French audiences' understanding and expectations of 'Irish' films with an empirically informed consideration of how this indigenous cinema and its filmmakers have been critiqued in the French-language press. With reference to a large number of sources, Le Corff traces similarities of critical observation and notes certain tendencies in vagaries of misunderstanding. She moves to her conclusion by offering some explanations for the misconceptions and confusions arising out of, among others, a general propensity to consider Irish cinema under the 'British' label and to consider its language as rendering it culturally closer to an international (American) mainstream.

In Chapter 15, the adaptation procedure is again considered with a non-Irish audience in mind as Noélia Borges regards the extent to which J. B. Keane's play *The Field* was transformed for screen by Jim Sheridan in his 1990 reworking. Considering the problematic nature of the process, and the difficulties owing to its subsequent adjudication in terms of fidelity to, or respect for, the 'original', Borges approaches her analysis in much the same way that Brigitte Bastiat did with *Mickybo and Me* (Chapter 12). Borges uses Dudley Andrews' writing on adaptation as a starting point for establishing her own analytical parameters, and then considers elements of the film's revisions of characterization, dialogue and setting, less to adjudicate on the relative merit of Sheridan's product, than as a means to interrogate the value of the process of remediation in a more general way. In the final chapter of this section, Ciara Chambers and I offer a context for a consideration of a differently motivated perspective on Irish film from abroad (in this case from Rome, Italy). By focusing on the personal project of one of Irish cinema's more enthusiastic cultural ambassadors in Europe – the creative director of the Rome Irish Film Festa, Susanna Pellis – the chapter begins by providing a brief history of the inception and development of that festival, before offering an extended interview with Pellis. In it, Chambers and I hope to have uncovered some insights into how Irish cinema – its cultural practice and industrial mechanisms – is perceived from another European perspective and, by offering the access to certain personal reflections on the state of our current indigenous film industry by someone involved in its presentation (and regarding it from a helpful distance), our aim has been to cast some light on an alternative viewpoint, and invite questions of further critique and reasons for optimism.

Part I

Politics of Home, Space and Place

1

'Nothin' But a Wee Humble Cottage': At Home in Irish Cinema

Conn Holohan

In September 2011, an *Irish Times* article on the unfinished 'ghost estates' that were blighting the post-Celtic Tiger Irish landscape cited the statistic that over the previous four years, Ireland had experienced the worst crash in house prices in the world since the Second World War (Holland, 2011). This fact, alongside the 2,881 incomplete housing estates that the Department of Environment calculated to be in existence around the country at the time, rendered in strikingly concrete terms the loss of economic sovereignty that had been experienced both individually and collectively since Ireland's economic boom had come to a dramatic end three years previously. The dominant role that the construction industry had played within the Irish economy over the previous ten years, constituting as much as 21% of national income by 2006/2007 (Kelly, 2009), as well as the personal spending power that inflated house prices had granted to large sections of the Irish population, ensured that the subsequent mass devaluation of domestic property now functioned as a powerful index of economic decline. In the aftermath of the crash, the home became increasingly associated with burden within popular and media discourse as large numbers of people struggled to cope with unaffordable mortgages on houses now worth significantly less than the amount that had been paid for them. Nevertheless, as numerous contemporary commentators would suggest, the collective trauma of this experience could not be explained entirely in economic terms. The particular emotional relationship that Irish culture has sustained with private property, evident as far back as the 19th-century peasant struggles for land rights, ensured that the collapse of the Irish economy, and more specifically that of the Irish property market, was perceived as a crisis at the very heart of Irish identity. This interpretative tendency was given succinct, if hyperbolic, expression in an *Irish Times* editorial (18 November 2011) on the morning after the Irish government applied for economic assistance from the International Monetary Fund, in which, echoing W. B. Yeats, it wondered 'was it for this' surrender of national sovereignty that the men of 1916 had died?

Writing of the centrality of the home within the Irish cultural imaginary, Sean O'Tuama asserts:

> One will probably find a reverential feeling for home-place in every country – and in every literature – throughout the world [...] It is unlikely, however, that feeling for place (including feeling for home-place) is found so deeply rooted, and so widely celebrated, in any western European culture as it is in Irish culture. It seems to have made its presence felt in Irish literature at every level and in every era from early historic times to the present day.
>
> (1995: 248–9)

O'Tuama traces this intense 'feeling for place' from Irish-language poetry of the 17th century, through folksongs and ballads, and into the writings of 20th-century poets such as Patrick Kavanagh and Seamus Heaney. The physical anchoring of national identity in the home-place has not been limited to Irish literature, however, but has also been prevalent within a wider cultural and political discourse that found apt expression in de Valera's famous image of Ireland as a countryside 'bright with cosy homesteads'. Extending analysis of this discourse into the domain of visual art, Tricia Cusack argues that the idea of home, given expression in images of the country cottage in the work of painters such as Paul Henry, functioned as a mundane but powerful articulation of a particular form of Irish national identity and belonging in the first half of the 20th century. Through its everyday presence and its visual form, she asserts, the cottage conflated a specific set of nationalist values and 'reinforced the claims of the new state to represent a people whose self-image enshrined homely and pious rural values' (Cusack, 2001: 234). Similarly, in a discussion about the gendered landscapes of Irish cultural nationalism, Catherine Nash suggests the particular power of the cottage to function as an indexical expression of cultural ideals as 'the realization, both in the physical fabric of the landscape and in the moral and spiritual domain, of the ideal form of Irish society' (1993: 49). It is in the context of such a cultural tradition that the image of an Ireland scarred by unfinished housing developments and a populace weighed down by property-related debt has functioned to express so potently a wider social and cultural malaise.

Writing on the expressive function of the home in Hollywood cinema, Elisabeth Bronfen insists that we consider home a fictive rather than an actually existing place. The home is, she argues, 'a symbolic fiction' that functions to mediate our relationship to the external world and 'makes one's actual place of habitation bearable' (Bronfen, 2004: 73). For Bronfen, home is an image of belonging; a utopian fantasy that confers order and stability upon the transient spaces of everyday life that we inhabit. While the imaginative act of home-making is intensely personalized in the relationships that we construct to our own spaces of habitation, the symbolic potency of the home-place within Irish cultural and political discourse suggests that the understanding of what it means to be 'at home' is always also a shared one. As J. Macgregor Wise argues, 'cultures are ways of territorializing, the ways one makes oneself at home' (2000: 300); it is through a shared understanding of belonging that a space becomes one in which we may collectively belong. However, as an examination of Irish cultural discourses over the past decades reveals, that understanding necessarily shifts over time in response to wider social, economic and cultural changes. In the pages that follow, this chapter will trace how such shifts have found expression within Irish cinema and how cinema as a medium has articulated a changing relationship to the 'symbolic fiction' that is home. In particular, it will track a movement within Irish films from the traditional association of home with a specific, bounded place, to the image of an Ireland that conceives of itself inhabiting a fluctuating global space. It will suggest that both these images of belonging express a tension between what might be termed 'local' and 'global' perspectives on space; indeed, that the purpose of home as an imaginative construct is to negotiate between those two seemingly divergent understandings of the physical and social spaces in which we live our everyday lives. Furthermore, in the troubled home-places of recent Irish cinema, it will discern a collapse of home's comforting fictions as Irish society experiences a visceral encounter with the economic forces that determine our ability to imagine a space in which we can belong.

The 'humble cottage'

In the opening moments of *The Quiet Man* (Ford, 1952) – that most iconic cinematic expression of what it means to be at home in Ireland –

John Ford succinctly captures the spatial qualities that have long characterized the home within the Irish cultural imagination. Having arrived
by train to the bucolic Irish countryside, Sean Thornton (John Wayne),
a returning American emigrant, finds himself momentarily waylaid by
a squabbling set of locals as he endeavours to acquire directions to
the nearby village of Innisfree. Suddenly, an enigmatic figure strolls
into shot, picks up Thornton's bags and serenely announces, 'Innisfree,
this way'. As Thornton and his newly acquired escort depart by horse-
drawn cart, Ford cuts to a wide shot of the green landscape, bisected
by the perpendicular trajectories of two contrasting modes of transport.
Advancing towards the camera is the train that Thornton has presumably just vacated; its mechanical nature emphasized by the several shrill
blasts of steam that it emits. Meanwhile, the horse and cart upon which
the American now travels ambles from right to left across the bottom
of the screen, before disappearing into a tunnel just as the train passes
by overhead. Through this simple spatial arrangement, Ford succeeds
in establishing what will be the key characteristic of Innisfree and what
renders it uniquely suitable as a space in which to make oneself at home.
It is not simply that the countryside where Thornton now finds himself is a space of tradition, of an older way of life where the horse and
cart supplants the train as a means of transportation. Equally significant
as the qualities ascribed to it is the simple fact that this space is qual-
itatively different, that to cross its boundaries is to ensure a different
mode of experience, indeed a different relationship to space and time
themselves. As the geographer Doreen Massey asserts, the experience
of place as home is generally rooted in 'the security of [...] stability and an apparently reassuring boundedness' (1994: 169). Despite an
occasional subversion of its idealized vision of Irish rural life, the film
does nonetheless present the village of Innisfree as one that is, above
all, distinct and bounded. In the shot immediately following the one
described above, we see Thornton and his guide seated on the cart in
mid-shot, the landscape passing behind them as the noise of the train
gradually fades from the soundtrack. As the train's final whistle sounds,
Thornton casts a last glance backwards before settling contentedly into
his seat and lighting a cigarette. Having passed through the tunnel, neither Thornton nor the film itself will return to the mechanized world of
modern life that has been left behind. The irreversibility of this journey from train to village suggests that it is not a simple movement
in space that Thornton is undertaking, but a transformative encounter
with place. Thus, when, a few moments later, Thornton first sets his eyes
on the 'wee humble cottage' that was his childhood home, its presence
in 'the physical fabric of the landscape' functions, to echo Nash, as a

synecdochical manifestation of an idealized Irish society, as seemingly stable and natural as the cottage's rustic whitewashed walls.

Critics such as Luke Gibbons and Martin McLoone have argued that *The Quiet Man* is less concerned with any actual place called Ireland than with a particular emigrant fantasy of return (Gibbons, 1988; McLoone, 2000). What Sean Thornton seeks in the film is a sense of place that seems to have been denied him in the 'steel and pig iron furnaces' of Pittsburgh; the promise of which Ford locates in the imagined space of Ireland's rural west. Unlike the alienating city-spaces of modernity, Ireland is here offered as a bucolic space of community in which everyone can find a place in which to feel at home. As Gibbons points out, however, Ford's vision is continuous with a long-established European romantic tradition that found in Ireland 'all the attributes of a vanished pre-industrial era' (Gibbons, 1988: 204). To compound the idealized essentialism, this was an image equally embraced internally by Irish cultural nationalism, which located in Ireland's western seaboard the markers of national difference that legitimized the pursuit of an independent Irish state. Thus, the space of rural Ireland has long offered a nationally specific image of belonging that has been predicated upon its separation from the flux and uncertainty of modern, industrialized life. In *The Quiet Man*, as Thornton becomes increasingly entwined in the communal structures of Innisfree, the village acquires for him what Gaston Bachelard labels 'the intimate values of inside space' (1994: 3); a feeling of belonging within a space that is perceived as materially distinct from that which lies beyond its borders. This seductive promise of the intimate rural space can be traced through the history of Irish film, from the earliest Kalem productions, filmed in Cork and Kerry in the 1910s, to the restorative power of the rural homecoming suggested by the very title of 1992's *Into the West* (Newell). Indeed, this strong association of the rural with intimacy and homecoming persists into such recent genre films as *Perrier's Bounty* (FitzGibbon, 2010), at the end of which a petty Dublin criminal escapes the crime-ridden city to reunite with his estranged mother on the coastline of County Clare. However, it is an image of belonging that has increasingly seemed to clash with Ireland's self-image as a cosmopolitan participant in a global cultural and economic space.

A global space

Writing on the changing meanings of Irishness during the years of the economic boom, Diane Negra argues that, from the mid-1990s, the cultural construction of Ireland as a space that remained apart from economic modernity was replaced with 'a new discursive formulation that emphasise[d] the integration of Irishness and globalization' (2010: 836). Correspondingly, in contrast to a representational tradition that conflated Ireland with images of its rural west, film and television productions from this period display a new focus on the city as a space where the Irish are at home. In the urban spaces of Dublin in particular, Celtic Tiger cinema locates what Martin McLoone labels 'a kind of transglobal cool [...] of luxurious apartments and well-appointed offices' (2008: 46); a global, cosmopolitan culture that seemingly transcends any narrowly local sense of place. In a range of films such as these, we encounter characters who move comfortably through a variety of urban spaces and whose identities are less bound to any particular geographical location than to the transnational flows of capital and culture that shape their urban lives. The representation of space in these films is markedly different from that which characterizes the carefully constructed sense of place in cinema's rural Ireland. In the example from *The Quiet Man* above, we see how *mise en scène*, narrative structure and dialogue function to demarcate the rural spaces of the film as bounded and distinct. The urban spaces of Celtic Tiger cinema, by contrast, are integrated into a transnational cosmopolitan space, characterized primarily by consumerism and sexual liberalism, and are marked by constant movement and change. An illustrative example is the opening title sequence of *Cowboys and Angels* (Gleeson, 2003) that introduces us to the cityscape of Limerick with a series of helicopter shots, and pans and crash zooms across its crowded city streets. These establishing visuals are underscored with the jaunty, upbeat soundtrack of a morning radio show. Movement is constant in this opening sequence; an aesthetic quality that clearly signifies the city as a vibrant space of personal encounters. Furthermore, the images that immediately follow these suggest the erotic potential of these encounters and the ability of the city to open us up to, as yet unknown, sexual pleasures. As the music fades, a young man wanders into shot, while a voice-over asks us if we have ever felt that there was something missing from life. A reverse shot frames three young women in slow motion as they brush past the young protagonist, suggesting quite clearly what the insinuated something might be. From these few images, the changing relationship to space occasioned by the shift to the city can be deduced. While the rural promises a stable set of inter-personal relationships within a clearly defined place, the city offers fulfilment in much more individualistic terms, through the fortuitous encounters forged by the individual's own trajectory through the mutable urban space.

Above all, these city-located films celebrate the potential for self-realization expressed in the spatial trope of circulation. In films such as *About Adam* (Stembridge, 2001) and *Goldfish Memory* (Gill, 2003), characters circulate between sexual partners and sexual orientation with dizzying regularity in narratives of self-discovery that they experience as overwhelmingly positive. Furthermore, the images of the city presented in these films constantly evoke movement and fluidity, emphasizing the circulation of water and people. In *Goldfish Memory*, the shots of the city that act as punctuation for the film's cyclical storylines return repeatedly to images of the River Liffey, to the bridges traversing it, and to the Customs House and Liberty Hall, which are both set on the riverbank. We see the city's revitalized Dockland area, now a paean to the promises of international capital; even the bar that serves as one of the primary settings in the film is located on the Liffey Basin. The streets flow with attractive young Dubliners, whose chance encounters drive its convoluted romantic plot. It is as if, in the shift from the rural to the urban as its primary narrative location, Irish cinema relinquishes the pleasures of place for the possibilities of a semantically open space. Identity in these films is tied less to the inhabitation of a particular geographic location than to the ability to move comfortably through a range of different milieux, primarily those of work, consumption and sexual pursuit. The shift to the city implies a loss of organic community, of the ties to the soil that bind Sean Thornton to the cottage of his youth, and yet the ease with which the 'hip-hedonists' of Celtic Tiger cinema circulate through the urban space ensures that they always feel at home.

As suggested above, we can understand this reimagining of the cinematic home-place in the context of a wider repositioning of Ireland as a model open economy, in which 'Irish' and 'global' are no longer mutually exclusive terms. Unlike the traditional, bounded image of home – clearly marking the distinction between within and without, between those who belong and those who do not – inside and outside now cease to be competing terms. In the celebratory cinema of Celtic Tiger Ireland, the country's urban landscape is reimagined as a home that is open to all – gay, straight, black, white – in a rhetoric of non-exclusion, even as the actual experience of exclusion which persists in the country is somewhat evaded. The urban is the site that perfectly expresses such a society, as it offers a sense of place that is both local and cosmopolitan, that offers the experience of being inside and outside the national space simultaneously. The cinematic city renders the nation visible through urban landmarks and a recognizable local space, yet, in the same moment, it expresses a transcendence of the parochial, a connection to the network of global metropolises that supersedes any narrowly national concerns.

As commentators such as Ruth Barton have pointed out, however, one of the difficulties that these films encountered was that critics and audiences regretted the deficit of identifiable local markers. Indeed, Barton describes *About Adam*, a romantic comedy set in middle-class Dublin, as illustrative of 'a culturally specific desire not to be culturally specific' (2004: 112), as a film that deliberately refuses the limiting set of images that had defined Ireland cinematically, but which thereby provokes anxious questions as to which markers of Irishness ultimately remain. This echoes a wider anxiety, expressed constantly in media discourses throughout the years of economic boom: namely, that in the process of modernization, Ireland had sacrificed a distinctive sense-of-self. Within this discourse, the cosmopolitan city becomes a space that gives concrete form to these nebulous fears. Discussing the planning and architectural changes that took place in Dublin throughout the Celtic Tiger years, Diane Negra describes 'the metallic sheen of a new Dublin landscape that showcases generic, postmodern features such as the Spire, the Luas, the refurbished Connolly Rail Station, and new financial districts/cultural quarters such as the International Financial Services Centre and the Docklands' (2010: 844). She contrasts this newly constituted city space with locations like Bewleys, the long-standing coffee shop that had been so central to Dublin's cultural identity in a previous era and spoke to a far more local sense of place. As she points out, in this spatial reconstruction of the city, 'traditional conceptions of the social geography of Ireland' are replaced with a new 'flexible' Irishness, 'celebrated for its ability to behave like global capital itself' (Negra, 2010: 839).

Indeed, such is the erasure of Ireland's traditional spatial imagery in both the urban cinematic images of the late 1990s and early 2000s, and in the urban spaces themselves, that they seem to aspire to what anthropologist Marc Augé has labelled the 'non-place'. He uses this term to describe 'the spaces of supermodernity', such as shopping malls, airports and motorways, in which any sense of the local or of history are sacrificed for a homogeneity of purpose which is ultimately determined by the social and economic structures of global capitalism (Augé, 2009). He distinguishes between such non-places and 'anthropological places' that 'can be defined as relational, historical and concerned with identity' (Augé, 2009: 63), mirroring the distinction that I have drawn between the bounded home-place of the Irish rural imaginary and the capital-infused spaces of individual fulfilment that come to stand for the city within Irish visual discourse. If anthropological places suggest an organic social structure, Augé goes on to state, then non-places are governed by a 'solitary contractuality' (2009: 76); an individual relationship to space that is predicated upon the promise of personal gratification. In the non-place, history is deliberately evacuated – these spaces are defined by their purpose rather than their historical genesis – and they offer the utopian promise of access to all. In fact, the utopian nature of these spaces depends upon their refusal of history, as they offer the promise of personal reinvention through consumption and the transcendence of place. In Celtic Tiger Dublin's cinematic cityscape, we see just such a promise of escape from history. In the films discussed above, the city is visually and narratively constructed as a space in which identity can be reconstituted and in which transformative encounters are always just around the corner. The films, therefore, speak to an Irish society that seeks to redefine itself, to escape the spatial limitations expressed in the image of the traditional rural home-place. No longer defined by its ties to the land and tradition, by its exclusion from modernity, it is a society that imagines itself as comfortably inhabiting the globe.

The loss of place?

Writing on the changing perception of place in an era of speeded up communications and free movement of capital, Massey outlines the common critical position that these changes 'have undermined an older sense of a "place-called-home", and left us placeless and disorientated' (1994: 163). It is just such a shift that seems to be traced in the changing cinematic representations of Ireland discussed above; a move from economic isolation and cultural exceptionalism to integration within a global social and economic space that is cause for both celebration and anxiety. However, such a narrative relies upon what Massey elsewhere labels the 'dubious' duality 'so popular and persistent – between space and place' (2005: 68). As Massey points out, these terms are persistently counterposed within a set of oppositions such as global/local and objective/subjective (1994: 183) that function to valorize the 'authentic' experience of place and decry its denigration into mere empty, abstract space. However, if the contemporary urban image expresses the fantasy of a frictionless non-place of personal fulfilment (an image inseparable from the consumerist logic of global capitalism), then the bounded authenticity of rural place is, of course, no less suffused with fantasy, and no less implicated within the transnational movements of capital and culture, as the genesis of *The Quiet Man* in an Irish-American emigrant imaginary makes clear. As Massey argues, to insist on the actuality of place implies an understanding of space 'as somehow originarily regionalized, as always-already divided up' (2005: 6), and avoids the acknowledgement that our experience of place is always in process, constituted through a network of relations and interactions 'from the immensity of the global to the intimately tiny' (2005: 9). Any sense of place, therefore, is always determined by 'the specificity of its interactions with "the outside" ' (Massey, 1994: 169), even, and especially, when the felt authenticity of that place is predicated upon a denial of such interactions.

Home is the site that most strikingly expresses this disjunction between the inside experience of spatial autonomy and the determining reality of wider spatial and economic structures. As homeowners who fail to meet their mortgage payments forcefully experience, the private intimacy of the home-place is at all times penetrated by the abstract seeming forces of global economic exchange. At a collective level, since its rapid decline in economic fortunes in 2008, Ireland's cultural understanding of itself as a place of belonging has been doubly disrupted by an inescapable awareness of the structures that sustain any fiction of home. As the cost of borrowing on international markets became a daily news item in Irish media, the reality of Ireland's imbrication within a set of global financial structures was unavoidably pressed upon the national consciousness. Thus, the comforting fiction of Ireland as a place apart is no longer a viable one, although it lingers in the tourist images designed to market the country abroad, and in occasional US film productions such as *Leap Year* (Tucker, 2010), for which Ireland remains a bucolic fantasy rather than an actual existing place. Meanwhile, the confident equation of urban Ireland with a cosmopolitan culture that transcends geographical borders has been undermined by an international media discourse in which Ireland has become a nationally specific signifier of global financial collapse. At the same time, the visceral effects of that collapse have ensured the visibility of those structures of exclusion and inequality occluded by a celebratory Celtic Tiger culture, while the very act of inhabiting Ireland has become a possibility denied to the many thousands of mostly young people forced to emigrate in search of employment.

In this context, we might usefully ask how recent Irish cinema has approached the image of home, both in its representations of domestic space and in its wider expression of Ireland as a shared space of belonging. A brief survey of the films to emerge from Ireland over recent years would suggest that these images of home have become troubled. Since the mid-2000s, the horror genre has enjoyed something of an ascent within the Irish film industry, with films such as *Isolation* (O'Brien, 2005), *The Daisy Chain* (Walsh, 2008) and *Wake Wood* (Keating, 2010) produced with support from the Irish Film Board. In many of these films, the rural itself is the source of horror, whether due to the animals that inhabit it or the anachronistic beliefs and practices that it sustains. Frequently, it is the house upon which the horror centres, as the possibility of domestic life is denied by the atavistic forces that invade it. While this trope is by no means unique to Irish film, it does reinforce the shift in representation of the Irish rural landscape from a place of community and belonging to a site of alienation and oppression. Meanwhile, the city is increasingly figured as a space of relentless movement that, instead of expressing the promise of future fulfilment, functions to deny the possibility of home. While more critical images of the city, such as Lenny Abrahamson's *Adam and Paul* (2004), did offer a counterbalance to the celebratory city films of the Celtic Tiger era, the placelessness of that film's central protagonists has prefigured many of the recent images of Irish urban space. In *Parked* (Byrne, 2010), the disenfranchisement of the Irish male caused by economic recession is directly expressed through an image of precarious habitation. Its central character, Fred (Colm Meaney), resides in a car parked on the outskirts of Dublin city and is unable to organize the world around him in a meaningful way without the physical space of home in which to settle. Physically and emotionally inadequate homes populate *Between the Canals* (O'Connor, 2011), which is set around a Dublin inner-city flat complex, the inhabitants of which are forced to seek refuge from their difficult domestic lives in the transient pleasures of drugs and alcohol available in the city's streets. Interestingly, even in an upbeat romantic comedy like Rob and Ronan Burke's *Standby* (2014), which situates its amorous encounters in the city's streets, Dublin is frequently disparaged in the dialogue as lacking in culture and as a site of personal un-fulfilment. While this is obviously just a small sample of the films that have emerged from Ireland over the past few years, these titles are, I would suggest, representative of a wider sense of dislocation that has permeated Irish culture and media discourse in that period. Collectively, they suggest a shift in our understanding of what it means to inhabit Irish society, as they explore the consequences for identity when our shared images of belonging begin to break down.

2

Gangland Geometries: Space, Mobility and Transgression in the Veronica Guerin Films

Jenny Knell

The Celtic Tiger boom years (1995–2007) witnessed a disproportionately high percentage of Irish films that addressed themselves to Dublin's representation as a 'gangland'. Of these, fewer than five productions, all released in the period between 1998 and 2003, were based upon or alternatively contain as a supporting character, the notorious underworld figure of Martin Cahill. *The General* (Boorman, 1998), the BBC's *Vicious Circle* (Blair, 1999) and *Ordinary Decent Criminal* (O'Sullivan, 2000) each falls into the former category, as Cahill, or a thinly disguised version of that real-life character, inspires their narratives. The remaining two films, which have garnered significantly less academic attention than the Cahill adaptations, are *When the Sky Falls* (Mackenzie, 1999) and *Veronica Guerin* (Schumacher, 2003). Rather than adopting the gangster as their central trope, these films explore Dublin's criminal underworld through the journalistic perspective of Veronica Guerin (or, as in Mackenzie's film, her fictional incarnation Sinead Hamilton). Given the global outlook of these films, I consider the impact of genre upon the sense of place conveyed, specifically in terms of how the city becomes constituted by interlocking, yet discrete, social worlds. Enabled by the 'mobilities paradigm' (Sheller & Urry, 2006; Cresswell, 2010), this chapter will examine how the Guerin/Hamilton character is shown to transgress the boundaries between these spaces and, in doing so, exposes the fault lines of gender/class in Dublin's landscape.

Bodies, mobilities and class

Tim Cresswell observes that the effect of being 'in place/out of place' is 'not simply a geographical matter. It always intersects with sociocultural

24

expectations' (Cresswell, 1996: 8). The belief that 'something or someone *belongs* in one place and not in another' underpins the social constructedness of a 'normative geography'. Calling upon Pierre Bourdieu's concept of *doxa* to establish his argument, Cresswell posits that the established social order (re)produces itself through the naturalization of common sense, or 'taken-for-granted' assumptions about the world. It is through acts of transgression, specifically not acting in accordance with common-sense *doxa*, that ideology becomes mapped onto place. Because Cresswell is concerned primarily with ideology, however, it is useful to synthesize his ideas with the more 'bodily-informed' concerns of feminist geographers such as Nirmal Puwar and Doreen Massey. Puwar, like Cresswell, draws heavily on the idea that places become inscribed with socio-cultural meaning, but foregrounds the role of 'dissonant bodies' (for her purposes, women and racialized minorities) in destabilizing the 'invisible, unmarked and undeclared somatic norm' of white masculinity (2004: 8). She asserts:

> There is a connection between bodies and space, which is built, repeated and contested over time. While all can, in theory, enter, it is certain types of bodies that are tacitly designated as being the 'natural' occupants of specific positions. Some bodies are deemed as having the right to belong, while others are marked out as trespassers, who are, in accordance with how both spaces and bodies are imagined (politically, historically and conceptually), circumscribed as being 'out of place'.
>
> (Puwar, 2004: 8)

Mobility, as enacted and experienced subjectively through the body, fundamentally enables any subversion of the dominant spatial regime. The interrelationship between bodies and space emerges as particularly salient in relation to the urban because, as Elizabeth Grosz notes, the city is 'the condition and milieu in which corporeality is socially, sexually, and discursively produced' (1999: 382). Although Grosz's framework productively interrogates how bodies transform, contest and reinscribe boundaries within the urban landscape, mobility must also be considered as a function of the socio-economic; that is, hierarchies of inequality and power (Sheller, 2014). Massey suggests that 'power-geometries' position individuals and social groups in distinct ways in relation to global capital, such that 'some are more on the receiving end of it than others; some are effectively imprisoned by it' (1993: 61). Thus, mobility not only becomes a question of movement, but also 'immobilities and moorings' (Hannam, Sheller & Urry, 2006).

The visibility of a 'power-geometry' became especially pronounced during the Celtic Tiger era, as socio-economic polarity increased despite the unprecedented level of wealth circulating within the country (Allen, 2000). Success, within the neoliberal era, assumed a gendered dimension, as women were posited as the 'privileged subjects of social change' (McRobbie, 2009: 15). If, ostensibly, women became the Celtic Tiger's 'winners' in terms of social advances (meanwhile being pathologized for availing of these new opportunities), men emerged as the 'losers' under the new socio-economic regime. Because they deal with the 'underclass', both films engage with American gangster mythology that proffered crime as the only viable route for upward social mobility for those on the class and/or ethnic margins of the capitalist system. In the Dublin context, the material rewards from organized crime enabled the drug barons (all hailing from similarly disadvantaged, working-class backgrounds) to occupy the privileged spaces of the elite, thus undermining the established 'power-geometry'. The films' interrogation of the spatial dilemmas raised by such 'illegitimate' social mobility, in conjunction with Guerin/Hamilton's entry into spaces that would normally be exclusionary to her on the basis of class/gender, serves to expose the 'somatic norms' inscribed upon urban space.

Generic worlds

Before assessing how bodies move through space, however, the differing production contexts of the films must be considered. Mackenzie's *When the Sky Falls*, released just three years after Guerin's death, began as a collaborative writing project between journalist Michael Sheridan and Guerin, and sought to address the disturbing escalation of drugs and violent crime in Dublin. Guerin's death prior to the completion of the script led to the involvement of two other writers – Ronan Gallagher and the novelist Colum McCann – and precipitated its shift in focus from the crime bosses to her own martyrdom; the key element then driving the revised storyline. Mackenzie's filtering of the narrative through the more televisual, 'local', aesthetic of the crime thriller genre (in contrast to Schumacher's larger-than-life biopic) facilitates a more explicit social critique of Celtic Tiger Dublin. As Mackenzie recalls in relation to his iconic gangster film *The Long Good Friday* (1980), *When the Sky Falls* was produced 'with a specific era and a city' in mind (20th Century Fox/Sky Pictures, 2000):

In a way it reminded me of *The Long Good Friday* because the London of the 1980s was a bit like that, a city on the rise, affluent, looking good, and along with that comes all this crime, which always seems to happen. So that was what attracted me, because I don't think it had been seen in films before. They all look a bit black and white to me, with cobble-stoned streets and horses pulling Guinness carts.

(Linehan, 2000: B47)

It is significant that Mackenzie transposes the storyline from 1996 to (then contemporaneous) 1999, in order to situate the narrative more firmly within the Celtic Tiger milieu. While the film is heavily reliant on a 'glass and steel' aesthetic to convey a sense of urban progress (this is underscored by the locational substitutes employed: for example, newly built Docklands' offices stand in for the typically aging exteriors of civil service buildings), Mackenzie (alongside accomplished cinematographer Seamus Deasy) consciously breaks with these older, more sentimental-ized representational regimes of the city in order to present Dublin as a modern, yet crime-ridden capital. The film's opening sequence, a fast-paced montage overlaid by a pulsating electronic score, exempli-fies this shift. Opening with an aerial shot of the Bailey Lighthouse in Howth (later a meeting point for Hamilton and the IRA), the image dis-solves into a panning shot of the East Link Bridge and the surrounding industrial landscape of the Docklands. This is followed by a montage of images depicting a journalistic representation of the underworld: shadowy figures with redacted eyes that simulate the long-angle lens photography consistent with surveillance and various newspaper-style sepia-infused images with words like 'dangerous', 'drug smuggler' and 'Dublin city'. The built environment of the inner city is represented through rapid zooms under the O'Connell Street and Ha'Penny Bridges and, later, the Guinness factory, which break with the representational conventions of these structures as Bord Fáilte images, instead portray-ing them as menacing urban spaces in which drug deals occur. The sense that the city has been devoured by drugs is concretized in a later scene in which Shaughnessy, overlooking a nocturnal, twinkling Dublin from Killiney Hill, observes that 'there's a needle for every point of light'.

Veronica Guerin, the Jerry Bruckheimer-produced, big-budget Hollywood blockbuster, is less concerned with Dublin's Celtic Tiger re-imaging than emplacing its universal narrative of individual heroism and sacrifice within an equally legible urban landscape. Schumacher's film imme-diately announces itself as the more cinematic of the two, opening with an aerial tracking shot of the Poolbeg chimneys before moving in towards the port, where Gilligan's dealers are unloading the trafficked drugs from containers and preparing them for distribution in the flats. Arguably, in what Pat Brereton has deemed the film's 'Americanisation of urban Irish identity' (2009: 110), Schumacher condenses Dublin's drug problem to a stage-like flat complex in the inner city (the fictional Ballymartin), not unlike Chicago or New York's 'projects', that serves to explicate the underworld's vice grip upon these communities. When Guerin enters the flats, she encounters two young children playing with used syringes on the kerb while, in the stairwell, a young mother in the throes of addiction neglects the infant clinging to her. The dramatic impact of these heavy-handed images of 'lost innocence' is heightened by the film's score, which relies upon the unmistakably Celtic sounds of the *uilleann* pipes to convey the drug problem as a national tragedy, while also serving to ally Guerin with 'a potent journalistic mythos of heroic sacrifice, which emanates through a noble line of Irish martyrs' (Brereton, 2009: 114). Thus, although the narrative is undeniably fixed in the local, these stock urban images are shot and contextualized to facilitate an unproblematic translation to an international audience.

In this sense, *where* the films emplace the drug problem is instructive. Whereas Schumacher characterizes the drug issue as one exclusively arising from the disadvantaged inner city, arguably in order for the film to resonate with the more universal experience of urban deprivation, Mackenzie's representation underscores how drugs (not simply restricted to heroin) have permeated every social strata of Irish society. *When the Sky Falls* shows Jamie, a young junkie who is later framed by the police and beaten to death, shooting heroin between his toes in a dilapidated Georgian flat, but equally, unlike *Veronica Guerin's* overly simplified take on the socio-cultural impact of drugs, depicts the emergent rave subculture of the 1990s (Hackett's club is modelled after the infamous Asylum Club on O'Connell Street) that crucially became fuelled by 'middle-class' (or 'lifestyle') drugs such as cocaine and ecstasy. While *Veronica Guerin's* evasion of the Celtic Tiger drug subculture enables the film to focus more resolutely on the protagonist as a lone crusader in pursuit of the truth, Mackenzie's less mythic and more socially conscious portrayal of Celtic Tiger excess enables an overt discourse to emerge in relation to Dublin's class-biased approach to the drug issue. Hamilton forcefully asserts in response to a fellow journalist's apathy in relation to escalating levels of heroin addiction in the inner city:

This shit's been happening for fifteen years and did you report it then? No. Why? Because it was working-class kids passing this stuff amongst themselves. Who gives a flying fuck about them? But now it's the middle-classes finding a package of smack in their teenage daughter's knicker drawer. Ah, that's news.

Transgressive bodies, destabilized spaces?

This quotation segues neatly into Cresswell's notion of 'socio-cultural expectations' and the question of how both filmmakers divide the city into three discrete social worlds with boundaries that are both challenged and reified through Guerin/Hamilton's intervention. These are the working-class inner city that becomes ground zero for the drug trade, the middle-class exurban environment in which Guerin/Hamilton lives with her family and the nouveaux riche spaces of the drug barons. Guerin/Hamilton's status as a middle-class woman intervening into the male-dominated, working-class spaces of the drug barons is a crucial dynamic for exploring, and ultimately transgressing, the normative classed/gendered divisions of the urban landscape. Although the concern of this chapter rests primarily with class, the fact that Guerin/Hamilton is a woman operating within a 'man's world' generates issues in relation to the collapse of public/private space, historically constituted as male/female; questions that would not be raised if not for her gender. Significantly, in both films, Guerin/Hamilton's collapse of the boundaries between her personal and professional life is encapsulated in the fact that she has no office: she works from home or, more symbolically, in terms of her automobility through the urban landscape in her red sports car. Her spatial freedom in this regard enables her association more with the 'physical infrastructure of mobility' (Sheller & Urry, 2000: 740); places such as motorways and roundabouts are given priority over the more traditional feminine realm of 'immobile, place-bound domesticity' (Skeggs, 2004: 51). Furthermore, the fact that Guerin/Hamilton is killed by a motorcycle assassin on the Naas dual carriageway underscores how automobility – itself a function of her privileged class position – becomes the agent of her own demise precisely because movement enables these spatial transgressions.

Guerin/Hamilton's entry into spaces in which she, as a woman, is deemed to be 'out of place' (both literally and figuratively) causes her to be vilified in a gendered context through allegations of unethical conduct and maternal irresponsibility. Although also present in *Veronica Guerin* both sets of issues are more forcefully articulated in *When the Sky*

Falls. Unlike Schumacher's Guerin, Hamilton wilfully draws her family into the underworld spaces of her investigation, for example, when she brings her young son Colum on a late-night stakeout in which he literally tumbles out onto Dublin's mean streets as an opportunistic thief opens their unlocked car door. This behaviour is again repeated when Hamilton brings Colum to an anti-drug march in Summerhill, which results in a row with her husband over her commitment to her work at the expense of the family's safety. Ironically, and seemingly underscoring the gendered double bind faced by Hamilton as a working woman, she is later told by a colleague to 'take up a placard for women who leave their kids home alone'. In this sense, her 'gall' in attempting to negotiate a work and family life, in addition to the belief that she is chasing celebrity status, encourages her demonization within her own professional circle. Although the 'bad mother' discourse is less prominent in *Veronica Guerin*, Schumacher's protagonist is deemed by a female competitor to have 'some balls' to shoot herself in the leg for publicity (following Traynor's physical attempt to immobilize her), thus denying her the professional respectability intrinsically afforded to men in her field. By extension, the charge that Guerin/Hamilton lacks femininity and her refusal to 'perform' as such leads her to become derisively coded as masculine.

Revealingly, this ascription is reversed when Guerin/Hamilton enters the working-class, male-dominated spaces of the criminal underworld. Here, the power dynamics of class and gender are revealed through the process of destabilization. In *When the Sky Falls*, Hamilton, likewise denied her credibility as a professional journalist, becomes overtly sexualized in an attempt to reconstitute the class/gender power balance. For instance, in one particularly instructive scene, Hamilton's presence in a working-class suburb is met with contempt by a group of low-level dealers who physically attempt to block her access to this space. Immediately 'othered' (underscored by Mackenzie's lingering shots of the male gaze upon her), Hamilton produces her press badge only to be told that her credentials are 'shag all use around here, press wankers'. Significantly, within this dynamic, Hamilton is not masculinized (as in her professional world), but her identity is reduced to her sexual objectification. Before his behaviour is 'corrected' by O'Fagan (the character inspired by Traynor who subsequently reveals himself as sexually motivated in his dealings with Hamilton), Tattoo refers to her as a 'bit of gash'. Thus, what this scene highlights is that in the absence of economic capital, the working-class men perform hypermasculine identities in order to dominate a female who holds a superior class position. Again, this point is reinforced when the same collective of men drink champagne in a hot tub while watching Hamilton's interview on television. Closing in on her image, and manipulating Hamilton's words relating to her exposure of the criminal underworld, Tattoo drops his towel and comments that he will 'expose himself' to her. By comparison, *Veronica Guerin* downplays this misogynistic discourse (although present in a scene in which Meehan labels a female guard as a lesbian because she fails to appreciate his form) and thus sidesteps the class/gender problematics raised by Mackenzie.

The sexual hostility directed towards Hamilton (a symbolic attempt to put her 'in place') cannot be read without reference to Mackenzie and Schumacher's reversal of the traditional male gaze of the gangster film. As a woman of privileged means, Hamilton/Guerin's presence within a world in which female subordination is normalized makes strange the embedded gender and power relations of this space. In both films, women's prescribed roles are delineated as the wives/girlfriends/mistresses of the gangsters or the prostitutes/strippers at the brothels; their limited use-value commodified in explicitly material terms. *When the Sky Falls* articulates this dynamic through O'Fagan's girlfriend. With her limited access to the 'power-geometry' juxtaposed against Hamilton's greater one, Mary moonlights as the lounge singer at the night club and becomes the victim of O'Fagan's abuse when he stubs cigarettes out into her skin. That Mary ultimately reveals O'Fagan's role in shooting Hamilton and gives voice to her abuse before fleeing to Liverpool runs contrary to the paradigmatic logic of the gangster film, in which females remain submissive to the male characters. Similarly, in Schumacher's film, Guerin and Traynor's girlfriend engage in a mutual recognition of their precarious position as regards their safety within a homosocial underworld marked by violence (symbolic and physical) against women. Although this character does not feature to the same extent as Mackenzie's incarnation, the abuse of women comes to the forefront in the film's extended closing sequence in which a prostitute, presumably watching the news footage of Guerin's death, is shown crying on the floor of a wrecked hotel room while Gilligan coldly stares into the distance. In this sense, the genre's reframing through the female body underscores (while still enabling) a critique of the way in which women have been traditionally dominated/disempowered (in other words, kept 'in place') within such narratives.

In addition to questions of gendered bodies/spaces discussed above, the films also construct a triad of urban worlds, the working-class inner city, Guerin/Hamilton's middle-class exurban milieu and the nouveaux riche spaces of the drug barons that inscribe class upon space through the depiction of bodies 'out of place'. Although the predominant displacement considered by both films is predicated on Guerin/Hamilton's gender and privileged class position, it is also instructive to consider how the illegitimate social mobility of the gangster disrupts the normative spatialization of class within the urban landscape. Echoing Pierre Bourdieu's theory of distinction (1984), both films underscore the 'out of placeness' of the drug lords within the spaces of Dublin's wealthy elite by contesting their legitimacy through their cultural capital, or lack thereof; an aspect that marks them out as imposters in this world. For example, in *Veronica Guerin*, Gilligan's attempt to 'perform' wealth by inviting a series of upper-crust British horse enthusiasts to his Jessborough Equestrian Centre comes undone when he makes the following low-brow joke in response to a guest's comment on the impressive size of the property: 'Said the nun to the sailor!' Although this comment is met with an uncomfortable silence, Gilligan's wife follows with the proud claim that the 'champers' and caviar are imported. As *Veronica Guerin*'s production designer Nathan Crowley recalls of Jessborough, 'I tried to find somewhere that was really gaudy. These people had lots of money, no values and bad taste' (Touchstone Pictures, 2003: 11). Crowley's assertion is also borne out through scenes that, for example, depict Traynor indulging his vanity in a tanning booth and Meehan confrontationally tossing his designer watch at the guards during a strip search, boasting that its value outstrips their annual salaries. In this sense, although the criminals are shown to have the economic means to gain access to the elite spaces of wealth, class, as a socio-cultural concept, remains resilient against this 'breach'.

Likewise, although with a more clichéd approach informed by Hollywood gangster archetypes, *When the Sky Falls* emphasizes the vulgarity with which the criminals flaunt their newly acquired wealth. Hackett, for instance, is met with a limousine, champagne and arrangements for his sexual needs to be sated upon his release from prison. In the latter scene, Mackenzie's tight framing of Hackett's sweaty face foregrounds the grotesqueness not only of his character, but also the culture of excess adopted by the drug barons. Indeed, the majority of the film's underworld dealers are depicted as inner city 'hard men' (iconically indexed as such through accent, track-suited bodies and cropped haircuts), which inherently facilitates their reading as 'out of place' in the monied Celtic Tiger milieu and – again recalling Bourdieu's theory of distinction – refined culture. Cosgrave, however, emerges as more layered in this regard and challenges this dynamic. When Hamilton meets the 'Runner' at his art deco home in Sandycove (an exclusive coastal village in South County Dublin), she discovers that although he enjoys the trappings of wealth, as evidenced by his penchant for expensive jet skis, he sardonically claims to live a modest lifestyle. As the scene continues, Hamilton watches as Cosgrave hits golf balls into the Irish Sea (his self-appropriated driving range) while commenting that he would love to 'hit that bollix out there on his yacht'. Cosgrave's refusal to align himself with the culture of the space he now inhabits underscores the inscription of class upon the urban landscape. In comparison to other characters that remain passively 'othered', Cosgrave actively 'others' himself by subverting the authority of this space, a tactic, as Cresswell notes, that is associated with dispossessed social groups (1996: 46): for the most part Dublin's 'underclass' whose marginalization encouraged the development of a criminal culture that, in the Celtic Tiger years, permeated the mainstream.

Conclusion

Both Mackenzie and Schumacher employ the trope of the female journalist in order to explore Dublin's fractured socio-spatial terrain. Hamilton/Guerin's 'normative' spatialization in a middle-class exurban idyll is strengthened by her 'othering'; through hyper-sexualization, within spaces marked out as exclusively masculine and working class. Likewise, although the criminals are shown to have destabilized spatial boundaries by their movement from disadvantaged areas of the city to economically exclusive spaces, their bodies remain inscribed as working class and further lacking the cultural capital that would normalize them within this world. As such, these representations effect a 'criminalization' of the working class that taps into a broader cultural discourse branding working-class wealth as 'aberrant' and its male subjects 'backward' and 'crude'. Further evidencing the resilience of such class/gender stereotypes, both films show how the city's socio-spatial boundaries are contested by mobility (either Hamilton/Guerin's or the criminals') but ultimately resistant to transgression. Although *When the Sky Falls*, engages directly with the Celtic Tiger context, *Veronica Guerin* emerges as the more cinematically realized and legible film in terms of Schumacher's articulation of the city through a series of (classed and gendered) worlds. In this sense, the film's (over)simplification of the urban landscape is advantageous as the connections between the aforementioned worlds are more clearly defined than in Mackenzie's well-meaning but uncertain rendering of Dublin's 'gangland'.

3
'Don't Use Your Own Accents!': Representations of Dublin's Accents in Contemporary Film

Nicholas O'Riordan

> Accent is one of the most intimate and powerful markers of group identity and solidarity as well as of individual difference.
>
> (Nacify, quoted in Barton, 2006: 174)

Against a history of misrepresentation in Irish film, whether it be the recurrence of the 'stage Irishman' in early Irish cinema, to the challenged representations and romanticization of the Irish landscape on screen, or images of violence (Rockett, Gibbons & Hill, 1988), public interest and commentary on Irish cinema is wrought with criticism of 'false' representations of Ireland and its people. However, more than any other of these criticized aspects of cinematic Ireland, representations and misrepresentations of the Irish accent have sparked some of the most sustained and common popular criticism. With post-Celtic Tiger Irish cinema frequently utilizing a more socio-realist aesthetic, the fact remains that both anecdotal and online evidence (to mention the broadest reference Internet sweep) shows that the words 'Irish film accent' generate pages of search results that all seem to follow the same theme: 'The Worst Irish Accents in Hollywood Movies' (Corrigan, 2015), 'Begorrah, Sure Is That for Real? Ten Worst Irish Accents in Film' (Phelan, 2014), 'Top 10 Dreadful Fake Irish Accents in Films' (Lee, 2013) and 'The Worst Irish Accents in Film History' (Selby, 2014) being representative examples. The sheer volume of popular criticism of portrayals of Irish accents on screen indicates both a massive popular interest, but also an area so relatively under-analysed within Irish film studies. In the public sphere, considerations of accent in Irish film are marked by an overarching negativity (with 'poor' Irish accents constantly criticized) and stand as perhaps the most commented upon feature of misrepresentation of Ireland on screen. This chapter examines the dissociative culture of the developments in accent in the Irish context over the past 25 years and the associated representations in recent Irish film. There is historical precedent for motivating this discourse, ideologically and politically, and to trace this detail will necessarily shift my attention momentarily from accent to language. Although this requires a historical leap of almost one century, this chapter will presuppose that the significance of the diachronic comparison is adequately justified in ideological readings of national protectionism and essentialized identity construction.

Identitarian language and the national self

On 25 November 1892, Douglas Hyde delivered a speech before the Irish National Literary Society in Dublin, stressing the 'Necessity for De-Anglicising Ireland' (cited in Duffy, Sigerson & Hyde, 1973: 117). At a period of significant linguistic change in Ireland, with the Irish language under threat of being overtaken by English, and with Gaeilge strategically and deliberately mobilized as a cultural and political anti-colonial weapon, Hyde warned of the dangers of 'neglecting what is Irish, and hastening to adopt, pell-mell, and indiscriminately, everything that is English' (cited in Duffy, Sigerson & Hyde, 1973: 117).

With heavily preservationist and nationalist overtones, Hyde's address demonstrated the perceived inseparability of language and identity, about which George Steiner notes that 'when a language dies, a way of understanding the world dies with it, a way of looking at the world' (cited in Olaziregi, White & Addis, 2004: 13). The central focus of Hyde's speech is the identification of national qualities of the Irish language with his overarching call for the importance of keeping Ireland essentially unique, with language serving as a marker of national individuality. This was echoed much later by Jones who, in a 2001 article, stated that 'the active achievement of national identity through social practices like language helps individuals to believe that they belong to the nation' (2001: 1064). Hyde's cultural protectionism is embedded in the concept of Irish 'cultural nationalism' which Irish cultural commentator Martin McLoone identifies as a 'set of assumptions about the nature of Irish identity [which] came to dominate the cultural agenda' in the late 19th and early 20th centuries (2000: 11). These assumptions included mainstream oppositional notions of an essentialist bent, namely that the nation was '*Irish-speaking* in language',

'*Gaelic* in culture', and that this culture was 'rural', 'catholic' and 'should aspire to *self-sufficiency* both economic and cultural' (McLoone, 2000: 12). With the increasing influence of English culture on Irish society in the late 19th century, advocates for Irish language and culture, including Douglas Hyde, wrote and spoke of the dangers of foreign influences both disrupting Irish cultural uniqueness and national identity.

In the 1930s, there was again significant public discussion surrounding language in Ireland, this time relating directly to the influence of cinema on linguistic behaviour, with 'American and British accents provid[ing] a rude shock to those who had been engaged in an ideological struggle to establish a distinctive cultural identity' (Rockett, Gibbons & Hill, 1988: 52). Kevin Rockett, in the seminal work *Cinema and Ireland*, makes reference to Oliver St John Gogarty, who, speaking in the Seanad on a bill relating to the censorship of films, commented that the talkies 'use a cosmopolitan lingo which is always degrading, and which is distracting the English speaking nations from the source of the language and from its own centre' (Rockett, Gibbons & Hill, 1988: 52). In this debate, Gogarty and colleagues warned that:

[i]f we allow talkies – this international lingo of vulgarity to be added to the cinema palaces we will do the country an incalculable harm, because, in my opinion, what is most precious to the nation is that the emotional nature of the nation be kept within its own confines. (1930)

This preservationist, more sceptical message echoes Hyde's speech of more than 40 years earlier. Delivered before the Irish Literary Society, Hyde's choice of audience demonstrates and identifies the tangible link between a national artistic output and linguistic behaviour in the country, with Hyde warning that we 'must set our face sternly against penny dreadfuls, shilling shockers, and still more, the garbage of vulgar English weeklies' (1973: 159). However, in spite of both of these, and more striking warnings, this influence of the media on linguistic behaviour has grown significantly, with Sackett, in 1979, writing that '[n]ever before in linguistic history has a cultural force been so comprehensively enveloping and pervasive as are the mass media today' (237). While this is immediately evident in discourses around, and performances within, contemporary representations of 'Irishness' on screen, it is not without historical precedent.

Especially significant in his warning against foreign cultural influence, particularly when considered from a contemporary perspective, is Hyde's aside, in which he asks the audience to:

> suppose for a moment [...] that there were to arise a series of Cromwells in England for the space of one hundred years [...] making Ireland a land of wealth and factories, whilst they extinguished every thought and every idea that was Irish, and left us, at last, after a hundred years of good government, fat, wealthy and populous, but with all our characteristics gone, with every external that at present differentiates us from the English lost or dropped [...] our Irish intonation changed, as far as possible [...] the fact that we were not of Saxon origin dropped out of sight and memory.
>
> (1973: 121–2)

Transposing Hyde's argument onto the contemporary moment, by adopting the viewpoint that accent holds the status which language held in the late 19th century, many correlations become evident between the protectionist panic over the Irish language in the 1890s and the proliferation of commonplace discourses and critique of ideologies of identitarianism of Irish accents one century earlier. These may be suggestive, as both are strongly linked to comparable notions of identification. In this seminal speech, Hyde argues that 'the Irish race is at present [in 1892] in the most anomalous position, imitating England and yet apparently hating it', asking '[h]ow can it produce anything good in literature, art, or institutions as long as it is actuated by motives so contradictory?' (1973: 121). This anomalous position of Irish identity is mirrored in contemporary performances of accent and, as this chapter proposes, the complex and deliberate cinematic framing of accent.

Accent in contemporary Ireland

Over the past 25 years, Dublin has been the setting of a major shift in accent. While traditionally viewed as a primarily geographical marker, accent began to be substantially differently infused by distinctions in identity and class. This shift can largely be attributed to a process of swift economic growth known as the 'Celtic Tiger', which led to arguably the greatest socio-economic and therefore socio-cultural changes and social identitarian stratification in recent Irish history. With increased wealth, a nouveau riche culture of south Dubliners emerged at the time: a social group that could be identified as more 'globalized', or 'Americanized' than as 'traditionally Irish'. With comments on the Americanization of Irish culture noted as early as 1924, 'Ireland's first Film Censor in 1924 James Montgomery declared that the greatest danger to Ireland came not from the Anglicization of Ireland, but from the Los Angelesation of Ireland' (Rockett, 1991: 18). With fashion, materialism, sexuality and other forms of identity expression (including accent) showing unprecedentedly significant signs of global influence, perhaps the most striking shift in identity expression was the notable shift in accent, about which Hickey and Moore have written at length (Hickey, 2005, 2007, 2011; Moore, 2011).

Demonstrating a rising critical interest in identity discourses, Raymond Hickey identifies a twofold division in accents in Dublin in the Celtic Tiger years. The first of these accents, the 'local' form of speech, is widely utilized by 'speakers who use the historically continuous vernacular [and] show strongest identification with traditional Dublin life of which the accent is very much a part' (cited in Moore, 2011: 47). This accent is significantly historically rooted and its users are often characterized as working-class Northside Dubliners. In opposition to this accent, a 'new' accent emerged: the 'D4' accent, which stands as a signifier of the nouveau riche class who 'do not identify with what they see as a narrow and restricted local culture' (Hickey, 2007: 354). Hickey labels this group, associated with the affluent Southside of Dublin, as 'new' (2007: 354). This is a social group of individuals who aim to rid themselves of signs of local Dublin, drawing cultural and social inspiration from outside of a (then perceived) 'backwards' Ireland.

Referencing Terence Dolan, Ed Power writes that '[e]ncouraged by the economic transformation of the past decade to shun all that is provincial and idiosyncratically Irish, an entire generation is tripping over itself to embrace a way of speaking it perceives to be modern, progressive and fashionable' (2005). A television advert for the mobile telephone operator Esat Digifone, which aired in the late 1990s on Irish national television, showcases the broad cultural perceptions of accent in the Celtic Tiger years. In this advert, after acquiring the phone number of an attractive young woman who passes it to him as she leaves a stylish urban bar, the stylish male protagonist walks outside to phone the woman. Having not formally met, and with no verbal exchanges up to this point, the humorous pay-off of the advert comes as he exits the bar to phone her, and with a very strong, Kerry/Cork 'local' accent: 'Hiya Kate, it's me, the guy from the bar ... no, honestly it is ... Hello?' In an article in the *Irish Independent*, Simon Moore is quoted as stating that '[t]here are some bars in Dublin where people wouldn't be caught dead sounding the way their parents do. They want to fit in, and that means sounding like you are American, [...] if our accents are integral to who we are then Ireland is suffering a collective identity crisis' (Power, 2005). With a stylish, romantic aesthetic and cosmopolitan *mise en scène*, reinforced by the extra-diegetic soundtrack of the American song 'Somethin' Stupid', this advert showcases both the type of bar and the cultural moment that Moore references. Hickey writes that '[f]or all young people who do not identify themselves linguistically with their own locality, [...this] new pronunciation is their phonological norm' (2007: 360). As this advert showcases, anything other than this new phonological norm is laughable or, as it suggests, just simply 'stupid'. In an explicit instance of what Lippi-Green terms 'dialectism' (language-based discrimination) (cited in Steffensen, 2012: 518), this advert transmits the message that to get ahead in Ireland, it is not enough to adopt some of the 'new' markers of identity (such as wearing stylish clothes, haunting fashionable bars and consuming trendy drinks): rather, to succeed, one must fully abandon one's Irishness, including voice (with the acquisition of the female in this advert reflecting acquisition of the modern society's acceptance).

Hickey (2000: 303) terms the linguistic equivalent of this rejection of local culture 'dissociation'; a process where 'younger newly affluent speakers "hive off" from the masses, by avoiding pronunciations seen as emblematic either of working class Dublin identity or of rural Irish provincialism' (Moore, 2011: 42). Questioning the origins of this new accent, Moore writes that

> Debate rages on in the newspapers and in the Irish media as to whether [this new accent] looks to America or England for phonological inspiration [...] even though they can't agree on what D4 is in imitation of, all seem to agree that it is in imitation – that it is, in fact, imitation as opposed to 'real' or authentic.
>
> (2011: 49)

The notion that accents can be perceived as 'authentic' is one that is recurrent in both popular and academic commentary. Although the notion of the 'authentic' accent has been debunked as an 'idealistic' attribute, with 'contemporary social science [...] radically skeptical about the feasibility of authentic experience' (Coupland, 2007: 180), an example of this discursive contact with notions of 'authenticity' is evident in a recent press release from Jana Bennett at the BBC. In relation to the company's efforts to become more linguistically inclusive, the press release states that there is a belief that 'a genuine sense of place and community will help draw an audience into a story and win their hearts', and they hope to do this by delivering 'distinctive voices with an authentic sense of place' (Bennett, 2010).

In the Irish context, the ideological use of accent to portray a sense of solidarity and inclusivity has been used to significant marketing effect in advertisements for 'Brennan's Bread', a campaign which Helen Kelly Holmes has assessed by focusing on the linguistic elements. Holmes talks of a 'process of informalization' whereby 'traditional barriers between different speech domains have been blurred and weakened, and thus we find [...] informal speech on what is generally a formal medium' (2005: 375). Holmes writes that 'motivations behind this move are based in the idea of constructing the speaker as one of us, rather than one of them', often using 'anachronistic language [...] that seems to relate to an earlier time' serving to situate the speaker as a more 'authentic' or 'locally situated' member of society (2005: 375). This linguistic 'informalization' (Holmes, 2005: 375) has recently been heard in Irish film, particularly in a post/counter-Celtic Tiger context. In what can be read as a reaction to the proliferation of images (and sounds) of a 'new' Dublin brought about by the increased wealth, infrastructure and general globalization associated with the Celtic Tiger years. In a post-Celtic Tiger context, the perceived 'artificiality' of the associated culture has led to a situation where the very accent which signified stagnancy, poverty and an 'old', 'irrelevant' Ireland, became the accent to signify 'authenticity', the 'real Ireland', and one that served as a strong, tangible marker of the Irishness, and nationalism, lost in the boom years. This has been used recently to strong effect in 'counter-Celtic Tiger' films including *Kisses* (Daly, 2010), *Dollhouse* (Sheridan, 2012), *Adam and Paul* (Abrahamson, 2004), *Stalker* (O'Connor, 2012), *Between the Canals* (O'Connor, 2011), *Parked* (Byrne, 2013), *Life's a Breeze* (Daly, 2013) and in television dramas including *Love/Hate* (Carolan, 2010–14).

Accent in recent Irish film

In his seminal publication *Style: Language Variation and Identity*, Nikolas Coupland introduces the term 'voicing' to explain 'how a speaker represents or implies ownership of an utterance or a way of speaking', stating that 'speakers often quote or reconstruct the words of other people, and in doing so they can inflect those source voices in various ways, giving them particular identity traits and qualities' (2007: 114). This phenomenon is widespread in Irish film, with characters often 'putting on' other voices for ideological reasons, and I propose that this voicing reflects a similar, more wide-ranging situation evident in accents in contemporary Irish culture.

Kieron J. Walsh's *When Brendan Met Trudy* (2000) bases its narrative on protagonist Brendan, who is often heard reciting quotations in the voice of Hollywood heroes such as John Wayne. In this less subtle instance of voicing, the performance of accent is framed within a meta-cinematic aesthetic. However, the narrative and characterization point to a feeling that something is lacking in Brendan's opinion of his own Irish identity, perhaps relating to a crisis in gendered and national identity at the time. Through Brendan's employment of other voices, he performs his desired personality: when teaching, for example, Brendan raises his tone and uses an almost stereotypical philosophical voicing. When he performs the voices of his favourite movie stars, the device signifies his temporary and escapist change in identity, particularly in relation to his newfound sexual prowess.

In an earlier example, similar voicing of the accent of the 'other' comes into play in a prominent and memorable scene from the Alan Parker adaptation of Roddy Doyle's novel, *The Commitments*. In a significant scene, the protagonist Jimmy Rabbitt is managing a rehearsal of the eponymous band. As *The Commitments* (1991) explores themes of local identity, marginalization and the working-class struggle, it makes references throughout to the importance of pride in one's locality and one's local identity, with Rabbitt famously claiming that the Irish are the 'blacks of Europe' and that the band should be 'black and proud'. With identity thus positioned as a core thematic concern, several moments allude to the desire of the Irish to appear un-Irish, or to admire non-Irish values or stars. Jimmy's father, played by Colm Meaney, makes constant references to his love for Elvis, even performing the character by singing imitatively with a classically 'Elvis' lilt. Similarly, in a montage sequence when Jimmy auditions prospective band members, we see a collection of different Dublin teens calling to the protagonist's door. Through costume, characterization and voice, we are presented with a youth culture influenced heavily by outside images and sounds, with many of these characters imitating other, specifically non-Irish identities in both appearance and accent. However, the most prominent and explicit reference to this linguistic quality comes with the voiced acknowledgement of the incapability of the Irish accent to fit in with the 'cool' music that they are singing. As the backing vocalists of the band sing the refrain from 'Mustang Sally', they voice the lyrics 'Ride, Sally, Ride' in strongly 'local' Dublin accents. Jimmy quickly steps in to demand that the singers 'don't use [their] own accents', and that it's pronounced 'Ride, Sally, Ride', not '*Roy-ad*, Sally, *Roy-ad*'.

Examples of this kind of voicing, deliberately performed by characters and thus framed on screen, are seen in several other recent Irish films, including *Adam and Paul*. In one scene, one of the dual protagonists approaches a café counter as his partner sits at a table and scouts the location for possible things of value to steal. While attempting to 'fit in' to the environment that he perceives as of more exclusive social status than his own heroin-addicted persona, Paul asks for 'a pot of tea, please' in a voice that attempts to be more 'correct' than that of his regular speech. The moment reflects his realization of the less socially desirable (and contextually betraying) nature of his own strongly 'local' accent. As was the case with the instances mentioned above from the film *When Brendan Met Trudy*, these allusions to the negative prestige of the local Irish accent may well identify a new collective crisis of socially stratified identity, prominent in an Ireland that was quickly modernizing as the economic gap between the 'haves' and the 'have-nots' stretched.

Moving further in his explanation of 'voicing', Coupland writes of 'processes of imitation and parody' (2007: 114). Examples of this abound in many instances of contemporary Irish film, the frequency of which points to a general tone of individuals' uncertainty surrounding 'traditional', or 'local' Irish accents. The character of Gerry Boyle (Colm Meaney) in *Intermission* (Crowley, 2003) again signifies this feeling of general 'inadequacy' through his performance of identity, both when he voices and performs a generic 'other' as the American reality TV detective. Through this performance, Boyle makes frequent references to his inspirations, and his performance of identity is framed as overtly constructed and 'played up for the camera'. Although his accent is not intensely affected, because of his use of phrasing and recognizably American colloquialisms, his performance can be read as both an indication and recognition of north Dublin 'local' accents as 'authentic', 'real' and 'historically rooted'. With his use of Americanisms comes a suggestion that Irish identity is not 'cool' enough for modern media, a fact that may imply that Ireland and Irish characters are suffering somewhat of a desire to break from traditional modes of identity performance as they identify the American identity as a more desirable alternative. Although another accent is not substantially employed by Boyle, he does change his speaking voice when performing 'the maverick detective'; one that has hints of an American twang, with a more belaboured, 'cinematic' vocal performance. This is mirrored by supermarket manager

Mr Henderson's use of American phrases when attempting to appear more attractive and 'cooler' in front of his staff, often quoting the line 'as they say in the States', again referencing the aura of esteem around that other culture.

In the opening sequences of Lenny Abrahamson's examination of the new Dublin class, *What Richard Did* (2012), we are given an explicit example of 'voicing' through imitation or parody, when the middle-class nouveau riche protagonists overtly mock perceptibly working-class characters. This new social group employed 'stylistic operations around accent and dialect [... to] express class-relevant distinctiveness and relations in their talk' (Coupland, 2009: 312) in order to diverge from what they perceive as a 'narrow and restricted local culture' (Hickey, 2007: 354). In this scene, Richard and his friends purchase food at a Dublin supermarket and overhear a conversation between the cashier and a colleague who both speak in heavy 'local' Dublin accents. As the boys walk away, they imitate the voices of the two working-class characters in mockery of them. Although the boys repeat only the words of the characters, accent is the target of their imitation, referencing both the negative esteem placed on the working-class accent and in turn establishing a pride in their 'new' middle-class accents. In a cinematic context, this marks a significant shift in characterization in Irish cinema, with this form of dialectism not so explicitly seen before in Irish film, pointing to a counter-Celtic Tiger sensibility in the film.

In a 2005 article in the *Irish Independent*, Ed Power refers to a contemporary trend that emerged in the post-Celtic Tiger environment, in which accent has again been used on a large scale for dissociative intentions (2005). '[A]ccent tourism' is a 'trend amongst the children of the extremely well off to speak in exaggerated working-class accents' (Power, 2005). The motivations behind this accent shift lie in a widespread cultural exposure of the 'shallow' nature of the lifestyles brought about by the boom years in which long-standing aspects of local culture, of which accent is very much a part, were replaced by more homogenized, global, uniform features of identity. With the rapid uptake of the D4 accent in the Celtic Tiger years, its usage was seen to spread far beyond the isoglosses of south Dublin, something Power acknowledges when he states that 'From Kerry to Carnsore, the south Dublin uplift is being adopted as a badge of progressiveness, an explicit rejection of provincial "backwardness"' (2005). In a similar vein, Terence Dolan, author of *A Dictionary of Hiberno-English*, comments: 'I was in Roscommon recently and hear two young ladies who I imagine had never been outside of the place in their life, and they were speaking in perfect Dublin 4 accents' (cited in Power, 2005). Due to the over-exposure of the 'new' accent, the increasing cultural realization of the 'faux' nature of the accent, and popular parodies of the D4 class in Irish literature and television, with the popular Ross O'Carroll Kelly series of books, and the *Damo & Ivor* (Quinn et al., 2013) television show, a cultural rejection of this accent began to emerge. Ed Power has noted that '[t]he speakers aren't plucky outsiders from the rough side of town, but the progeny of doctors and lawyers for whom a rough-hewn accent represents a subtle form of rebellion' (Power, 2005). Essentially, the youth culture in Ireland had developed into a culture which felt no connection to its own nationality, taking inspiration from international (with television and film playing a large role in the dissemination of these) sources, and in a post-Celtic Tiger context, a reversion of this is underway.

Kirsten Sheridan's *Dollhouse* (2012) signifies an ostensible address to accent in Irish film, featuring the phenomenon of 'accent tourism', as it references the cultural shift in attitudes towards accent and acknowledges attitudes towards the class divide heightened during the boom years. The narrative of *Dollhouse* centres on a group of working-class Northside Dublin youths, who break into an expensive beachside house to wreak havoc and party for the night. The narrative unfolds through a series of revelations. The most linguistically, and narratively significant, of these relates to the fact that the protagonist, Jeannie, is not actually 'one of them', but is a Southside Dublin youth from a wealthy family, dissatisfied with her wealthy family and social life. Through accent, Jeannie passes as a working-class Dubliner, with her 'natural' speaking accent revealed to be that of the 'Dublin 4' stereotype later in the film. Sheridan interestingly places the working-class accent as the accent of social prestige in the film with the 'Dublin 4' characters, Jeannie and Robbie, ridiculed for their accents. The other characters use 'voicing' to mock and imitate the 'middle-class' characters for their accents, including Jack Reynor, who also performs the archetypal south Dublin youth as he had done in *What Richard Did*. Jeannie's use of voicing, or downward accent 'accommodation' (Coupland, 2007: 62), is striking in this film, as it is the first instance of such a phenomenon in Irish cinema and can be read to demonstrate a highly subversive counter-Celtic Tiger sensibility by representing the linguistic behaviour known as 'accent tourism' (Power, 2005).

Conclusion

Against a history of misrepresentation of Irish accents in cinema, the current cinematic moment has demonstrated significant developments in its ideological use of accent as a marker of identity. With the increasingly complex and deliberate framing of accent in indigenous Irish film, cases such as *The Commitments, Dollhouse, Adam and Paul, What Richard Did, When Brendan Met Trudy* and others have both served to represent accent in a more considered and socially relevant manner. In extra-textual – and often intertextual – considerations of accent in Irish film, commentaries often point to misrepresentations of the indigenous accent by (most frequently) American stars. When problematized by de-essentializing notions of hybridity and performativity, certain questions emerge around the ideological validity and value judgements that are often bestowed upon notions of accuracy, authenticity and precision in the on-screen rendering of a regional accent. This very flexibility is borne out infrequently in contemporary Irish film (echoing very real sociological changes) and in how a number of these films address, apply or manifestly play with this tonal elasticity, thus allowing many of the linguistic categories of performance that I have evoked in this chapter including voicing, accent accommodation, linguistic dissociation and accent tourism.

4
Beyond Horror: Surviving Sexual Abuse in Carmel Winters' *Snap*

Kathleen Vejvoda

In the traditional ghost story, the cause of the haunting is frequently revealed to be the neglect, abuse or murder of a child. This preoccupation with the victimization of children carries over into horror literature and films, in which children are abusers, as well as abused haunters, as well as haunted.[1] The genre has a history of unsettling the notion of childhood innocence through the trope of the 'evil child', whose malevolence may be inherent or the result of familial or social influences. But while evil children who terrorize adults have pervaded popular culture since the second half of the 20th century,[2] vile adults who menace children have always been a staple of ghost stories and horror films. Usually male with supernatural powers, this figure – whom I label the 'spectral abuser' – cannot be defeated. Through the spectral abuser's indestructibility, horror films incite our fears about the spectre of child abuse, particularly about our ability, as individuals and in a wider social and cultural context, to protect children. Horror films do the cultural work of addressing child abuse, primarily by invoking it and suggesting the inability to eradicate it, thus containing our fears within the sensational world of the narrative and enabling us to dismiss them, to some extent, as the stuff of scary movies.

Outside of the horror genre, feature films about child abuse are relatively rare.[3] Historical dramas about clerical and institutional abuse, such as *The Magdalene Sisters* (Mullan, 2002) or *Song for a Raggy Boy* (Walsh, 2003), tend to rely heavily on gothic conventions. Based on historical or (auto)biographical accounts, clerical abuse dramas necessarily frame the traumatic events and even their reverberations as having happened in the past: they typically include an extra-diegetic, textual coda explaining how the abuse was brought to light and what happened to the real people on whom the characters are based, who may be alluded to as tragic, unknowable entities. While the coda may not suggest that justice has been served, it reassures us that we are now beyond the benighted era depicted in the film.

Critics have pointed to the radical economic, demographic and cultural changes in Ireland since the Celtic Tiger, followed by the economic collapse of 2008, to account for the turn to horror in Irish cinema since the early 2000s.[4] The clerical abuse scandal has played a part as well: revelations of clerical abuse began to erupt in the late 1990s, resulting in a media obsession with child abuse that has not abated.[5] While I cannot survey the ways in which Irish cinema has addressed the child abuse scandal, I would like to begin with a brief discussion of how this history is incorporated in the Irish horror film *Shrooms* (Breathnach, 2007). As Emma Radley has argued, this wry, self-reflexive slasher film exemplifies the 'transpositions' that can occur when Irish filmmakers set their films in an Irish context yet rely on transnational, or Hollywood, genre conventions (2013). In *Shrooms*, a group of American students travels to Ireland on a quest for psychedelic mushrooms. Their guide is Jake, a British former exchange student with whom Tara, an Irish-American girl, is infatuated. Jake leads them deep into the woods somewhere in Cork, where Tara discovers that he is not interested in her, eats the wrong mushroom and has a very bad trip, murdering all of her friends, including Jake.

While it turns out that there are no supernatural forces at work in *Shrooms*, it is the Englishman's campfire story that goads the hallucinating Tara into paranoid terror. A nearby ruin, Jake tells the Americans, was once a reform school where young 'offenders' were sent; he goes on to enumerate the horrors that took place at this institution run by a 'religious order kind of like the Christian Brothers'. *Shrooms* takes the history of institutional abuse in Ireland – already sensational enough, as testimonies such as those in the Ryan Report reveal – and embellishes it: the Irish industrial school becomes the ruined mental asylum of Hollywood horror films, and Ireland's clerical abusers are converted into one composite, supernaturally evil, monkish Freddy Krueger called 'the Black Brother', who not only tortures children, but commits mushroom-induced mass murder.

Citing Roddy Flynn's (2008) complaint that 'the spectre of industrial schools' in *Shrooms* lacks any depth or political resonance, Radley counters that, like other horror filmmakers, Breathnach comments on Ireland's history through his film's formal elements, which include an 'explicit, tangible, and persistent' rendering of the 'horror of the industrial school'. Radley continues: 'Metaphorical, allegorical or heavy-handed, the horror film's business is exploiting trauma, and in the case of *Shrooms* this trauma has specific [Irish] cultural resonances that, while perhaps not explicitly rendered, cannot be evaded' (2013: 119). In a scene that appears to be a satire of late Victorian colonialism and its anxieties about the primitive 'Other', two ragged, filthy locals (Bernie and Ernie) emerge from the trees, and one of the Americans says 'What is this, the Island of Dr Moreau?' Jake replies, 'I think that's what we call the indigenous people.' As Radley argues, Bernie and Ernie evoke the stereotype of the Irish as simian and savage and transform pastoral images of the Irish peasantry through the cliché of 'the inbred, back-wards redneck' (2013: 122). But Bernie and Ernie are not just rustics: they are former inmates at the industrial school in Jake's ghost story. When one of the American tourists stumbles upon their shack in the forest, they talk about copulating with pigs and bull calves, and their shelves are full of the mushrooms to which they are addicted. *Shrooms* suggests that 'indigenous [Irish] people' – especially those who have been abused – are damaged beyond repair by their history. As in many other horror films, the abused invariably become monsters themselves, irretrievably Othered and outcast.

From an ethical standpoint, the representation of abuse survivors as monstrous and doomed is deeply troubling, especially given the wide distribution and popularity of horror films. Superimposing the conventions of horror cinema onto Ireland's history of industrial school abuse, horrific as that history may be, implies that we do not need to care about or even believe such narratives *as* history; evident in Jake's later dismissal of his tale: 'It's just a story.' While there is a certain grim honesty in imagining child abuse as a nightmare without end (at least on a societal level), there is also a need to imagine ways of coping with that recurring nightmare, particularly at this juncture in Irish history.

Snap (2010), the début feature film by award-winning playwright and director Carmel Winters, a native of County Cork, was filmed in Cork City in 2009. After garnering critical praise and awards at European film festivals in 2010, it was released in 2011 in Ireland, where it received Best Irish Film and Best Irish Director awards from the Dublin Film Critics Circle.[6] Classified by many reviewers as a thriller, *Snap* is also one of the most thoughtful and demanding films – Irish or otherwise – about child sexual abuse. Winters tackles a difficult subject: as clinical psychologists Whitelock, Lamb and Rentfrow recently observed, child sexual abuse 'is widely viewed as a psychological and physical trauma [...]

associated with more severely negative long-term outcomes for victims than any other type of child maltreatment' (2013: 351). *Snap* raises vital and timely questions about genre and the ethics of cinematic representation, relying on a documentary realism that subtly evokes and troubles the conventions of horror.[7] Acknowledging that Irish films about child abuse tend to be clerical abuse dramas, Winters has said that in *Snap*, her purpose was to eschew gothic sensationalism:

> I'm so tired of abuse being sensationally dealt with, and with people not trusting their audience, hastening to convince them that the film is PC and prove that 'oh we're horrified by this as well!' They end up lying about the characters and doing them a great disservice in portraying the complexity of their story.
>
> (McDermott, 2011)

The narrative of *Snap* is 'fracture[d] [...] into dozens of fragments' (Maguire, 2011): it is a film within a film within a film, with additional cuts to flashbacks, Super 8 home movies and footage from mobile phones and security cameras. Through this meta-cinematic layering, Winters explores the nature of trauma, memory and recognition, gradually revealing one family's history of multigenerational sexual abuse. In many ways, this is a film that gestures towards the fraught historical relationship between cinema and childhood.[8] In *Snap*, filmmaking itself plays a paradoxical role: it can be child pornography, or it can be a therapeutic practice for the abuse survivor. But in the end, filmmaking provides an ethic and aesthetic of transparency that makes it possible for Stephen, and possibly his mother Sandra, to move on after trauma.

Sandra (Aisling O'Sullivan) is a single mother who agrees to be filmed talking about a crime committed three years before by her son Stephen (Stephen Moran), who at 15 abducted a toddler (Adam Duggan) and kept him in his grandfather's house for five days. She is defensive, angry and sardonic, railing at the camera, behind which (we later realize) is Stephen, now 18. She has endured years of scrutiny by the media as well as hate mail from an outraged public. Stephen's social worker has suggested that filming his mother would help them both to 'set the record straight'; he uses sophisticated equipment and has a sound technician (John Crean), suggesting that he might be pursuing a future in filmmaking.

The title of the film stresses the connection between filmmaking and memory. The word 'snap' refers to the action of taking a picture, but it also describes what can happen when a traumatic memory is triggered: Stephen 'snaps' emotionally and kidnaps the child after his grandfather (Pascal Scott) has a stroke. Sandra forces Stephen to visit him in the hospital and go to his house to take care of his dog. Over the course of *Snap*, we piece together the family's history. At 15, Sandra gave birth to a baby girl, whom she gave up for adoption; in a flashback, she lies weeping in a hospital bed as her father dotes on the newborn. While her father appears to be supportive and loving, eventually we realize that he has molested both his daughter and his grandson. As the narrative develops, so do the disturbing implications: Sandra was routinely raped by her father, perhaps after the death of her mother, and her father most likely sired not only her first child, but perhaps also Stephen, who is named after him. Consequently, Sandra has had a lifetime of alcohol addiction and problems with intimacy.[9] When Stephen is two years old, she has a breakdown and cannot take care of him, so she gives him to her father. Trying to justify this decision, she complains to the camera/Stephen about the inadequacy of social services: 'Where are they when you need them? My dad was the only taker.' When the technician asks Sandra to dub this part of the film due to sound problems, she must repeat her own words. Watching and listening to herself on film causes her to scream: 'The camera *does* lie! It does fuckin' lie!' The take with her defiant claim 'my dad was the only taker' reappears at the end of the film as part of a montage of chilling, revelatory moments. As with other eerie manipulations of Sandra's image and voice – speeding up and slowing down, repeating and reversing her movements, and at one point, slowing down her voice to sound like a demonic growl – we are meant to understand this montage as Stephen's editing. It is his 'unseen hand' that 'pauses and rewinds the raw documentary footage, looking for unguarded moments' (Maguire, 2011).

Sandra's history of childhood sexual abuse is suggested in a sequence in which she picks up an old drunk (veteran actor Mick Lally, in his last film) at a Chinese takeaway. The ensuing bedroom scene includes full-frontal male nudity: Sandra forces the hapless man to strip, refusing to allow him to turn off the light as she watches him defiantly. The nudity of this older man (who is about her father's age) renders him the disempowered object of her gaze and ours. As Winters observed in an e-mail response to this author, Lally beautifully conveys his character's vulnerability (2013). Sandra does not enjoy sex, but uses it to gain a temporary sense of control. After their brief sexual encounter, he dozes; she puts her arm around him and regards him tenderly before she too falls asleep. *Snap* does not oversimplify the complex emotional repercussions of childhood sexual abuse: we realize here that she still loves her hospitalized father. When she wakes up, however, she pushes the stranger out of her bed and yells: 'Get out! And if you break my Child of Prague, I'll break your bony arse!' Fetishizing symbols of purity such as the Infant of Prague, she reveals earlier that she always wanted to be a nun: 'Sister Immaculata.'

Sandra's denial of her own childhood sexual abuse enables her father to abuse her son: for 11 years, from age 2 to age 13, Stephen lives with his grandfather, who molests him and films this molestation. Stephen's suffering is compounded by his mother's inability to express, and at times to feel, maternal affection. While *Snap* does not make it easy to sympathize with either Stephen or Sandra, I would contend that we identify more with Sandra because we share her perplexity about Stephen. She cries to Chris: 'I'm scared! I'm scared shitless of my own son!' Stephen is suspect from the beginning, as is filmmaking: his constant filming is a sinister reminder of his grandfather ('Shovin' cameras in people's faces! You know who you're like, don't ya?' Sandra accuses). *Snap* begins with an image of a father and his toddler son playing by a pond in a park; we see them through the viewfinder of a video camera and hear the cameraman's breathing as he adjusts the focus and zooms in on them. Forced to watch this family from the perspective of someone filming them surreptitiously, we are instantly uneasy. When the child's ball falls into the pond and the father goes to retrieve it, the cameraman quickly approaches the child, whom we see in the handheld camera's unsteady frame, which then fills with the blurry movement of the ground as he races away with the child.

Stephen uses the boy as an alter ego or instrument in a desperate attempt to recreate himself as the prelapsarian child, the person he was before he was sexually abused. Significantly named Adam, the child is two years old, the same age as Stephen when he was first abused. Since returning to live with his mother, Stephen has avoided his grandfather. Now, forced to return to the scene of his childhood trauma, he brings Adam with him as a kind of talisman or symbol of innocence, but also as a scapegoat for his anger and self-loathing, alternating ominously between baby talk and verbal hostility towards Adam. When a neighbour asks Stephen who the boy is, he says he is his brother, also named Stephen.

As Maguire notes, throughout *Snap*, 'the director maintains a mood of imminent horror, a sense that the awful things that have been revealed are nothing when placed against what remains hidden' (Maguire, 2011). Central to this 'imminent horror' is our anxiety about whether Stephen molests or hurts the child, a question the film does not answer until the end. In this way, Winters manipulates audience assumptions about the doubleness of abused children, whose potential for malice is the subject of so many horror films.

In *Snap*'s climactic sequence, Stephen realizes consciously for the first time that he has been molested. This devastating scene is intercut with a scene in which Sandra, doing laundry, finds a milk-bottle nipple in his pocket and deduces that he took the missing child. In his grandfather's living room, Stephen strips both himself and Adam to their underwear and puts a videotape in the VCR (one of many home movies, this one titled 'Stephen age 2'), and we watch Stephen as he watches it. Eventually, we realize that he is watching a film of his two-year-old self being molested in the bathtub. While we worry about what might happen in the foreground – where Stephen sits sweating in his briefs, staring impassively at the television screen, as Adam, his childhood double, pats his shoulder, trying to get his attention – the real horror unfolds in the background, in the grainy fragments of a home movie.

We see only brief shots of the face and torso of baby Stephen. We do not see the grandfather, who is more a voice than an image; his heavy breathing being the clearest indicator of what is happening. As he watches this pornographic film of which he says he is the 'star', Stephen becomes disoriented and Adam instinctively hides from him. In a low-angle, handheld camera shot from the child's point of view, we see Stephen searching the room for the child, calling him 'Adam' now instead of 'Stephen', implying that he no longer identifies himself with the unmolested child. 'Do you want to go home lookin' like a porn star?' Stephen demands of the hiding boy, which suggests that he is preparing to return Adam to his parents. He sobs: 'I amn't going to touch you. I just wanna change your stupid nappy!' Overcome with shame, hunched on the floor, Stephen wails 'I'm sorry!' Just as his mother breaks into the house to rescue the toddler, Stephen hurls himself down the stairs. Sandra hears a baby crying and rushes into the living room, only to see that the crying child is two-year-old Stephen: the video of her father molesting her son is still playing. She takes all the videotapes and photographs out into the yard and destroys them in a bonfire; an act that reveals the wilfulness of her continuing denial. (Her son, meanwhile, overdoses on pills from the medicine cabinet.) *Snap* suggests that it is not enough to repress or destroy such images: new memories, new images must replace them. One reason that Stephen films so obsessively is to crowd out these spectral images from the past.[10]

One might argue that the grandfather is a spectral abuser: through the home movies, he is a pervasive presence, and often we hear the ghostly echo of his insinuating voice, bubbling over with babytalk ('Upsy-daisy!'). But *Snap* ultimately rejects the trope of the spectral abuser and the suggestion of lasting power that goes with it: instead it is the abused child and the *memory* of abuse that are spectral. When Stephen is in the hospital recovering from his overdose, he wakes to see his grandfather sitting beside him, stroking his hair and softly singing 'You Are My Sunshine'. But Stephen only stares at him and then whispers, 'You hurt me'. His grandfather seems puzzled at first, but then slowly withdraws his hand from Stephen's hair. The scene is bathed in the fluorescent light of a hospital room: there is no melodrama here. If *Snap* foregrounds the fact that child sexual abuse can occur in seemingly everyday contexts, it also suggests that such abuse can be confronted in the plain light of day. This vital scene marks the beginning of Stephen's long process of healing. While it does not appear that the accusation ever results in a criminal complaint, the grandfather's fate is left ambiguous, suggesting that for Stephen, who has turned resolutely away from him, he is as good as dead. As a baby, he was the powerless object of the camera's gaze, but he is not so in *Snap*.

In an interview with Edel Coffey, Winters discusses the 'burden' of survivors who were abused by someone they loved and trusted rather than by a 'demon':

> A 15-year-old boy who was sexually abused by the only person who took 'good care' of him, the one person who loved him, that's a far greater burden for him to carry than the sensationalized demonised story. It's a much greater story for him to sift through that and wonder what he'll be like as [a] carer of young people or his fears about who he might become.
>
> (2011: 20)

Like Sandra, the audience spends most of the film wondering what Stephen might have done to the child. Is Stephen a monster? One of my film students said that she found the abduction plot outrageous because most survivors of sexual abuse would not commit such a crime. In John Michael McDonagh's recent celebrated film *Calvary* (2014), a survivor of clerical sexual abuse (played by Chris O'Dowd) premeditates the murder of an innocent priest, yet critics have not found this device to be exploitative. Like so many horror films, *Calvary* – essentially a spaghetti Western – invokes the trauma of abuse but does not attempt to represent viable ways of coping with it. In contrast to these genre films, *Snap* confronts seriously pressing social questions such as: What are the lifelong effects of child sexual abuse? Why are some abuse survivors more resilient than others? Researchers in clinical psychology, social work and neuroscience are still debating answers, but recent findings are optimistic: 'Clearly, nonnegative outcomes after [child sexual abuse] are not only possible but may actually be common' (Whitelock, Lamb & Rentfrow, 2013: 358). Winters sugarcoats nothing, but she rightly suggests that it is possible for abuse survivors to rebuild their lives.

At the end of *Snap*, mother and son are together in the same park from which Stephen abducted Adam at the beginning. He films Sandra feeding ducks with a boy of about five (the age Adam would be at this point). Stephen reviews the footage in his viewfinder, freezing it on the image of her touching the boy's outstretched hand, obviously still craving his mother's love. While filming her is his way of trying to establish intimacy, it is also of course a barrier to intimacy. The toddler goes off with its parent, and Sandra sits on the bench beside Stephen and produces a photograph, the one image she has saved from the conflagration. Believing it to be a picture of Stephen as a baby, she shows it to him and says: 'The hair on you ... like candy-floss!' Then, suddenly and jarringly, she demands, 'Did you hurt that child?' When he says 'No', her whole body relaxes for the first time in the film: Stephen has not continued the cycle of sexual abuse. We share her relief, and Stephen's humanity and loneliness are palpable as he crumples up against his mother's chest in tears. But she literally pushes him away. Before he rises to leave, he stacks in a neat pile on the bench the tapes containing the films he has shot of her ('MAM #5', etc.) and says quietly: 'The kid with the candy-floss hair wasn't me, Ma. It was you.' The scene cuts to Stephen's montage of his mother's most revealing moments, followed by a shot of her still sitting on the bench, staring pensively into the distance: this montage does not so much represent, as enact, Sandra's comprehension of her own childhood abuse. *Snap* ends with a close-up of Sandra as a toddler in a home movie, moving on a swing in slow motion, gazing at the camera and us. The abused child is made visible: she appears like a ghost, signifying not horror, but terrible sadness.

The scene in the park at end of *Snap* is the first time that we see Sandra and Stephen together in a public space rather than in a claustrophobic domestic space, suggesting that they are beginning to function in the social world. The film begins and ends in a park, a place associated not only with children, but also with the dangers to them. While mother and son are both still isolated emotionally, Stephen has taken the first steps towards reclaiming his life, and he prompts his mother to do the same. In its diegetic treatment of the uses of filmmaking, *Snap* points to the important role of cinema in imagining what a recovery from the national as well as the private trauma of child abuse might look like.

Notes

1. We see this over-determined representation of the child in countless horror films and their progeny, from *The Exorcist* (Friedkin, 1973) and Stephen King adaptations, to Japanese horror and, most recently, *The Babadook* (Kent, 2014).
2. See Renner (2013: 1–27).
3. An interesting example is the sci-fi thriller *The Butterfly Effect* (Bress & Gruber, 2004).
4. See Crosson (2012) and Radley (2013).
5. The multivolume Ryan Commission Report, published in 2009, details the neglect and systematic physical, sexual and emotional abuse of children in institutions run jointly by the state and Catholic Church throughout the 20th century.
6. Because the film has not yet been released on DVD (though it has recently been distributed by BrinkVision in Canada in VOD), I refer with permission to a copy from the Irish Film Archive.
7. *Park* (Carney & Hall, 1999), another Irish film that conjures the trauma of sexual abuse, is very different formally, particularly in its emphasis on the spectral abuser and its tragic outcome.
8. As Lebeau (2008) argues, early cinema was obsessed with capturing the spectacle of the child, with sometimes exploitative or abusive results; see pp. 7–10.
9. Whitelock, Lamb and Rentfrow cite research demonstrating that 'more "severe" abuse – characterized by its longer duration, use of force, the identity of the perpetrator as a father figure, and/or experience of penetration – tends to increase the likelihood of negative outcomes for survivors' (2013: 352).
10. Similarly, in *The Butterfly Effect* (Bress & Gruber, 2004), the scene of child pornography is the originary trauma that the protagonist repeatedly tries to undo.

Part II

Identities of Gender and Stardom

5
Black and White and Green All Over? Emergent Irish Female Stardom in Contemporary Popular Cinemas

Ciara Barrett

In this chapter, I will consider the historical incompatibility of female 'Irishness' with film stardom in relation to two contemporary female actors who self-identify as 'Irish'; Saoirse Ronan and Ruth Negga, who appear to be challenging established gendered paradigms of Irish representation in popular anglophone cinema and surrounding discourse. I posit that the history of Irish female stardom may be characterized as a history of absence, against which these actors' individual performances of Irishness and their developing star images-*as-Irish* must be analysed. In the light of Ronan and Negga's recent rise to prominence internationally, I will suggest that Irish female stardom is just now beginning to find embodiment on screen, while the image of 'Irish femininity' remains an unstable and revisable signifying category.[1]

First, however, it will be necessary to define the certain terms and propose specific theories on which I will be drawing, particularly the working definitions of 'Irishness' and 'stardom' that facilitate my qualitative analysis of performance. Irishness, in this case, will be contingent on 'indigenousness', or a physical and cognitive association with Ireland, as distinct from the more nebulous heritage Irishness associated with the hyphenated identities of the Irish diaspora. Furthermore, Irish female stardom will be discussed in the context of recognizability across popular anglophone cinema, as an amalgamation of the Hollywood and, to a lesser extent, Irish, British and Canadian film industries. In this capitalist system, contemporary film 'stardom' is contingent on international recognition, market accessibility, appeal and sell-ability. Theoretically, a 'star' is a composite sign or matrix comprised of various signifiers: the 'real person', the persona, the image and the star-as-commodity (Dyer, 1998). In practice, a film star is entrusted to open medium- to big-budget productions based on name and image recognition, which are a by-product of his or her visibility in the media. With these terms of reference thus established, I hope to explore why, historically, there have been, relatively, so few female Irish stars about whom the fulfilment of these criteria might be claimed.

Over the last 100 years or so, Irishness has held considerable signifying value in popular anglophone cinema. This is evidenced by the ubiquity of Irish-themed movies and Irish-identified characters in popular Hollywood films: ranging from James Cagney as the classic Irish-American gangster in *The Public Enemy* (Wellman, 1931) to the 'Oirish' man-candy love interests of *The Matchmaker* (Joffe, 1997), *P.S. I Love You* (LaGravenese, 2007) and *Leap Year* (Tucker, 2010). All these films represent Irish men as powerfully seductive and desirable, their gendered and ethnic characteristics working dialectically towards the affirmation of their erotic appeal. As has been noted by Irish film scholars Ruth Barton and Luke Gibbons, it has been relatively easy, historically, for Irish male actors (rather than for females) to succeed in Hollywood or internationally as so-called film 'stars' (Barton, 2006: 224–5): Irish masculinity has thus been perennially constructed as 'sexy'.

Major Irish or Irish-associated female stars, however, are few and far between across the course of Hollywood film history. They are limited to a handful, comprising Mary Pickford (1892–1972), Colleen Moore (1899–1988), Maureen O'Sullivan (1911–98), Maureen O'Hara (b.1920) and Constance Smith (1928–2003). In the wake of O'Hara's career throughout the post-classical Hollywood period and into the 21st century, no indigenous Irish female actor has made the leap to international film stardom (despite the significant critical acclaim that has been afforded to such performers as Brenda Fricker and Sinéad Cusack). By contrast, a partial list of Irish-identified male stars who have risen to prominence since 1960 includes Peter O'Toole, Gabriel Byrne, Pierce Brosnan, Liam Neeson, Colin Farrell, Cillian Murphy, Jonathan Rhys Myers, Michael Fassbender and Jamie Dornan.[2] Regardless of their characters' nationality or ethnicity, these actors' Irishness is generally emphasized in publicity materials and affirmed towards the production of their images as positively masculine and stereotypically 'sexy'. An equivalent representational paradigm has not, however, existed for female Irish actors.

With a view to addressing this imbalance, Barton (2006) has suggested that the Irish female actor-performer has been disadvantaged
by the popular shift away from idealizing de-ethnicized or 'unproblematic' female whiteness in stars, with a tendency towards desiring images
of 'mixed-race', 'off-white' (Negra, 2001b), or even non-white female
beauty. Gibbons (cited in Barton, 2006: xviii) has further proposed
that Irish actors' performance style – which, historically, has tended
to eschew close-ups and bodily expressiveness – has almost disqualified
Irish actresses from attaining true stardom; for a star's (particularly a
female's) image(ing) is predicated to some degree on the acceptance of
a glorifying/scopophilic gaze.[3] Overall, Irishness has seldom been represented *through* femininity, and thus it has not been deployed as a
fetishizable cultural signifier among women to the same extent that
Irishness has been employed by male actors (or their public relations
machines) towards the establishment of a desirable image.

Where, for men, Irishness functions frequently to connote a certain kind of earthy sexuality and accessible sensuality, female actors'
Irishness has tended to work towards the invocation of girlishness and
pre-sexuality (if not full *a*sexuality). As Gaylyn Studlar and Christopher
Shannon have shown, Mary Pickford consciously invoked her Irish
heritage in films and publicity to mitigate her erotic appeal as underde-
veloped, latent and/or sexually in-active, thus to preserve a conservative
fan base (Studlar, 2002; Shannon, 2009). Similarly, Colleen Moore's
Irishness may be seen to have tempered her association with a liber-
alized flapper culture such that her female unruliness was seen to be
located in innocence and immaturity rather than transgression (Negra,
2001b). Such associations were further borne out and referenced (albeit
with flashes of subversion and inconsistencies of ethnic characterization) in the careers of Maureen O'Sullivan and Maureen O'Hara (Barton,
2006; McLoone, 2008).

Indeed, the composite image of traditional Irish femininity has, both
within and beyond Ireland, been a bodiless one. Over the history of Irish
visual and literary culture – which has been associated predominantly
with *Catholic* Irish visual and literary culture (the dominant inflection
of Irishness at least in the eyes of the outside world) – the Irish woman
has been denied a basic, earthly embodiment, tending instead to be figured as a de-sexualized religious or political symbol (the Virgin Mary
or Kathleen Ni Houlihan). With the exceptions of the aforementioned
Irish girl-stars, female sexuality and/or the female body has tended to be
contained within, or restricted to, domestic maternity and traditionally

maternal roles on film (quintessentially, though not uniquely, the ever-pregnant Brenda Fricker of *My Left Foot* [Sheridan, 1989]). Alternatively, when the sexually active female has *not* been contained within a domestic role, she has been posited as dangerous for, disruptive to, or otherwise transgressive of, patriarchal Irish-Catholic society (taking, for example, the 'problem' of unwed mothers Goretti in *Hush-a-Bye Baby* [Harkin, 1992] and Sharon in *The Snapper* [Frears, 1993]). Whereas the film star – and certainly and perhaps especially the female film star – is necessarily 'of the body', and thusly highly image-able, the Irish woman as represented historically in traditional popular culture has been decidedly not. If not *unimaginable*, as such, the desirable (that is, sexual or sexualizable), young Irish woman has been almost un*image*-able. Irishness as cultural currency, or as a potential star attribute, has been effectively incompatible with 'femininity' in popular media. Irishness, in the traditional sense, does not belong to the female body and, in another sense, is not physically 'of the female'. Indeed, the composite image of Irishness upheld and developed by audiences historically has been both gendered and overtly sexed *away* from 'the feminine' and the female, excepting where femininity has been contained via bodily negation.

The lack of significant starring and lead roles for Irish female actors in indigenously-made Irish films has only compounded this problem, contributing to a low rate of retention for Irish female talent in the film industry, when compared with their theatrical counterparts. This is further exacerbated by the proximity of Ireland to Britain, which has encouraged young female acting talent to emigrate prior to establishing a strong national profile (and, following that, international recognition) as 'Irish stars' (Guiney, 2013). And it is also perpetuated by the casting, typically, of non-Irish female stars in high-profile 'Irish' roles, such as Kate Hudson (American) in *About Adam* (Stembridge, 2000), Kelly MacDonald and Shirley Henderson (Scottish) in *Intermission* (Crowley, 2003) and more recently, Judi Dench (English) in *Philomena* (Frears, 2013). Thus, in terms of raw material data – that is, Irish female protagonists within film narratives and/or Irish female stars in contemporary popular cinema – there is little of 'Irish female stardom' to analyse. Despite the obvious fact that Irish womanhood exists, Irish media and cinema have resisted being 'peopled' with women. In the meantime, Irish male actors like Colin Farrell, Cillian Murphy and Michael Fassbender remain ubiquitous on screen and in the press, providing fertile ground for scholarly analyses of Irish masculinity on film (Holohan & Tracy, 2014) without a requisite gender balance. Critically, theoretically and in praxis, Irishness has, as Negra has observed, 'correlate[d] with depictions of male centrality and ancillary femininity' (2009: 280). Thus, 'Irishness' in contemporary popular cinema has remained largely the province of male actor-stars into the 21st century, while Irish female stars and representations of Irish femininity have been under-represented. 'Irishness' as an ethnic and cultural marker has, for the most part, been understood and made appreciable as a star attribute (and thus commodifiable and consumable for a mass market) when it is gendered male.

Nevertheless, since 2000, two indigenous Irish film actors, Saoirse Ronan and Ruth Negga, have achieved notable mainstream recognition outside of Ireland. For this reason, I wish to explore how these actresses' rise to stardom or potential stardom (in the case of Negga) reflects present changing cultural attitudes towards Irish femininity both within and outside the nation itself. In the context of a nascently multi-cultural, or as Edna Longley and Declan Kiberd would have it, 'inter-cultural' Ireland (2001: 10), the stability of the meaning of Irishness is breaking down. This leaves room for the evolution of a new concept of Irish stardom and a new understanding of Irishness as gendered and 'coloured' away from the traditionalist, masculinist concept of Irishness.

Below, I examine the various means by which, both in film and press appearances, these actors have negotiated their Irishness alongside their ascendancy as stars, albeit in crucially different ways. In particular, I wish to underscore how the more traditionally 'Irish-looking' Saoirse Ronan has often suppressed the Irish side of her image in the construction of her star image-persona. On the other hand, in the case of ethnically 'off-white' (borrowing the term from Negra, 2001) Irish actress Ruth Negga, the nationality of the actor has rather been *highlighted* and re-affirmed in surrounding star discourses as a means of solidifying her cultural identity, thus satisfying another prerequisite of stardom. In contrasting these actors' differing performative negotiations of subscription to 'Irishness', I will further demonstrate Irish female stars' potential to destabilize traditionally held views of Irishness as 'white' and, more specifically, Irish femininity as domestic/maternal, or indeed, conventional at all.

Ronan, born in America to Irish parents in 1994 and raised in County Carlow, first gained international acclaim for her Oscar-nominated appearance in a supporting role in *Atonement* (Wright, 2007). Since then, she has appeared in a number of similar prestige dramas, including *The Lovely Bones* (Jackson, 2009), *Hanna* (Wright, 2011) and *The Grand Budapest Hotel* (Anderson, 2014), as well as starring in the teen-oriented

Hollywood would-be blockbuster *The Host* (Niccol, 2013), evidencing an assumed currency within the Hollywood star-production system. Negga, on the other hand, 12 years older than Ronan – born in Ethiopia in 1982 to an Irish mother and Ethiopian father and thereafter raised in Dublin – has been slower to make the transition into big-budget international productions. Negga first rose to prominence as an Irish actor on a number of Irish television series, eventually breaking into Irish cinema in Neil Jordan's *Breakfast on Pluto* (2005) and to British television with the *Misfits* in 2010, and the Shirley Bassey biopic *Shirley* in 2011 (Teague). In 2012, she took the leading role in the low-budget Canadian crime drama *Fury* (David Weaver), also known as *The Samaritan*, which was released in the UK but did not pick up international distribution. Since then, she has shot scenes for major Hollywood productions *12 Years a Slave* (McQueen, 2013) and *World War Z* (Forster, 2013), showing evidence of a building international star profile, but was notably largely cut out of both releases. Unlike Ronan, Negga has not appeared on the American chat-show circuit in promotion of her films and star image, though she has done so more recently in Britain.

At this point it will be interesting to consider how Ronan and Negga's respective 'Irishness' has been employed (or not) in the mediation of their star images, by virtue of the different meanings generated in the intersection of their individual 'races' and ethnicity: Ronan represents traditional Irish femininity as white, while Negga is more problematically an Irish woman, but black. This presents a problem for each in the negotiation of her emergent star image: for Ronan, how to present her physicality in the light of – or in spite of – her Irishness as a female; for Negga, how to affirm a national identity that her physical presence would traditionally, semiotically contradict, in order to concretize a coherent and marketable star image.

I would argue that Ronan, the more established 'Hollywood star' of the two, has been engaged in a subtle process of Irish-disavowal, by which her Irishness has consistently and systematically been disembodied or shifted from her body-image, both through performative means and as represented through promotional discourses. This may be observed through her fluid performance of non-Irish accents, both in films and in interviews, which has worked to put her Irish-specific nationality at a distance from her more generalized whiteness. This has facilitated her appearance as simultaneously ethnic and *non*-ethnic, and has re-affirmed her ability – as a white woman – to perform (or masquerade) as multiple nationalities without limitation: her non-ethnic whiteness thus providing a relative 'blank slate' for performance.[4] Her

embodiment of Irishness is secondly denied in recourse to a fixation on –
and, indeed, fetishization of – her Irish name in publicity appearances.
This has functioned to contain her Irishness in a verbal form, to distance her Irish ethnicity further from the physical and present fact of her
performing body, with which her Irishness-cum-femaleness might otherwise be in conflict (or would be unable to accommodate satisfactorily
in terms of star representation).

In appearances on talk shows during and since the promotion of
her star vehicle *Hanna* in 2011, Ronan may be seen as engaged in
an ongoing process of simultaneous fetishization and disavowal of her
Irish ethnicity. This has manifested itself in a tendency to poke fun at
the Irish (although slightly Anglicized, as 'SER-sha' rather than 'SEER-
sha') pronunciation of her first name, firstly towards acknowledging
her ethnicity, and secondly, towards compartmentalizing the significance of that ethnicity within her name-as-sign. As a means, then,
of disavowing the practical limitations of her ethnicity – which, as
I have shown, for a female actor, is traditionally founded in a process
of bodily negation – she tends to engage in a series of performances
of accents, thus re-claiming her ethnicity-as-Irish as significant of a generalized pan-whiteness – a *lack* of ethnic identification – rather than
of a commodifiable ethnic identity and image. This may be seen in
a number of appearances on chat shows in Britain and America during her promotional tour for *Hanna*, including an interview with Ellen
Degeneres from April 2011,[5] during which she insists upon the pronunciation of her Irish-spelled name as 'Sersha' while making fun of a
number of common mispronunciations of the Irish name. As prompted
by Degeneres, she then performs a series of regional American accents,
as if in the same breath denying the specific Irishness-of-image that her
name would purport to indicate. In such a way, I would argue, Ronan's
performative star image is constructed as nominally Irish. Practicably
and personally, however, it remains undefined or malleable, and thus
more subscriptive to a protean 'whiteness' than to a 'true' or specific
ethnicity.

This is in keeping with the essential paradigm of Irish femininity that
I have reviewed above, by which physicality – a prerequisite of star
performance – and traditional white 'Irishness' are seen as incompatible
within the female body. For Ronan, adhering to this representational
paradigm, performing Irishness may be seen to detract from her image
as a star to be looked at and desired. Because Ronan is white, however,
her Irish ethnicity is easily erasable; once fetishized and simultaneously disavowed in/by the verbal/aural packages of her name and voice.

Her white body becomes a sort of *tabula rasa* on which any number of performed ethnicities may be inscribed and thereby signified by, or channelled through, her speech (a figurative 'colourlessness' perfectly echoed in/by the nationless *Hanna*). In most of her film roles and in her extra-textual appearances, Ronan appears to be engaged in a conspicuous performance of alternative white ethnicities and, arguably, a corollary under-performance of her white ethnicity-as-Irish. With the exception of her role in *The Grand Budapest Hotel* in 2014, Ronan has not appeared as 'Irish' in a single film since (and including) her breakout performance in *Atonement*.[6] She performs in accent almost always as either British or American, depending on narrative context.[7]

Ruth Negga, on the other hand, does not appear to have had the same performative flexibility of image and identity, precisely and ironically because her race and ethnicity are, at least on the visual outset, more ambiguous. Negga's appearance as 'mixed race' is such that her Irishness is not immediately or stereotypically visually marked. The fact that Negga speaks with an Irish accent but *looks* 'black' – and so 'not Irish' in any traditional sense – has evidently been a source of fascination for many interviewers, who time and again (and with varying degrees of subtlety) have asked that Negga explicate her ethnic and national origins in relation to her various dramatic roles. For instance, when prompted to review her ethnic background in an interview with the BBC in 2011[8] to promote her role as Shirley Bassey in a made-for-TV movie, Negga declares unequivocally, 'I'm Irish', before relating her genealogical history. In print interviews with Negga, the ostensible mismatch between her visual and aural image has furthermore been made explicit: as noted in the London *Metro* in September 2011, for instance, her looks are described as 'striking', being the 'result of an Irish mother and Ethiopian father' (thus euphemistically referring to the 'exoticism' of her ethnic lineage) at the same time as her accent is noted as a 'pronounced [...] soft Irish brogue' (Watson, 2011). Negga may thus be observed consistently re-affirming her Irishness in media appearances, having to declare or call herself out repeatedly *as* Irish, towards the rendering of a coherent star image. The apparent 'need' for such clarification thus speaks to the historical location-cum-ossification of Irishness within whiteness, and further to the challenge to gendered norms of ethnic and racial identity that the 'off-white' Negga presents.

Indeed, Negga's ethnic background is consistently interrogated in her public appearances, seemingly as a means of solidifying or identifying her problematic image as an 'off-white' Irish star who, though she subscribes to the cultural heritage of Irishness, nevertheless physically and unavoidably speaks *against* the bodily effacement which has been seen to go hand in hand with traditional Irish femininity. The incongruousness of Negga's visual appearance, compounded by the mismatch of her Irish-sounding voice, appears to necessitate interrogation when she performs 'as herself' in a public forum. I would argue that it has made Negga's casting in international productions such as the aforementioned *12 Years A Slave* and *World War Z* relatively dubious (accepting as well the unfair disadvantage at which performers of colour are always already poised when competing for high-profile roles). As evidenced by Negga's relative success in being cast in British and Irish television programmes and in supporting roles in films (most recently the British–Irish co-production *Jimi: All Is by My Side* [Ridley, 2013] and Irish production *Noble* [Bradley, 2014]), her star profile appears as yet only comfortably established in the British Isles by virtue of her local recognizability and reputation as an actor. It would appear that Negga's success as a star is contingent first on the negotiation of her ethnic identity within national specificity – Irish or assimilated as British – before she may be marketed more broadly internationally. Until then, the signified values of her physical off-whiteness and nominal Irishness as a female actor may not be satisfactorily reconciled into a commodifiable star image.

Addressing the possibility of a performed redefinition of female Irishness in contemporary film and media, Charlotte McIvor has provided a useful analysis of Negga's imagistic function as 'forc[ing] the audience towards a contemporary engagement with a transnational Irish history that illuminates the history of a "global Irish"' (2009: 30). While perhaps not done consciously on the part of casting directors in Irish films and television shows such as *Love/Hate* (Carolan, 2010–14), Negga's bodily presence on screen as a non-white Irish female nevertheless serves as a constant reminder of, and commentary on, her national identity and indeed the unstable definition of Irish femininity. Negga's unavoidable (and very much in quotation marks) 'colouredness' thus requires repeated definition and explanation in media and press, while the reiteration of her Irishness over a breadth of interviews seems to amount to a composite image of her as Irish *but-not-white*. Such reiteration constantly draws attention back to her body, her physicality, firstly as a non-white woman and secondly, *as a woman*. Thus, for Negga, Irishness, as a component of her star image, functions as a complement to her physicality as a performer and as an asset – however incongruous and self-contradictory – towards the concretization of a star image. For Ronan, meanwhile, the 'truth' of her ethnicity, even as she talks about it to Ellen Degeneres, is repeatedly disavowed or denied in the physical casting off of the signifiers of Irishness through her vocal performance or mimicry of accents commonly ascribed to other white ethnicities. It remains to be seen, however, how Negga might be further 'packaged' by Hollywood, ethnically and racially, as she develops her image as an increasingly and unavoidably *visible* Irish female star.

Conclusion

In this chapter, I have detailed how stardom on behalf of the Irish female performer has been made all but impossible in popular and mainstream cinema due to the cultural associations of Irishness-cum-femininity with stereotypical whiteness, bodilessness and asexuality, as well as a failure on behalf of the Irish film industry to promote indigenous female talent both nationally and abroad. However, as I have traced the rise to prominence of two talented film actors in the last decade, Saoirse Ronan and Ruth Negga, I would suggest that the palpable absence of Irish femininity from popular cinema and visual media is currently in a state of redress. Furthermore, in the light of Negga's a-typical performative affect as Irish but 'off-white', I have argued that she poses a particular problem to the signifying value of Irishness in the film texts and media in which she appears – which cannot be contained in the same way that the 'problem' of Ronan's Irish ethnicity in relation to her female stardom can be disavowed or indeed performed-against.

The distinction between Negga's and Ronan's various (re)presentations of Irishness therefore appears to be between Irishness-by-subscription on Negga's part, versus Irishness-in-containment on Ronan's. For Negga, the seeming incompatibility of her ethnic signifiers – visual versus aural affects – invites consideration of her (semiotically problematic) body. Meanwhile for Ronan, fetishization of her Irish moniker serves as an outlet almost for her ethnic identification as 'Irish', which might otherwise disallow focus on her physicality as a star. In this sense, Saoirse Ronan may be seen to perform *against* her Irish ethnicity, whereas Negga – whose body itself would seem to speak an 'Other' ethnicity – literally speaks *for* Irish-identification, but through new visual signifiers. Therefore, while Ronan's trajectory as a female performer in Hollywood is unlikely to see her promoted internationally as an 'Irish star', in keeping with an established representational paradigm, Negga's Irishness may continue to be invoked in explication of her visually and aurally incoherent or problematic star image. In that her image's incoherence is predicated on the mismatch of her body with the established cultural significations of Irish femininity, Negga thus embodies a 'new' sort of Irish female star, insistently – if problematically – self-identified and 'called out' as such, at the same time as she self-consciously performs, and is represented as, 'to-be-looked-at'.

Notes

1. I am limiting my discussion to these actresses' film work – accepting that Negga, in particular, has built up an impressive résumé of critically acclaimed stage roles – in that such stage work, by nature of its medium, is inherently local, or place-and-time-specific, and is not immediately reconcilable with the discussion of international stardom with which I am concerned here.
2. Male Irish stars like Farrell and Neeson open or are expected to open (would-be) blockbusters such as *Total Recall* (Wiseman, 2012) and *Non-Stop* (Collet-Serra, 2014). Meanwhile, Michael Fassbender works consistently as a second lead in blockbuster films (*X-Men: First Class* [Vaughan, 2011], *12 Years a Slave*) and takes top billing in high-profile independent and European-arthouse movies that get considerable press in the American market (*A Dangerous Method* [Cronenberg, 2011], *Shame* [McQueen, 2011]).
3. I am taking the theory of 'to-be-looked-at-ness' inherent to the female star/image from Laura Mulvey's theory of the gendered politics of viewing, founded in 'Visual Pleasure and Narrative Cinema' (1975). It should be noted that feminist film criticism since the 1970s has expanded on – and at times diverged from – Mulveyan apparatus theory to accommodate discussions of female agency, authorship and phenomenological impact, such as in the work of Tania Modleski and Gaylyn Studlar. Nevertheless, it remains a given within contemporary film and star studies that the image of woman has been constructed through the classical Hollywood style (with exception and notwithstanding certain evident strategies of subversion) as 'pure image', as put by Lucy Fischer in 'The Image of Woman as Image: The Optical Politics of "Dames"' (1976).
4. As Dyer (1997) has argued, whiteness in popular culture has come to represent an absence or even liberation from racial/ethnic specificity: an absence of 'colouration' in both literal and figurative terms.
5. Accessible at: https://www.youtube.com/watch?v=Ggx0qSjnbME.
6. It is important to note I designate Ronan's performance 'as Irish' in *The Grand Budapest Hotel* by virtue only of the aural signifier of her accent: her character is ostensibly Eastern European, a generic ethnic identity reminiscent of her role in *Hanna*. Ronan's performance through the Irish accent results from Anderson's tendency as a director to encourage actors to perform in their 'real' accents. Narratively, then, Ronan's performance is not intended to be read 'as Irish'; however, in that the integrity of her ethnic image is thus aurally preserved, I would argue her representation and performance as a star in

   this film goes some way towards contradicting/counteracting her extra-textual performative de-ethnicization.
7. Interestingly, however, Ronan is currently slated to star in John Crowley and Nick Hornby's adaptation of Colm Toibín's novel *Brooklyn*, to be released in 2015, in which she will play an Irish immigrant to America.
8. Accessible at: https://www.youtube.com/watch?v=Ggx0qSjnbME.

6
Transcending Parochial Borders? Jonathan Rhys Meyers *Is* Henry VIII

Liz Carville

Lingering in popular memory as one of history's most violent men, Henry Tudor was infamous for marrying and executing multiple wives in succession while severing all religious ties between England and Papal Rome. On being approached by the popular US Network *Showtime* to create a period soap opera based on the Tudor dynasty, writer Michael Hirst agreed, on condition that he could rewrite Henry VIII, not so much by altering the tyrant's character, but by seriously reinventing his appearance:

> I pitched Henry as a young, glamorous, athletic, sexy [...] etc., king because I was fed up of his English iconic version as a fat, bearded monster with a vast ego and vaster sexual appetite. Holbein's tyrant! He had everything! He was in fact a keen intelligence – and for me there was nothing more fascinating or sexy than getting him involved in the big political and religious issues of his day.
>
> (2007: xii)

It is true that the motivation to dramatize the Tudor reign is not surprising in itself. The scandalous reputation of the historical Henry VIII alone was both bizarre and outrageous enough to fuel the serialization the network desired. What is noteworthy, however, is that of all the talented and popular British (or even American) actors available, Hirst selected Irish actor, Jonathan Rhys Meyers, to render his interpretation of history:

> An actor had to come along who could not only play him, but embody him. It's ironic, given the rough history between our nations

71

that the man in question is an Irishman! But Jonathan Rhys Meyers, as an actor, easily transcends parochial borders. Indeed it was this refusal to accept limitations of any kind that connected him with the young king. And Jonathan recognized this, just as he instinctually recognized that Henry's love for his first wife, Katherine of Aragon, was never totally destroyed by his tearing passion for his second, Anne Boleyn. Such deep emotional attachments are not necessarily guided by the script but have to be felt in the performance.

(2007: xiv)

The 'rough history' that Hirst refers to concerns a religious and territorial conflict that has had major consequences for both Irish and English people. Historically, the Tudor entitlement to Ireland derived from a papal grant that proclaimed Henry II 'lord of Ireland'. However, Henry VIII was forced to revive this claim in 1540 once his dissolution of his first marriage ended England's allegiance to papal authority (Somerset Fry & Somerset Fry, 1991). Relations between England and Ireland had remained stable under Henry VII through the king's conciliatory relationship with his deputy in Ireland, the 9th Earl of Kildare, Gerald Fitzgerald (Campbell, 1995). Such accord ended when Fitzgerald was charged with arms offenses and imprisoned in the Tower of London, inciting his son, 'Silken Thomas', to initiate a rebellion against the English king (Somerset Fry & Somerset Fry, 1991). When, in 1535, Thomas' army took control of Maynooth Castle, Henry dispatched a new deputy, William Skeffington, with military to subdue the revolt. Once Thomas' forces were defeated, the young earl and five of his uncles were executed in London (Somerset Fry & Somerset Fry, 1991). With the downfall of the Fitzgeralds, the wealthiest power in Ireland at the time, there was little to prevent Henry from laying claim to Ireland in 1540, an occupation that had been too expensive for English kings before him (Somerset Fry & Somerset Fry, 1991). The Silken Thomas affair is not dealt with in the drama, but that is not to say that Irishness does not factor into the meanings the series produced: in casting Meyers as Henry VIII, Hirst was not only altering popular perception of a notorious icon in English history, but undermining four centuries of sectarian conflict for which that icon was responsible. What follows then, will isolate the kind of violent character that Meyers plays and determine to what extent the actor's ethnicity and star persona intersect with the Henry VIII of Hirst's series. This chapter will begin by considering the familiar stereotype of Irish violence and discuss its relevance to Meyers' recognition as an actor. Finally, it will consider examples from the series in order to understand the possible reasoning behind Hirst's decision to communicate the dark and inauspicious side of the English monarchic past through the commodifiable body of one of Ireland's latest sex symbols.

While the specific details of colonization in Ireland cannot be considered general knowledge, popular culture has to a certain degree cannibalized specific historical facts, which have subsequently become culturally embedded. As Colin Graham has stated, 'Ireland becomes a plenitude of images replicating itself for continual consumption and at times achieving an oversatiation. It is here that the "Ireland", which is excessive, topples into an Ireland of ceaseless reproduction and commodification' (2001: 2). Irishness has frequently functioned as shorthand for expressions of anger and physical aggression in male-centred narratives, to the extent that violence often appears as biologically atavistic in Irish people, rather than a response to political conflict, where 'a proclivity to violence was seen as a tragic flaw of the Irish themselves' (McLoone, 2000: 34). Ireland was constructed as the antithesis of England's propriety. The English, as Kiberd has pointed out, 'presented themselves to the world as controlled, refined and rooted; and so it suited them to find the Irish hot-headed, rude and nomadic, the perfect foil to set off their own virtues' (2002: 9).

Contemporary representations of Irish violence have originated and developed through four particular formulae. The first concerns localized images of Irish violence, which extended from English or occasionally Irish sources, and are referred to as 'Troubles' films. These films predominantly take a critical stance against Irish violence, specifically as it arose in relation to the civil conflict over Northern Ireland. The films centre on the period from the resurgence of intense political conflict in Northern Ireland from the 1970s to the middle of the 1990s, however, very few, if any, focus on the political motives concerned. Typically, these films cast the Troubles as a consequence of a pathological predisposition of the Irish to violent action.

The USA has been the second source of films relating to the Troubles and Irish violence. In the majority of those movies based on the political conflict between North and South, the Troubles have served as a narrative framework to resolve essentially American dramas following the conclusion of the Cold War, with *Patriot Games* (Noyce, 1992), *Blown Away* (Hopkins, 1994) and *The Devil's Own* (Pakula, 1997) among the most popular examples from the 1990s (McLoone, 2000). Thirdly, the predisposition of the Irish to violence has also emerged in a less obvious, but equally pervasive way, through the actions of Irish-American characters in Hollywood such as gangsters, firemen or law enforcers. In these instances, signifiers of Irishness such as red hair, a typically Irish surname, or even a Celtic soundtrack are taken as explanation for the unruly conduct of Irish-American characters. Finally, the appropriation of the gangster genre by indigenous Irish filmmakers has led to numerous films based on the criminal activities of the urban underworld in Ireland's major cities, predominantly set in Dublin, such as *I Went Down* (Breathnach, 1997), *The General* (Boorman, 1998), *Ordinary Decent Criminal* (O'Sullivan, 2000), *Disco Pigs* (Sheridan, 2001), *Intermission* (Crowley, 2003) and *In Bruges* (McDonagh, 2008). To a certain extent, these films glorify the violence perpetrated through the sarcasm and sharp wit of the male protagonists, in that the crime and gangland rivalries portrayed function as arenas in which to test and prove the characters' masculinity.

Given the volume of representations concerning Irish violence, alongside the political conflict that dominated the relationship between people in the North and South of Ireland, it is reasonable to consider that the stereotype correlating Irishness with violence impacted Hirst's decision to cast an Irish actor such as Meyers as Henry VIII. This is particularly suggested when taking Meyers' public recognition leading up to and throughout the initial airing of the first series. According to Hirst, one of the reasons the writer favoured Meyers for the role was due to the similarities that he saw between the actor and the character Hirst wished to present:

> Jonathan Rhys Meyers who played Henry VIII, shared quite a lot of traits with his character. So I could play to Johnny's temperament, for example Johnny has a short attention span, he has a kind of nerviness, and a sense of dangerousness. You can feel it in the atmosphere when he walks into the room. Like Henry, he has a short attention span and wants to be engaged and interested. I would play to this in scenes where I would have Henry come into the room and move between people and conversations, showing how he changed between being bored, interested, flirty, and angry. To me they were so similar in that way.
>
> (Hirst, cited in Potter, 2012)

For over ten years prior to his casting, Meyers had gradually been making a name for himself, with three characteristics principally shaping his public image. Firstly, Meyers' particular kind of good looks, with his chiselled jaw, his almost aquiline facial features and slender figure, made him highly popular as a male model. Meyers was selected as the icon for the popular men's fragrance and clothing brand *Hugo Boss*, and the young Irish actor featured in several of their advertising campaigns from 2005. Secondly, Meyers' career was crafted through parts involving attractive, mysterious but deeply unstable male characters often in historical dramas, films or mini-series set in a distant time or location, such as *Samson and Delilah* (Roeg, 1996), *The Governess* (Goldbacher, 1998), *Ride with the Devil* (Lee, 1999), *Titus* (Taymor, 1999), *Gormenghast* (Wilson, 2000), *The Emperor's Wife* (Vrebos, 2003), *Lionheart* (Konchalovskiy, 2003), *Vanity Fair* (Nair, 2004), *Alexander* (Stone, 2005) and *Elvis: The Early Years* (Sadwith, 2005). Thus, Meyers' role in *The Tudors* (Hirst, 2007) was very much in keeping with the kind of character that the young actor had played throughout his career to that date. In the majority of the films mentioned, Meyers plays characters that capitalize on his groomed appearance and, where applicable, his ability to replicate the English accent convincingly. However, since the millennium, the actor's ethnicity has become progressively more integrated into his roles and public image, and this is particularly apparent when considering the three major films of Meyers' career before his role in Hirst's series: *Alexander, Match Point* (Allen, 2005) and *Elvis: The Early Years*. In *Alexander*, Meyers played the effeminate Macedonian soldier, Cassander, in a film criticized because of director Oliver Stone's decision to use a cast of Irish actors as a means of employing Irishness as a metaphor for the Celticism of the Macedonian people. In *Match Point*, he was cast as a fortune-hunting Irish tennis player who goes to brutal lengths to sustain a loveless marriage for material benefit, while as Elvis, Meyers received a Golden Globe for his convincing portrayal of the troubled Hollywood icon. In this case, there was much media attention surrounding the decision to cast an Irish actor for the part, and Meyers frequently responded to questions when interviewed by drawing comparisons between his own impoverished background and that of his character (Harrington, 2005). As a result, by 2005, Meyers was not only becoming recognized as a credible dramatic actor, but also one noted for being of Irish extraction.

Thirdly, Meyers' image was deeply affected by his addiction to drugs and alcohol, predominantly as the actor made headlines for reacting violently to attempts to curb his behaviour when intoxicated. Throughout his career, Meyers has been noted for his excessive drinking habits and drug abuse, and was dropped by *Hugo Boss* for gaining negative publicity due to his reckless behaviour in his personal life. While it is not unusual for Hollywood stars to become the subject of scandal during their careers, incidents involving Irish actors and alcohol have been treated as indicative of an ethnic trait. Meyers' addiction has continued to punctuate his film career, and the actor has been arrested on numerous occasions for acting violently when intoxicated, most notably on three occasions while at airports in Dublin in 2007, Paris in 2009 and the USA in 2010, and also following a domestic dispute in 2006. The numerous portrayals concerning Irish violence in British, Irish and Hollywood cinema, the political conflict that dominated the relationship between Catholics and Protestants in the North and South of Ireland, as well as Meyers' expanding reputation as a serious actor with a deeply troubled personal life, are indicative of how the stereotype correlating Irishness with violence and Meyers' specific star persona affected Hirst's decision to cast the Irish actor as Henry VIII. It is therefore worth making note of the specific attributes that define the Henry VIII of Hirst's series. In this respect, it is interesting to consider the fact that one of the most resounding characteristics apparent in the first series is the way in which Henry's policies on warfare are frequently directed to serve personal rather than political ends.

The first major decision that Henry makes in the pilot episode is to declare war on France. On this occasion, it is in response to the murder of his uncle by French insurgents, but throughout the series, Henry displays what Cardinal Wolsey describes as 'an appetite for war' (Hirst, 2007: 42). For example, the king voices his disappointment when it is suggested he find a peaceful solution to the French assassination by exclaiming 'What! No battles? No glory?' (Hirst, 2007: 65). Throughout the series, Henry favours leisure pursuits that involve competition, such as jousting and tennis, or violence, such as hunting and archery, and Henry's personal predilections are integrated into his political decisions. Soon after agreeing a truce with France, he resumes his initial plan for war against the French. He forms another alliance with the king of Spain in order to invade France, and becomes 'increasingly excited' by the preparations. It is also worth noting that his only objective when initially considering peace with France is as a means of historical recognition. Arguably, however, the strongest example of Henry's perspective on warfare is stated in conversation with the king's close friend, former tutor and Lord Chancellor, Thomas More.

Frequently, More attempts to act as Henry's moral conscience by advocating humanist objectives and solutions to political predicaments. On a particular occasion in the pilot episode of the first series, Henry visits More in his home in Chelsea and the two men walk side by side along the river to discuss matters in confidence. More's objective in the conversation is to persuade Henry against a war with France by appealing to him to put his resources to better the lives of his people 'instead of spending ruinous amounts of money on war' (Hirst, 2007: 56). Henry's response, however, is not only indicative of his partiality for war, but also conveys the motivation behind Henry's decisions that Hirst wished to articulate:

> Thomas, I swear to you I intend to be a just ruler. But tell me this: Why is Henry V remembered? Because he endowed universities and built alm houses for the destitute? No. He is remembered because he won the battle of Agincourt. Three thousand English bowmen against sixty thousand French. The flower of French chivalry destroyed in four hours. That victory made him famous, Thomas. It made him immortal!
>
> (Hirst, 2007: 56)

Henry's response confirms both his preference and reasons for using warfare as a means to settle international grievances and raises an important aspect in relation to the character that Hirst wished to portray. The above quotation from the series leaves no room for speculation: Henry sees war as an opportunity for glory. More importantly, it reveals an intention on Hirst's part to present Henry's capacity for violence through his personality, rather than his body, and this aspect of the series is worth particular consideration.

When compared with previous dramatizations of Henry VIII, what arguably made Hirst's concept of Henry exceptional was the fact that, due to Meyers' rather lean build, he fails to cut an intimidating figure. In the opening episodes of the first series of *The Tudors*, several incidents occur that expose Meyers' Henry as a physically vulnerable king. In Episode 2, for example, Henry travels to France to sign a treaty with the French king, Francis, which, due to each man's dislike of the other, turns into a battle of one-upmanship. Both kings and their retinues gather in the Val D'Or, a dazzling palace constructed out of canvas and adorned with furnishings of silk and taffeta, where the continual goading of one king by the other eventually leads to a challenge of physical strength. Eager to prove that his kingdom possesses fighters of greater ability, Henry challenges King Francis to a wrestling match that proves foolhardy once Francis emerges victorious. Similarly, on another occasion in Episode 4, Henry is out hawking on horseback with his close friends, Knivert and Compton, and his usual train of servants, when a marsh impedes the riders' progress. Henry dismounts and, in a manner similar to that involving the king of France, is incited by his friends' insistence that the ditch cannot be crossed. Henry orders a flagpole and attempts to pole-vault over the marsh. However, when the pole snaps, the king almost suffocates, as he is submerged in mud and unable to breathe. In the same episode, Henry is nearly blinded when he omits to secure the protective visor for his face before competing in a joust and is wounded when knocked from his horse by Knivert; while in Episode 6, he is defeated in an arm-wrestling match against Charles Brandon. This incident is another in which Henry proposes a challenge that he is unable to fulfil: Brandon loses the king's favour when he elopes with Henry's sister, Margaret, and Henry challenges Brandon to the test of strength in order to win permission to return to court. It is worth noting that the actor who played Brandon, Henry Cavill, later went on to play superman in Zack Snyder's rendering of the superhero story, *Man of Steel* (2013), where the actor proved to be a credible successor to Christopher Reeve, with his lean but muscular frame. Meyers himself undertook a vigorous exercise regime for his role as Henry, but, with his biceps exposed, the arm-wrestling scene only serves to emphasize Cavill's greater strength, particularly when Meyers loses so definitively in the challenge. Henry's face contorts with rage and pressure and he appears far more tested by the encounter than Brandon does.

The previous examples not only demonstrate Meyers' lack of physicality in the role, but also reveal the kind of Henry that Hirst wished to present on screen. One of the most recognizable images of Henry VIII was the portrait created by the 16th-century artist Hans Holbein, which portrays the king as a man of thickset build with a bearded face characterized by a broad nose and heavy jowls. It was imperative that Hirst presented a credible Henry VIII with a capacity to threaten, if not in appearance, then with his menacing personality. Throughout the opening series, Meyers' Henry displays a volatile temper when events fail to go his way. For example, Henry is so outraged when defeated by the king of France in the wrestling match that he threatens to renege on signing the treaty uniting their two countries, until Thomas More intervenes to try to calm the situation:

All right. If you want the world to think that the king of England is easily changeable, shallow, intemperate, incapable of keeping his word – then, of course I'll go and tell them. After all, I am merely Your Majesty's humble servant.

(Hirst, 2007: 109)

While Henry does go through with the peace agreement, a violent tantrum before departing France reveals him to possess exactly those faults that More has accused him of, and Henry makes plans to negotiate with Spain almost immediately on returning to England. Given the thorough description in Hirst's final shooting script of the scene, it is informative to quote at length:

INT: KING'S APARTMENTS – PALACE OF ILLUSIONS – DAY

HENRY stands alone in his beautiful apartment, holding the Gospels in his hand. A long beat, then he hurls the book across the chambers, smashing something. Then seizing an ornamental axe from the wall, he starts to destroy the apartment. Because everything is so flimsy (the walls made of canvas and only painted to look like bricks), it is easier for him to wreak havoc. He tears the illusion to bits, his cold fury so great and terrifying as he hacks about him that no servant or groom dares approach. They back off, disappear... while HENRY grunts with concentration, destroying the dream.

(Hirst, 2007: 111)

As the scene demonstrates, Henry's ego frequently causes him to react in a volatile manner when denied what he wants or when diminished in pride by a rival or peer. For instance, before challenging Brandon to arm-wrestle for his place in court in Episode 6, Henry forces Brandon, who remains his closest friend until his death, to kneel and beg forgiveness. Similarly, on an earlier occasion in Episode 4, he reacts violently when demeaned in a pamphlet by the ecumenical reformer, Martin Luther. Luther accuses the king of 'raving like a strumpet in a tantrum' in a manuscript that Henry published damning Luther and his cause (Hirst, 2007: 209). Henry's rage at being described in such a degrading way by the priest provokes him to fling crockery across the room, declaring that Luther 'ought to be burned' (Hirst, 2007: 210). Equally revealing are the particularly cruel methods that Henry employs when dealing with those who displease him, for example, in the execution of Lord Buckingham in Episode 2. Buckingham believes that he is the rightful successor to the English throne and is sentenced to death once he is discovered plotting against Henry. Notwithstanding the way in which the series contains detailed scenes conveying the brutality of execution methods in Tudor England, the fact that Henry places a carriage clock in Buckingham's room on the eve of his execution, containing the inscription 'with humble, true heart' is particularly meaningful in the context of the episode

(Hirst, 2007: 131). The clock was a gift from Buckingham to Henry the previous Christmas, and the placement reveals Henry's spiteful attempt to rile the lord over and above the fatal sentence he has imposed. Similarly, in Episode 10, the king lulls Cardinal Wolsey into a false sense of security before removing him of his seal of office and confiscating his assets. Wolsey is subjected to several humiliations and the scene in which Henry rides off leaving Wolsey begging for the king is particularly affecting. Even in the case of his wife, Catherine of Aragon, Henry is so incensed at the queen's refusal to acquiesce to his wishes that he threatens to separate her from Mary, their daughter and only surviving child together, and the incident stands as another example of how Henry's character is presented as one capable of dealing cruelly with those who displease him.

In conclusion, it should be stated that the facts surrounding the actions of the historical Henry VIII reveal more serious examples of violence; namely, the execution of several of Henry's wives and his decision to seize the assets and subdue the occupants of Catholic monasteries in England. While the occasions cited – although examples of an unstable temper – are not comparable to such severely violent deeds for which the historical figure is most infamous, they are in a way more relevant when taking Hirst's portrayal into account. No amount of creative license on Hirst's part could extend to altering such documented facts as the beheading of Anne Boleyn, but how Hirst stages the way that Henry responds to less serious events, such as his defeat by Francis or Brandon or the insult by Luther, does indicate the kind of volatile man that Hirst wished to portray: namely, a king whose fury manifested itself in his tempestuous mentality rather than in physical displays of prowess. With his lean figure, effeminate appearance and Irish nationality, the casting of Jonathan Rhys Meyers as Henry VIII arguably challenged contemporary expectations of the series or any previous representations of the notorious English king. The casting reveals certain interesting points regarding the uses of Irishness in popular culture, and also the meanings attached to Irishness and Irish masculinity in popular discourse. In presenting egocentric motives behind historical events, Hirst created a character with a penchant for warfare as a means of solving personal conflicts, particularly when taking into account the fact that Meyers' body does not strike an intimidating figure in the series. This suggests that Hirst's intention for the character was a man whose ferocity was communicated through his volatile personality: a personality that Hirst claimed Meyers 'instinctively' possessed. Hirst's Henry VIII may not be played 'Irish', but the fact that Meyers was specifically selected to portray him does suggest an attempt to harness some aspect of Meyers' character which distinguished him from other eligible British actors who were perhaps more ethnically suitable for the role. According to Meyers:

> ...they saw something in me that they liked in their Henry. They wanted the fresh, youthful, impetuousness to this Henry that makes him do the things that he does and to create something that was quite different to anything that had been seen before. Barring the physical, you know? My Henry is not Keith Richard's or Richard Burton's or Ray Winston's – it's mine.
>
> ('Becoming Henry VIII' *The Tudors*, 2007 [DVD]
> Created by Michael Hirst USA: Showtime)

7

Old and New Irish Ethnics: Exploring Ethnic and Gender Representation in *P.S. I Love You*

Silvia Dibeltulo

In this chapter, I will analyse how Irish identity is expressed and signified in *P.S. I Love You* (LaGravenese, 2007), using it as a paradigmatic example of the portrayal of Irishness in contemporary mainstream American cinema. Specifically, I will focus on the contrast between 'old' and 'new' Irish ethnics and I will highlight the complexities associated with the representation of hyphenated identities as opposed to non-hyphenated ones. My approach will draw on Herbert J. Gans' influential theory of 'symbolic ethnicity' in order to examine the nostalgic attitude towards the 'old country' as a way of expressing ethnic identity and, thus, to illustrate Hollywood's vision of the relationship between Irish-Americans and their ancestral homeland, as well as its people. This chapter will also address issues of gender in relation to the representation of Irish masculinity in the film. In this context, I will analyse the intersection of ethnic and gender identity in the portrayal of the Irish male as a commodified object of sexual desire.

In his essay 'Symbolic Ethnicity: The Future of Ethnic Groups and Cultures in America' (1979), Herbert J. Gans argues that, for later-generation European-Americans, ethnic identity is something that can be assumed or dismissed at one's leisure rather than existing essentially as an inherent characteristic. As ethnic affiliation, for later-generation ethnics, can no longer be taken for granted, ethnicity needs to be expressed in novel ways. Gans observes that, since expressive behaviour often deploys symbols, such 'new ways of being ethnics' can be defined as 'symbolic ethnicity' (1979: 6). Symbolic ethnicity is intermittent and, as a consequence, it does not interfere with other practices and ways of life. Such a convenient way of expressing ethnic identity

allows later-generation ethnics to choose 'when and how to play ethnic roles' (Gans, 1979: 8), without compromising their assimilation
into the hosting society. Symbolic ethnicity works via the abstraction
of signs and symbols originating from the old ethnic culture: commu-
nicative elements that are de-contextualized and subsequently made
more easily recognizable indicators of that culture. One of the features of this expressive behaviour is, according to Gans, a nostalgic
attitude towards the 'old country'. The return to the diasporic homeland is one possible manifestation of this kind of nostalgia. Gans'
theory has been substantiated by Richard D. Alba and Mary C. Waters'
ethnographic studies on later-generation European-Americans (Alba,
1990; Waters, 1990). These sociologists stress the voluntary aspect of
ethnic identification at a time when being 'ethnic' is no longer placed
in contrast with being 'American'. Waters replaces the notion of ethnicity as something 'biological or primordial' with the idea of 'ethnic
self-identification' (1990: 16). The active approach towards ethnic identification described by the sociologists is evident in the film under
scrutiny here, to the extent that ethnic expression borders on ethnic
performance.

P.S. I Love You – a romantic comedy/drama based on the international
bestseller of the same title by Irish novelist Cecilia Ahern (2004) – tells
the story of a young widow, Holly (Hilary Swank), who receives letters which her late husband Gerry (Gerard Butler) had arranged to have
delivered to her after his death. The central narrative is punctuated by
flashbacks that retrace the couple's love story. Not surprisingly, apart
from being labelled 'an exercise in chick-flickery' (Anderson, 2007),
P.S. I Love You has been criticized for its weepiness, and has been
described as being replete with 'melodramatic excesses' (Dargis, 2007).
However, in spite of its poor critical reception,[1] the film has been relatively well received by audiences, grossing US$156,835,339 worldwide
(Box Office Mojo, 2014).

While in the novel all the characters are Irish and live in Dublin, the
film is set in New York City. Holly is a later-generation Irish-American,
whereas Gerry is a new immigrant, having only recently moved to the
United States. Among several changes, the film introduces the motif of
the Irish-American's return to the homeland of his/her ancestors. Obviously, the change in the location of the story and the nationality of
most of the characters entails issues of ethnic-identity representation
which are absent in the book. The film allows for a comparison between
an Irish-American and an Irish identity, more specifically, between a
hyphenated and a non-hyphenated form of Irishness. In this sense,

P.S. I Love You presents itself as an interesting case showing the points of contact and divergence in the way that contemporary Hollywood cinema represents these two forms of Irishness.

Gerry's Irish identity is established in the long pre-credit sequence, during which the couple has a heated fight. The first and most obvious indication of Gerry's Irishness is his accent.[2] Adding evidentially to that, his nationality is revealed by Holly when she complains: 'Why can't I be the cute, carefree Irish guy who sings all the time?' The function of Holly's remark is twofold: firstly, it marks Gerry's otherness; secondly, in its attempt to make Irishness instantly recognizable to the audience, it reinforces one of many long-established stereotypes about the Irish. At this stage, Holly is positioned as a 'non-hyphenated' American who is defining Gerry by virtue of his ethnic difference. In keeping with an inveterate cinematic and literary tradition, Gerry embodies the stereotypical Irish character: high-spirited, fiery, carefree, funny and entertaining. In addition, he plays the guitar and sings: a habit that Holly clearly associates with Irishness, as she asks, 'Do all Irishmen sing?' Holly's rhetorical question is adequate evidence of Noel MacLaughlin and Martin McLoone's observation that 'a key element in the range of stereotypes characteristically assigned to the Irish has been their natural proclivity for music and song' (2012: 181).

Another way of stressing Gerry's ethnic otherness is his use of Irish slang words and expressions, such as the ones uttered during an exchange at the beginning of the film:

Gerry: Oh, that's *me* bollocks!
Holly: Stop acting bilingual.
Gerry: Oh, kiss *me* arse.
Holly: Kiss mine, in English!

Interestingly, this conversation takes place at a particularly tense moment during the couple's fight in the pre-credit sequence, as if to signify that once Gerry has disengaged himself from the linguistic inhibitions that force him to communicate through 'Holly's English', his real self emerges from idiosyncratic ethnic language. Subsequently, as if this was not an eloquent enough display of Irishness, Gerry performs a striptease wearing a pair of shamrock-patterned boxer shorts. While accent and linguistic idiosyncrasies can be seen as two realistic features used to code the ethnic identity of a relatively recent immigrant, the further display of an ethnic symbol – the shamrock – for the same purpose betrays a representational pattern recurrent in stereotypical depictions.

From a diegetic point of view, the character should not need to deploy ethnic signifiers in order to affirm his Irishness, as this has already been established in the previous scenes. Countering the need for this narrative hyperbolic reiteration, we might review Gans, who has argued that 'ethnics have always had an ethnic identity, but in the past it was largely taken for granted' (1979: 8). First-generation European immigrants who migrated to America between the end of the 19th century and the first decades of the 20th century were not generally concerned with ethnic expression. Conversely, later-generation ethnics, who are no longer part of 'groups that anchor their ethnicity', need to make their ethnic identity 'more explicit than it was in the past, and must even look for ways of expressing it' (Gans, 1979: 8). If we consider the representation of Gerry's Irishness in the light of this observation, it becomes apparent that the character does not take his ethnic identity for granted, but he consciously expresses it through relevant symbols (such as the shamrock). This suggests that when it comes to the representation of ethnic identity, the 'new' immigrant is treated as if he were an 'old' immigrant (a later-generation ethnic). Such an excess of ethnic expression betrays an over-simplified vision of Irish identity which encompasses both hyphenated and non-hyphenated characters indiscriminately.

The presence of extra-diegetic 'striptease music' during the first part of the scene in question indicates that Gerry's performance is addressed to the audience as well as to Holly. The sequence ends with Holly's humorous remark: 'I can't believe I'm in love with a leprechaun!' Later on, a man dressed up as a leprechaun delivers one of Gerry's letters to Holly. This is the second Irish-themed performance organized by Gerry, although this time another character is performing. Even more clearly than the striptease scene, this episode signals a concept of ethnic identity as a costume, something that can be expressed through carnivalesque display. In this sense, the film makes no distinction between Irish and non-Irish individuals, as both Gerry and the deliveryman 'dress up as Irish'. Put differently, Irishness, as an ethnic costume, can be worn by anybody. The casting of a non-Irish actor for the role of Gerry corroborates the idea of ethnic identity as something that can be represented as a costume even further.

It is only after the opening credits that we realize that Holly is Irish-American. The narrative moves, through a flash-forward, to the wake of her husband who has recently died of a brain tumour. The sequence opens with an exterior shot of an Irish bar, with a harp-shaped neon sign hanging above the door. As the camera cuts to the inside, we see Holly's mother, Mrs Reilly (Kathy Bates), behind the counter in the process of having affairs arranged for the wake, and low Celtic music is audible in the background. Gerry's favourite song 'Fairytale of New York' by The Pogues is played at the ceremony. The guests honour the dead by drinking shots of Jameson (Irish) whiskey.[3] Many commentators have indicated The Pogues' association with the Irish diaspora's experience. MacLaughlin and McLoone have argued that the band 'address[es] the Irish emigrant through song narratives that offer an "in-betweenness"' (2012: 191). Similarly, Joe Cleary observes that The Pogues are linked to sentiments of 'emigrant nostalgia' (2007: 261). In this sense, the band's music works as an ethnic signifier, as it provides a widely recognizable manifestation of Irish America's diasporic identity. The film opens with another song performed (extra-diegetically) by The Pogues – 'Love You 'till the End' – which is later sung by Gerry and Holly. Thus, the film employs The Pogues' music as a transnational, or rather transatlantic, signifier of Irishness that can be simultaneously appropriated by both old and new Irish ethnics as a common ground for expressing their shared ethnic identity.

By comparing the ways in which Irish identity is expressed in the pre-credit sequence and in the wake sequence, we can see how Holly's Irishness is presented as something extrinsic, acquired, more like a family tradition than an inherent quality of the self, whereas Gerry's Irishness is unequivocally associated with the individual, rather than with social or familial practices and rituals. If, in the former instance, Holly perceives herself, and is perceived by the viewer, as 'American', especially because she highlights Gerry's ethnic otherness, in the latter she is seen as part of an ethnic family/community. The complexity of Holly's hyphenated identity is first manifest when she defines herself indisputably as Irish. After receiving Gerry's first letter on her birthday, Holly and her Irish-American friend Daniel try to figure out why 'God killed Gerry':

Daniel: Hey, you're Irish. Maybe it's an Irish curse or something.
Holly: Gerry and I did love the Yankees, which is pretty much against our religion.

Here, Holly's Irishness is equated with Gerry's via their shared religion: Catholicism. At the same time, their love for the New York Yankees baseball team stands for assimilation into the American society and as a betrayal of one's ethnic allegiance. Holly's 'ethnic explanation' suggests a polarization of the two sides of the hyphenated self, whereby affiliation with one – in this case the American side represented by the New York Yankees – implies disloyalty towards the other.

And yet, despite such overt manifestations of Irishness, Holly is coded as American when she is in Ireland. During one of her trips, Holly goes to Whelan's, Gerry's favourite pub. Here she meets an Irish man, William (Jeffrey Dean Morgan), who later turns out to be an old friend of Gerry's. Holly's friends, Sharon and Denise, try to convince her to introduce herself to him: 'You are American, you've got exotic stuff going,' Sharon says. 'There's nothing exotic about being American,' Holly replies. When she finally talks to William, he asks whether she is American, to which she replies in the affirmative. The whole sequence serves the purpose of establishing Holly's otherness in a quintessentially (stereotypical) Irish setting: the pub. Her Americanness is further underlined in the following sequence. During a boat trip on a lake, Denise encourages Holly to find William. She replies 'No!' and adds that William must believe she is an idiot since she left without saying goodbye to him. In an attempt to cheer her up, Denise remarks, 'You are an American. They expect us to be idiots'.

The fact that, depending on the geographical context, Holly is seen as either Irish or American is an implication of the complex relationship between the diasporas and their originating cultures. Stephanie Rains has observed:

> The 'sameness' which Irish-Americans are seen to have in relation to Ireland is a product of their positioning within wider American society, as a form of continuity with an inheritance from their common Irish cultural background. So this 'sameness' is a relative perception, made against the Irish-American diaspora's 'difference' from other ethnic and diasporic communities within the United States. Yet, seen against the reference point of contemporary Ireland, this same diasporic group is often seen in terms of its 'difference' from Irish culture, by virtue of both the cultural influence of those very American ethnic groups who identify the Irish-Americans as 'the same' as the Irish, and by the temporal and spatial ruptures inherent to their diasporic status.
>
> (2007: 204–5)

Indeed, Holly's ethnic identity only becomes visible when it is put in relation to a broader American context. When she is in Ireland, Holly never questions her Americanness, nor does she manifest her Irish ethnic background. In other words, her 'difference' is asserted at the expense of her 'sameness'. Nevertheless, when she is in America, her ethnic identity is challenged by Gerry's in that the 'wholeness' and purported 'purity' of his Irishness highlights how hers is hyphenated and, therefore, one supposes, compromised. As a result, Holly is presented as an American who, as Gans would put it, sometimes 'plays an ethnic role'. In this sense, the film's approach to ethnic identity reflects the emphasis Alba and Waters put on the voluntary nature of ethnic identification.

As I have noted above, Gans argues that the return to the ancestral homeland is 'another variety of symbolic ethnicity' (1979: 11). Holly visits Ireland three times. The scene at the beginning of her first visit is set in the Wicklow Mountains, where she meets and falls in love with Gerry. The idyllic country location and the exaltation of the landscape, through the use of artificially bright colours, reveal a romanticized vision of Ireland as a rural space. The cinematic tradition that has inspired this vision can be easily evidenced as an intertextual reworking of Sean Thornton's first encounter with Mary Kate Danaher in *The Quiet Man* (Ford, 1952). Gerry – a male version of the Irish colleen[4] – is seen emerging from the landscape just like Mary Kate, as if it was common for Irish people in the 21st century to *walk* through rural locations instead of driving or using any other modern form of transport. In this way, the film indicates that Hollywood still tends to depict Ireland as a rural and backward society, whose habitants live in perfect harmony with nature and, more significantly, in a pre-modern state.

Holly's second trip to Ireland is also set in the countryside. The country house in which she stays with her female friends embodies the quintessence of the (Irish-)American fairy-tale idea of Ireland as a land of ancestral memories, peacefulness and soulfulness.[5] The house is set in a bright green garden surrounded by fields populated with sheep. Ireland is presented as a 'magic' land of happiness, where people are, or become happy, by virtue of mere habitation. Indeed, on this occasion, Holly experiences her first moments of happiness, as well as a reawakening of her sexuality, since her husband's death. Her last visit is the film's most evident enactment of the trope of the immigrant's return to the ancestral home. This time Holly goes to Ireland to show her mother the land of their ancestors and, most importantly, to facilitate her rediscovery of happiness. Mrs Reilly, who has not laughed since her husband abandoned her and her daughters, finally bursts into laughter at a humorous and flattering remark made by an Irish man. The scene also hints at a happy ending as Holly is reunited with William.

Gans claims that the motif of the immigrant's return, as a manifestation of symbolic ethnicity, 'is characterized by a nostalgic allegiance to the culture of the immigrant generation, or that of the old country' (1979: 9). In *P.S. I Love You*, the sentimentality and nostalgia linked to the old country are heightened by the fact that it was in Ireland that Holly first met Gerry.[6] A recurring element of the narrative of the Irish-American's return to Ireland is the touristic attitude towards the country and its people. While analysing various Irish heritage products 'intended for the consumption by later-generation Irish-Americans', Rains concludes that 'the common factor [...] is clearly the process of commodifying Irishness and its representations for diasporic consumption' (2007: 102).[7] She points out that a certain kind of representation of the country has long been employed in both touristic and artistic representations:

> The depiction of Ireland in terms of a pre-modern idyll for visitors (and, by implication for the Irish too) is one of the most consistent recurring themes of the nation's tourist imagery. [...] The leisurely pace of Irish life, and its promise to the visitor of the opportunity to escape from the pressures of modern, work-dominated life, is also a central feature of Irish tourism's ongoing representation of the country.
>
> (Rains, 2007: 111)

As Rains notes, since the 1950s, Irish tourism has made a significant use of film narrative as a form of promotional material. At the same time, cinematic depictions have tended not to stray from already established images of the country in order to satisfy audiences' firmly entrenched expectations. Such a long-lasting exchange of mutual benefit between film and tourism has created a trend in which Irishness, as a commodified popular cultural product, can be as easily consumed by both tourists and film viewers. Indeed, the conflation of consumerism and longing for ethnicity characterizes a number of recent Irish-themed romantic comedies. Like *P.S. I Love You*, *The Matchmaker* (Joffe, 1997)[8] and *Leap Year* (Tucker, 2010) feature an American woman who travels to Ireland and falls in love with both the country and a local man.

It has been noted that one of the key aspects of the commodification of Irishness on film and through tourist images is the objectification of Irish people as one of the many 'treasures' of the country (Rains, 2007). *P.S. I Love You* articulates explicitly the notion that Irish people might be seen as souvenirs. When Denise first sees William, she exclaims, 'Please let me *buy* him as a *souvenir!'* Along the same lines, Sharon remarks: 'We don't have those in the States! They don't *make* those!' Although they are humorous, these comments convey unequivocally the concept of the Irish male as something that is *made* in order to be *bought* as a souvenir and brought back home to America. The context of these remarks reveals the erotic nature of this objectification: Holly has not had a sexual encounter in a long time; therefore, her friends are trying to arrange a date between her and William.

The theme of the Irish man as object of sexual desire appears earlier in the narrative. As I noted above, the beginning of the love story between Holly and Gerry recalls the dynamics of *The Quiet Man*, in which an Irish-American travels to Ireland and falls in love with a local person. In *The Quiet Man*, it is Sean, the Irish-American, who first catches sight of Mary Kate against a manifestly stereotypical Irish landscape: the scene is an example of the tendency illustrated by Laura Mulvey (1975), whereby classical mainstream cinema has tended to objectify the passive female character to satisfy the gaze of the male (spectator, character and filmmaker). In *P.S. I Love You*, the Irish-American, Holly, is not the bearer of the gaze and, by extension, the point of view. In a reiteration of the trend identified by Mulvey, Holly, as a female character, is the passive object of Gerry's (male) gaze.

The comparison between the two scenes shows that, even if Gerry is an object of sexual desire throughout the story, his objectification never entails feminization. Since Gerry is the bearer and not the object of the gaze, his masculinity is not questioned or jeopardized. With regard to this, Steve Neale (1992) argues that making a male character the recipient of a female look necessarily involves a process of feminization. Taking as an example Rock Hudson's on-screen persona in Douglas Sirk's melodramas, he observes that there are moments in which the actor is presented as the object of a female erotic look and that his 'body is *feminized* in those moments, an indication of the strength of those conventions which dictate that only women can function as the objects of an explicit erotic gaze' (Neale, 1992: 286, emphasis in original).

The film presents Gerry's as an ideal kind of masculinity, especially thanks to his sex appeal. Gerry, along with his replica, William, is portrayed as a better option for Holly compared with American (or other) men. From the beginning of the film, in the striptease scene, Gerry's ethnic identity is both exoticized and eroticized: via an accentuation of his Irishness, he is presented as an exotic object of love and sexual desire. The connection between sex appeal and ethnic identity could not have been more blatant, as Gerry wears a pair of shamrock-patterned boxer shorts. Gerry's sexuality is emphasized throughout the film through a conspicuous attention to his looks and especially his muscular, and frequently half-naked, body. In all of the scenes in which Holly imagines that Gerry is still 'around', he is seen bare-chested. When he is dressed, he usually wears tight T-shirts that highlight his biceps and pectoral muscles. This 'fixation' with the Irish male's body goes even further in a scene in which William, having had a shower, comes out of the bathroom completely naked while Holly, from another room, stares at him.

In recent times, Irish masculinity has been increasingly associated with sexiness and with a specific attention to the body. The most popular example of this trend is Irish-born actor Colin Farrell, whose sex-symbol/playboy status has often been linked to his Irishness. This eroticized type of Irish masculinity marks a shift towards a less aggressive type of Irish male, especially in comparison with the ever-recurring violent-prone Irish and Irish-American gangsters and criminals of the Hollywood cinematic tradition. At the same time, however, thanks to an association with sexual potency,[9] as indicated by the fetishization of underwear garments as signs of ethnic identity, the Irish male is not emasculated.

The Irish male's popularity needs to be analysed in relation to the wider context of a renewed appreciation of Irish ethnicity in post-9/11 America. Diane Negra (2006) argues that in the light of America's concern with ethnic otherness after the events of 9/11, Irishness has been employed as a means of exalting whiteness, while simultaneously showing America's tolerance and benevolence towards ethnics. Negra claims that 'Irishness may be more and more a pose that enables a hard, masculine Americanness a foray into sentiment and recollection without engendering any deviation from identity as stipulated' (2006: 363). Thus, the conflation of romance, sentimentality and sexually potent masculinity embodied by Gerry is, arguably, a reflection of a specific function of Irishness in contemporary American society. As Debbie Ging has rightly noted, the film's fascination with Gerry has to do to with the fact that he represents an 'idealised ethnic identity, both proud of its traditions and yet unequivocally confident in its sense of belonging to the dominant culture' (2013: 197). Ging's observation brings us back to Gans' notion of symbolic ethnicity as something which allows for ethnic identification while not being in conflict with mainstream Americanness.[10] The objectification of the Irish male as the personification of this kind of ethnicity mirrors the tendency to manifest ethnic identity as 'self-conscious consumption of goods and services', as described by Marilyn Halter (2000: 7). In the context of what she labels a 'postmodern ethnic revival' (Halter, 2000: 83) – a phenomenon of renewed interest in ethnicity in America that started in the 1990s – the nostalgic willingness to reclaim an ethnic identity is expressed through the consumption of ethnic-themed commercial and cultural products. Ultimately, the film indicates that popular culture constantly reinvents ethnicity even if it employs the same set of symbols for ethnic expression. Indeed, Irishness, as much as other ethnic identities, is constantly readjusted to new purposes, and is invested with novel meanings and multiple functions, which make the examination and interpretation of ethnic-identity representation an ongoing endeavour.

Notes

1. Rotten Tomatoes (2014) indicates that only 24% of the 101 film's reviews surveyed are positive.
2. The Scottish actor's stereotypical Irish accent has been harshly criticized by Irish film critics. For example, Michael Dwyer (2007) has claimed that Butler's accent is 'as authentic as a leprechaun'.
3. The scene bears a striking resemblance to a wake scene in one of the episodes of the American television series *The Wire* (2002–08), analysed by Gerardine Meaney: 'In an extraordinary wake scene in the third series of *The Wire*, the ritual mourning of a dead colleague involves laying him out at Kavanagh's Irish Pub, an oration, a great deal of drink, and the singing of The Pogues' 'Body of an American' by a group of colleagues [...]' (2007: 13). The use of two songs by The Pogues in both scenes confirms the band's association with the Irish diaspora's experience in popular culture.
4. As if to make the connection between Gerry and Maureen O' Hara's Mary Kate even more blatant, here Butler's hair is slightly reddish, whereas in the other scenes of the film it is black.
5. For an extensive discussion on the romanticization of Ireland in cinematic representations, see Luke Gibbons (1988) 'Romanticism, Realism and Irish Cinema' in Rockett, Gibbons and Hill (1998: 194–257).
6. The nostalgic attitude of Irish-Americans towards Ireland is also indicated in a scene set in the Irish Hunger Memorial in New York City. The choice of this location strengthens the notion of Irish America's enduring relationship with Ireland, as well as the awareness of the significance of its diasporic past.
7. On the commodification of Irishness and its market in the United States, see also Negra (2001a) 'Consuming Ireland: Lucky Charms Cereal, Irish Spring Soap, and 1–800-Shamrock'. *Cultural Studies*. 15(1), pp. 76–97; The 'Best Kept Secret in Retail, Selling Irishness in Contemporary America' (Casey, cited in Negra, 2006: 84–109).

8. In this respect, even if the female protagonist is not Irish-American, *The Matchmaker* (Joffe, 1997) can be seen as precursor of *P.S. I Love You*. In his analysis of the film, Barry Monahan argues that the film is pervaded by a sense that 'Irish culture has become [...] a commodified *end in itself*', so much so that 'the hyper-commodification of everything Irish provides a framework for much of the humor in the film' (Monahan, 2009a: 333, emphasis in original).

9. Gerardine Meaney (2007) has pointed out that sexual potency is a key factor in the ethnic definition of Tommy Gavin, the Irish-American fireman protagonist of the television series *Rescue Me* (Fortenberry et al., 2004–11).

10. While *P.S. I Love You* (LaGravenese, 2007) reflects Gans' vision of ethnicity, as it suggests that the two sides of Holly's hyphenated identity co-exist harmoniously, this is not the case for other films featuring ethnic characters. Specifically, gangster film has traditionally been the locus for the exploration of the conflict between ethnic and American identity, and between ethnic identification and assimilation, thus investing ethnicity with other meanings and connotations. Such a conflictual vision better reflects Werner Sollors' (1986) theory of ethnicity, which emphasizes the tensions inherent in hyphenated identities.

8

Mediating between *His & Hers*: An Exploration of Gender Representations and Self-Representations

Patricia Neville

By the time Ken Wardrop's 2009 film *His & Hers* received its Irish cinema release on 18 June 2010, there had already been considerable industry anticipation about the film. In May 2009, it won the 5th US Distributors Showcase, the Directors Finders Series 2009, which enabled the film to get a screening with a number of key US distributors and filmmakers (Wardrop & Freeman, 2009). The film also went on to have a successful festival season. It garnered many accolades, including the Feature Award in the Galway Film Fleadh (July 2009), where the film also had its début (Whitaker, 2009), the Audience Award at the Dublin International Film Festival, the Cinematography Award at the Sundance Film Festival and the George Morrison Feature Award for Best Documentary at the Irish Film and Television Awards (Element Pictures, 2010).

The Oscar-winning documentary filmmaker Michael Moore exclaimed that *His & Hers* was 'One of the most moving and original films I've seen this year. No one has ever made a documentary like this one. In a summer of tired and stale movies from Hollywood "His & Hers" is a breath of fresh air blowing in from the midlands of Ireland' (quoted in Element Pictures, 2010). The national press were equally glowing in their reviews. Lauded as 'Very possibly the best Irish film we'll see this year' by the *Irish Independent* (quoted in Element Pictures, 2010), the film and its content seemed to strike an affective note among its reviewers. This 'Impossibly charming, sweetly profound' film was deemed to have the ability to transform and affect even the most hardened viewer. Indeed, one critic remarked, 'You will need a heart of stone not to be moved by it. You will walk from the cinema with a smile on your face, and call your mother' (quoted in www.irishfilmboard.ie, 29 June 2010).

The documentary *His & Hers* offers access to one of the most intimate aspects of a woman's experience: her relationship with the men in her life. Through the contributions of 70 different women from the Irish midlands, the narrative takes a life-course approach, tracing the stories of the women's relationships with the opposite sex, first as young girls and daughters, and later as women, married or widowed. In this respect, the documentary breaks new ground in terms of its cinematic representation of Irish femininity. With a documentary lens, we are introduced to an array of 'real' and 'authentic' expositions about the minutiae of intimate relationships (Corner, 1996: 10). Despite the personal and gendered subject matter of the film, it proved a hit among Irish cinemagoers. It was released in a select number of Irish cinemas on 18 June 2010 (Murphy, 2010). Even though it only grossed €40,000 in its first week of general release, its popularity grew and, by its second week, *His & Hers* was being shown in ten cinemas and had entered the top ten of the EDI charts (Element Pictures, 2010). Twelve weeks later, it was still being shown in Irish cinemas and had amassed €300,000 in box-office sales. Such cinema returns were all the more striking when you consider that the film was produced on the meagre budget of €100,000 (Murphy, 2010; www.iftn.ie, 2010).

This chapter analyses the film in terms of its construction of Irish femininity and the personal and relational lives of the women it features. As a documentary, it has the potential to offer us an alternative viewpoint and perspective on the experiences of 'ordinary' Irish women. It considers the question: do the self-representations of the women in *His & Hers* present an alternative viewpoint on Irish femininity? The chapter is made of up to three parts: in the first, I will present a review of the representation of women in Irish society and film. Following on from this, I will consider the work of Ken Wardrop, his documentary style and career to date, and finally I will return to a more detailed analysis of *His & Hers*.

The representations of gender in Irish society and film

Much scholarship into the representations of gender in Ireland has directed its focus on the representation of women and the implications of their being constructed as the carriers of 'tradition, morality and virtue' (Ryan, 1998: 181) for the Irish state. Such a symbolic manipulation of women into the meta-narrative of Irish nationalism is not unique to Ireland. In fact, it is a common strategy among nationalist movements to mobilize women's behaviour and characteristics in order to reflect and strategically unify the body politic (Jayawardena, 1986; Anthias & Yuval-Davis, 1993; Innes, 1993; McClintock, 1993; Kandiyoti 1996a, 1996b, cited in Ryan, 1998: 182). In the Irish case, various ideological and legal devices were used to ingratiate a rigid construction of Irish femininity into the collective consciousness. First, the Irish Constitution of 1937 legally restricted the role and responsibilities of Irish women to the domestic sphere as wives and mothers (Clancy, cited in Ryan, 1998: 182). This domestification of Irish women meant that they were rendered powerless except for their sphere of influence over the family circle. Entrenched in this invisible and private reality, the notion of the 'selfless' woman and mother gained prominence, whose duty to care was directed elsewhere (Davidoff & Hall, 1987: 452). This reified construction of motherhood dovetails with the 'Marian' construction of femininity in Catholicism.

Second, locating Irish women's place in the patriarchal, marital home also supported the gendered ideology of Irish nationalism. It helped project the notion of 'Mother Éire': a mother who has sacrificed her children in the name of the nationalist project. The pairing of motherhood with loss also extends to her continued willingness to surrender her children to emigration. All in all, the ideological construction of Irish motherhood became one borne out of personal pain, sadness and suffering. Such a construction of Irish femininity as self-sacrificing and self-denying could only be made tenable/bearable if the act of motherhood itself became re-constituted and re-interpreted. As a consequence, women, and motherhood more specifically, were deemed to have the 'moral superiority' over men and fatherhood. Such a promotion of motherhood as a biological destiny and moral vocation was actively propagated by the Irish Catholic Church throughout the mid-20th century (Inglis, 1988).

Third, while the social and moral role of mother was central to this ideological arrangement, female fertility occupied a rather precarious position and status. On the one hand, fertile female bodies were needed to provide the next generation of Irish people. However, a robust sexuality was incompatible with the strict moral code of Catholicism as well as the 'quiet, modest, self-sacrificing role' (Valuilis, cited in Inglis, 2005: 20) of motherhood espoused by Irish nationalism. As a compromise, only one prototype of female sexuality was permitted, namely that of the sexually demure and chaste female. Any other expression of female sexuality was prohibited and punished. If any woman were found to contravene this strict social and moral code, then the consequences would be severe. Unmarried mothers, 'the sexually promiscuous, the sexually transgressive', were routinely singled out and enmeshed into 'Ireland's architecture of containment' (Smith, 2007: xiii). A variety of building locations such as the network of Magdalen laundries, mother and baby homes and industrial schools were established as specific places where 'unruly' women were placed until they were deemed to be 'fit' to re-join Irish society. These excessive measures were legitimated by the social need to uphold the narrative of chaste, Catholic and conservative Ireland (Smith, 2007: xiv).

It is clear that a maternal, sexually demure and domesticated notion of Irish femininity was promoted and maintained throughout the majority of the 20th century. This ideal was also conveyed in popular Irish and American films. Two cinematic representations of Irish motherhood emerged: the 'suffering mother' (Meaney, 1998: 243) whose sons died for Ireland's freedom and the 'Irish mammy' whose purpose was to restore their 'wayward sons' (Bracken & Radley, 2007: 158) and put them back on the straight and narrow. While such representations of Irish motherhood are clearly aligned with the nationalistic project, unmarried Irish women came to represent something more alluring and dramatic. Whether she is the 'Colleen Bawn' of the silent-film era, whose love can bridge social divides (Meaney, 1998: 238–9), or the 'wild Irish girl' of the 1940s, whose rebellious and tempestuous nature is ultimately tamed by the love of 'the right man' (Meaney, 1998: 240; Bracken & Radley, 2007: 158), the cinematic register appears to have more creative licence with female singlehood. Nevertheless, it is important to note that the spiritedness of female singlehood is eventually subdued by marriage. These cinematic examples force Meaney to conclude that 'tradition and/or nature as well as Ireland' feature prominently in the cinematic representation of femininity in Irish and American films of the 20th century (1998: 240). As a result, film has played an active role in perpetuating the meta-narrative of Irish femininity as dominant and nurturing figures in the life worlds they inhabit, but powerless in society.

The social value of documentaries

The previous section focused on how the ideological construction of Irish femininity in the 20th century was sustained and maintained by film. However, it is worth noting that not all media genres perpetuate the dominant hegemony unquestioningly. There is a strong media tradition that claims that documentaries can be thought of as 'films [that] cause trouble' by illuminating forgotten or hidden aspects of society (Winston, 2012: xvii–xviii). At the heart of the documentary genre is a core epistemological assumption, namely that 'a special relationship to the real is being achieved (indexical, evidential, revelatory)' (Corner, 1996: 10) by its particular mobilization of camera, microphone and the 'testimony of its participants' (Corner, 1996: 3). Through the use of real-world locations, unrehearsed dialogues and handheld cameras, these and other techniques are used 'to connote authenticity' (Chandler & Munday, 2011: 109). Such a concern with 'reflect[ing] and report[ing] on "the real" through the use of recorded images and sounds of actuality' (Corner, 1996: 2) increases the social and political effects of the film. By foregrounding the personal experiences of its subjects, the documentary format offers audiences an opportunity to connect personally with the participants' stories. However, as the genre tries to retell facts and information to the audience in a nuanced and direct way, these stories can also resonate as social or political topics of concern. It has been argued that documentaries create a 'discourse of sobriety' (Nichols, quoted in Bell, 2004: 89) as they attempt to weave connections between the participants' personal experiences and their political significance. In this way, the documentary genre has been found to inform as well as educate its audiences on many issues.

Much has been written of the ability of documentary to expose the scandals, controversies and contradictions that have plagued Irish society since the 1990s (MacKeogh & O'Connell, 2012: 2). Many commentators have pointed to the 1996 TV documentary *Dear Daughter* (Louis Lentin) about the physical and psychological abuse that occurred in Goldenbridge industrial schools, and to the seminal 1999 documentary *States of Fear* (Raftery), which documented the systematic abuse of children in Irish industrial schools, as watershed moments for Irish social change (Smith, 2007: 88). Kenny (2009) writes that TV documentaries also played an important role in raising awareness of child sex-abuse scandals in Ireland. As a result, Winston (2012: xvii) maintains that documentaries play a critical role in Irish society by offering us 'truth claims' (Corner, 1996: 3) from witnesses and survivor testimonies that strike at the very heart of the ideological pretence that has come to define our collective construction of reality.

While documentaries generally use facts to explain their story (Nichols, 2001: 132), not all documentaries are the same. Nichols identifies six documentary types: the poetic, the expository mode, the observational mode, the participatory mode, the reflexive mode and the performative mode (2001). *His & Hers* can be defined as a performative documentary. This documentary approach assumes that our construction of knowledge and reality are essentially subjective and emotional and not based on the existence of an objective reality (Nichols, 2001: 131; Bruzzi, 2011: 3). Performative documentaries offer a more expressive rather than factual account of their material and characters, encouraging the viewer to identify with their subjects (Nichols, 2001: 132). Although their impact is emotional, performative documentaries are also conscious of the fact that they are constructed, a fact that is demonstrated through a number of key stylistic features. In some instances, the documentary maker can become a figure within the diegesis, as 'author-performer', and can also contain 'the self conscious performance by it subjects', furthermore, the genre can also manifestly employ 'making of' footage as a part of the film; elements that might include the setting up of scenes or phoning up of potential subjects (Bruzzi, 2011: 2). In summary, performative documentaries are characterized by their 'emotional intensity and subjective expressiveness' (Nichols, 2001: 101).

Considering the main characteristics of the performative documentary mode, we might question anew the extent to which we can consider the self-representations of the women in *His & Hers* as 'authentic'. Nevertheless, as I have already stated in the introduction, *His & Hers* was particularly successful in igniting an emotional response and connection with its viewers. In the next section, we will consider in more detail the devices and strategies used by Wardrop to achieve such an effective response to the film. I will also assess the type of performances its subjects present and will evaluate their significance with regard to the representation of women in Irish film more broadly.

His & Hers as a performative documentary

To date, two creative influences have shaped Wardrop's career: women and the performative documentary mode. Wardrop's cinematic interest in women's lives first began with his graduating short film from the Dun Laoghaire Institute of Art, Design and Technology (IADT) *Undressing My Mother* (2004). In this short film, he presents his mother Ethel, naked, talking frankly about her life with her late husband (Parpart, 2011: 79). Wardrop uses both the narrative of Ethel as well as her 'aging maternal body' to offer an alternative and radical construction of cinematic femininity. Several devices are also used to dramatic effect 'from high-contrast lighting to asymmetrical framing and composition, frequent close-ups and elements of photographic abstractions' to achieve such an ambitious aim (Parpart, 2011: 79). *Undressing My Mother* is intended to 'flout conventional constructions of Irish femininity' (Parpart, 2011: 80) by giving a potentially radical voice to the ideological 'silent' and 'invisible' Irish mother. However, Parpart (2011) finds that this objective is limited by the fact that the film and the subject continually return to the topic of her relationship with her husband. As a result, the cinematic subject adopts a less radical positioning.

Wardrop took this interest in women further in *His & Hers*. 'It is layered with all sorts of characters but at the heart is the mother and the power that they have [...] that emotional strength that women have that men don't have' (quoted in O'Connell, 2012: 142). He states, '[f]or me it was more interesting to do the female story' (O'Connell, 2012: 143). He uses the performative documentary mode to bring to life such a substantive theme.

I have already stated that one of the characteristics of the performative documentary mode is the active role that the documentarian can have on the end product. While some performative documentary makers, such as Michael Moore, take on the persona of an 'actor-performer' in the documentary (Bruzzi, 2011: 2), Wardrop, on the other hand, makes his presence felt in the planning, scripting and staging of the film. He has said, 'I have never done documentary in its purest form because I have constructed all of my stories but I've used real people and real words, their statements of reality. I tend to play with the visuals and stuff' (quoted in O'Connell, 2012: 136–7). With *His & Hers*, Wardrop first wrote a script, and then he held castings to see if he could find women to fit in with his narrative. Prospective participants were then filmed for an hour in their homes and he used these films to decide whom to include in his project. Eventually, he settled on a cast of 70 contributors, filming each one for up to four hours. In addition to being the director, he also edited the contributions as the project evolved, omitting some elements depending on the narrative that he wanted to create/achieve (Wardrop, quoted in O'Connell, 2012: 142). One type of personal information that Wardrop removed from the film was any personal or traumatic life experience, such as teenage pregnancy or desertion. He did not include these testimonies in the film because he 'was interested in the ordinary' (O'Connell, 2012: 139).

Such a desire to present the 'ordinariness' of these women's lives also influenced the type of film and shooting style used. The use of Super 16 film and a forgoing of expensive stage production meant that there was distinctive framing used throughout the film, with the documentary being shot through doorways and windows. While O'Connell attributes this technique to establishing an aesthetic around the 'theme of emotional relationships between men and women' (2012: 137), Wardrop himself admits that it was used for both aesthetic as well as financial reasons. Admitting to his desire to use this technique 'to show the similarity between the worlds we all live in', it has to be acknowledged that keeping the film 'to one or two frames' is also a less expensive mode of direction (quoted in O'Connell, 2012: 138).

Wardrop set himself a mammoth creative task. On the one hand he wanted to 'celebrate' the uniqueness and singularity of women, yet, by his employment of the performative documentary mode, he is actively enforcing his particular pre-conceived image of womanhood in the film, through the selecting and scripting of its subjects. The only biodata permitted from the women is that which focuses on their relationships with men. This relationship with men is first presented in the context of a nurturing paternal relationship. Young children and teenagers talk about their fathers in loving and considerate tones. As the subjects move into early adulthood, the focus shifts to boyfriends and later, to partners and spouses. Again, the nature of the disclosures is positive in content. The film therefore trades in a catalogue of unproblematic female–male binaries as either female child–father or woman–man. In respect of the adult relationships, the film promotes a traditional definition of love as heterosexual. Such a focus on female heterosexual relations might be considered less surprising in the light of the target commercial and mass audience for whom this film was produced.

The documentary *His & Hers* clearly advances a conventional, heterosexual and sanitized version of female–male relationships. By foregrounding these types of relationships in the dialogue of the subjects, the film promotes a traditional understanding of femininity as being defined by its relationship to various male figures in the lives of the women presented. Interestingly, maternity and the value of female friendships do not figure in their disclosures. The decision to reduce women's lives to their relationship with men is a pointed ideological device, revealing Wardrop's potentially limited understanding of women's lives and womanhood. Several other issues are also conveniently absent from Wardrop's construction of women's lives (Lye, 1997/2008). There is no exploration of how the women feel about being a woman in contemporary society. No attempt is made to bridge their personal monologues with social, political or economic contexts that actively shape and influence their lives. No discussion is given over to finances, jobs and employment, the schooling of children, hobbies and leisure interests. Overall, *His & Hers* offers the audience a depoliticized and decontextualized ideological space – one nonetheless inevitably ideologically implicated – against which his contributors talk about their private lives. This socio-political muting is further assured by the way in which the women's contributions appear as staged expositions; sitting on a chair, or bed, in the home setting. Though Wardrop insists that this focus on the domestic setting is a means to celebrate the bond between all women, the domestic sphere is a potent ideological and discursive space that historically constrained, rather than empowered, Irish women. In this respect, the film serves to reiterate the 'active/male and passive/female' positioning of Irish women, already more universally expressed in Laura Mulvey's seminal essay (1975: 137).

Conclusions

Wardrop endeavoured to produce a film that was 'a celebration of women and motherhood' (O'Connell, 2012: 142). While the film is an emotionally compelling piece of cinema, it is important to remember that documentaries are unavoidably influenced by the personal and political viewpoints of the documentary maker (Barnouw, quoted in O'Brien, 2012: 15). As Wardrop designed his documentary in the performative mode, he worked as casting officer, writer, editor and director; a situation that allowed him full creative control over the subjects. Through their dialogue and the location of various domestic settings, he crafted a particular construction of womanhood and femininity where male relationships are prioritized and privileged. By affixing attention to their daughter–father and girlfriend–boyfriend, wife–husband roles and relations, the structural, political, economic and ideological dimensions of heterosexual relations are ignored. The gendered and emotional division of labour is not problematized or discussed at any length. Irigaray has commented: 'Love may perhaps require secrecy, but it also needs culture and a social context in order to last and develop' (1993/2007: 98). The film is also patriarchal as it does little to interrogate or challenge the conventions of Irish femininity in Irish film and society in general. For these reasons, I find that *His & Hers* caters for the 'pleasure and privilege of the "invisible guest"' (Mulvey, 1975: 141): of the heterosexual males' importance in the lives of the interviewed women, rather than foregrounding the validity and importance of the lives of 'ordinary women'. In this respect, this film does not offer an alternative viewpoint on women's experiences in Irish society. The emotional expressiveness of the text cleverly disguises a stereotypic representation of Irish womanhood.

Part III
Northern Ireland

9

From Belfast to Bamako: Cinema in the Era of Capitalist Realism

Stephen Baker and Greg McLaughlin

All films are ideological, whether they are configured as purely entertainment, or thought to transcend the world of politics to engage with some universal truth. However, typically when we talk about 'political cinema', we are referring to films that engage with political issues explicitly, questioning power and/or contesting dominant perceptions of the world. For these films, the 'triumph' of global capitalism and free-market theory has presented particular challenges. First of all, cinema audiences are increasingly configured as consumers, pursuing pleasure and untrammelled entertainment. Second, the scope for political films is greatly reduced when 'capitalist realism' means that it is easier to imagine the end of the world than it is to imagine the end of capitalism (Fisher, 2009: 2).

This chapter considers two very different types of cinematic response to the 'triumph' of global capitalism. It looks first of all at two films from Northern Ireland where the peace process has been underwritten by a 'peace dividend' that proposes the region's incorporation into the global free market after years of violent civil conflict made its full membership of that society impossible. Fittingly, films such as *The Boxer* (Sheridan, 1996) and *Divorcing Jack* (Caffery, 1998) offer stories of romantic restoration in which their protagonists escape from poisonous and deadly political spheres to the sanctuary of 'home'. In this way, both films concur with the 'official' narrative of the peace process, which, on the evidence of these films at least, is one that is imagined in terms of passive domesticity and a deep antipathy to politics, qualities that should ingratiate the region with global capitalism. This is in sharp contrast to Abderrahmane Sissako's *Bamako* (2006), made in the wake of the G8 conference at Gleneagles in 2005. It contrives a court case in the backyard of a multi-occupancy house in the eponymous Malian capital and puts on trial the International Monetary Fund (IMF) and World Bank, indicting them for the implementation of the structural adjustment policies (SAPs) that force upon African countries punitive public-spending cuts, privatization and the free market. This improbable courtroom drama intertwines with the everyday lives of the residents living around the yard, in a way that does not allow an easy separation of politics and domestic life.

The decision, here, to contrast films set in the North of Ireland with one located in north-west Africa might seem eccentric, but the geographical leap from Belfast to Bamako has a point. Since the beginning of the peace process, we have carried out research into the transformation of Northern Ireland's media image. During this time, we have had cause to wonder whether it was possible to imagine a cinema and broader media culture that is politically engaged at all. Despite the excitement that has accompanied the new dispensation and the achievement of political accord between Ulster unionism and Irish nationalism, 'ceasefire cinema'[1] has been a largely anodyne affair, in keeping with a broader media culture that has been determinedly banal and pusillanimous in tone. Our chance encounter with Sissako's *Bamako* reinforced our conviction that this need not, and should not, be the case, and that there is nothing archaic or strange about the idea of political cinema. It also highlights, by contrast, the taken-for-granted nature of capitalism in 'ceasefire cinema' at the very moment that Northern Ireland began its exposure to the global free-market proper.

The propaganda of peace

The Northern Ireland peace process was underscored by two narrative frameworks that worked in concert with each other: an explicit narrative of 'peace and reconciliation' and an implicit narrative that set about imagining Northern Ireland in terms conducive to its entry into the global free market.[2] This is well illustrated by two remarkable images that appeared at different moments in the peace process. The first was a rapturous symbol of peace and reconciliation, widely circulated in the media. It showed Bono, the lead singer of international rock group U2, standing between the leaders of moderate unionism and nationalism – David Trimble and John Hume – holding their arms aloft like two triumphant prizefighters at a concert at Belfast's Waterfront Hall, on 19 May 1998, three days before the referendum on the Good Friday Agreement. The image is frequently cited as a turning point in the campaign that helped to secure the 'yes' vote. Almost a decade later in December 2007, after years of crisis talks and protracted negotiations to save the agreement, a very different image emerged. Once again, it was a picture of the leaders of unionism and nationalism, but this time the personnel and surroundings had changed. Ian Paisley, the new first minister of Northern Ireland, and Martin McGuinness, the deputy first minister, once mortal enemies, were pictured seated beside each other on a sofa at the entrance of the newly opened IKEA in Belfast, framed by the corporate slogan in the background: 'Home is the most important place in the world.' The triumphalism of Trimble and Hume's 'Bono moment' was here superseded by the banality of Paisley and McGuinness' 'IKEA moment': the leaders of once militant republicanism and truculent loyalism, pacified and domesticated, endorsing a determinedly apolitical and nakedly consumerist brand identity (McLaughlin & Baker, 2010: 92).

In a sense, these two images bookend the ideological meaning of the peace process and expose its pretensions and limitations: how the 'historic' achievement of political accord gave way to the modest realization of Northern Ireland's proposed integration into global capitalism with its disavowal of politics in preference for consumer sovereignty. This is a world where, as David Harvey has pointed out, 'the neo-liberal ethic of intense, possessive individualism, and its political withdrawal from collective forms of action, becomes the template for human socialization' (2008: 31).

Belfast

A predilection for this sort of individualism and political abstention is explicit in the film *Divorcing Jack* (Caffery, 1998), an irreverent comedy that was released in the same year as the signing of the Good Friday Agreement. Set in an imagined, near future, a newly independent Northern Ireland is on the brink of peace and electing its first prime minister. Its protagonist, a cynical Belfast journalist, Dan Starkey, has a hunch that this is all too good to be true. It turns out Starkey is right to be sceptical: the favourite candidate to win the election, Michael Brinn, is concealing a violent past that utterly undermines his credentials as a peacemaker. In the meantime, one of Brinn's former comrades, the psychopathic paramilitary, 'Cow Pat' Keegan, is determined to expose the political front-runner's violent background. Starkey is then drawn into this world of political machinations through a mixture of happenstance and misadventure.

In *Divorcing Jack*, Northern Ireland's political sphere is universally dystopian, referred to by Starkey as a 'stupid fucking place'. As a consequence, the film advocates a withdrawal into domestic intimacy from the 'chaos out there'; a withdrawal demonstrated figuratively in a conversation between Starkey and a journalist colleague from the United States. The American asks Starkey what he prefers to call Northern Ireland: 'Ulster', 'the occupied six counties', 'the North' or 'the province'? Starkey tells him he just calls it 'home', avoiding the political and sectarian associations of the other designations. It is fitting then that most of the film is taken up with Starkey's efforts to rescue his home life after an act of marital infidelity plunges him into the world of political intrigue, estranges him from his wife and leads to her being kidnapped by unreconstructed republican, Keegan.

The climactic scene finds Starkey caught between the duplicitous politician, Brinn, and pathological Keegan, angrily admonishing them for their cynical disregard for individuals. These he defines as people able to think for themselves, go for a pint with the lads and, recalling his earlier affair, give 'the best fucking kiss in the world goodnight'. This last reference to romantic communion is significant, and a similar intimacy is evident in the final scene when Starkey and his wife are reconciled at home and make love on what he describes as their 'magic settee'. Such moments in cinema are described by Mas'ud Zavarzadeh as ones of 'plentitude, presence, and pellucidity: an instant in which the intimates are free from the mediating forces of culture and society and directly present to each other's consciousness, feelings, and perhaps bodies' (1991: 115). He argues that such intimacy naturalizes the notion of pan-historical and sovereign individuality, essential to contemporary capitalism. In this respect, the Starkeys' romantic intimacy transcends Northern Ireland's troublesome history and politics, while its location in the 'home', configured earlier by Dan Starkey as apolitical and benign, shelters them from the political maelstrom beyond their front door. It also serves as a sign of the possessive individualism that is characteristic of the propertied neo-liberal subject. Incidentally, this recovery of Dan Starkey's marriage on his 'magic settee' strikingly reprises the image of the pacified and domesticated Paisley and McGuinness on a sofa in IKEA. Meanwhile, the evocation of an inalienable and politically neutral space called 'home' chimes with IKEA's own commercially self-interested assertion of it being the 'most important place in the world'.

The privileging of domestic relations and negative depiction of politics is not peculiar to *Divorcing Jack*. Most films made in the period of the peace process make clear that their various protagonists can remain virtuous and safe only by standing apart from politics and public activism.

It is important to stress here that 'ceasefire cinema' has tended not to make any distinction between different types of politics. Politics are always bad because they are only ever conceived of as those of Northern Ireland's violent past. The antidote to that past is not new forms of political solidarity and community, but a depoliticized and unproblematic domesticity.

This is also the case in films like *Some Mother's Son* (George, 1996) and *Titanic Town* (Michell, 1998), in which naïve and embattled mothers become embroiled in the political sphere when their children and families are threatened. However, in the end they are returned to the domesticated lives they previously led, repelled by the deceptions and incomprehensibility of the world of politics. Children, on the other hand, are portrayed on screen in pre-lapsarian terms, with films like *Mickybo and Me* (Loane, 2004) and *The Mighty Celt* (Elliot, 2005) offering depictions of young protagonists whose innocence is endangered by the violent social world around them. Meanwhile, the success of lovers and entrepreneurs is dependent upon their being able to transcend politics in films like *The Most Fertile Man in Ireland* (Appleton, 1999) and *An Everlasting Piece* (Levinson, 2000). Even ex-combatants can be recuperated providing that they renounce political convictions and become family men.

This is the clear message of *The Boxer*, essentially a love story set against the backdrop of the struggle within the Irish republican movement, between those seeking a peaceful settlement of the conflict and those committed to physical force. Danny, a republican ex-prisoner, has turned his back on violence and his old comrades, a rejection made all the more emphatic by his determination to rekindle an affair with former lover, Maggie. She is already married to an IRA man still serving time in prison and Danny's advances towards her provoke consternation in the republican community. They also make him a target for Harry, a hardliner, hostile to the peace process, who considers Danny and Maggie's relationship a betrayal of her incarcerated husband. The two men then are set on a collision course, threatening Danny's relationship with Maggie and his very life.

In the end, it is only the violent intervention of Maggie's father, Joe Hamill, himself a leading republican and the chief architect of the peace strategy, which simultaneously saves the romantic couple and the ceasefire. He orders the assassination of Harry and the film concludes with Danny, Maggie and her son embracing, looking the very picture of domestic integrity. However, there is the more troubling scene of Harry's widow grieving over her dead husband's body. This emphasizes the film's moral message: that a commitment to political violence ultimately thwarts romantic and sexual desire, a long-standing trope of cinematic Ireland[3] and one that is evident from the beginning of the film when Danny is released from prison. This coincides with a wedding behind bars and the incongruous sight of a bride and groom taking their vows surrounded by a wedding party made up of prison officers. Afterwards at the reception, a group of prisoners' wives dance and sing along to The Rolling Stones' anthem to sexual frustration, '(I Can't Get No) Satisfaction'. From this point on, *The Boxer*, like *Divorcing Jack*, is about the recuperation of 'home', configured in terms of heterosexual intimacy and political neutrality.

In a scene deeply symbolic of this recuperation, Danny, shortly after his release from prison, returns to where he once lived. It is now a derelict, boarded up flat, so to get access, he takes a sledgehammer to the bricks that block his front door. His actions attract the concerned attention of British soldiers who ask him what he is doing. He simply points out that the flat is his home. No further explanation is necessary and indeed, throughout the film, when Danny is told he should leave Belfast for his own safety, he evokes the notion of 'home' as an inalienable right. The film closes with a scene in which Danny and Maggie are stopped at an RUC checkpoint where an officer asks them where they are going. 'We're going home,' says Maggie. Once again there are no further questions and the police officer waves them on their way. Even the RUC, ostensibly the malevolent foe of northern nationalism, cannot object to such a natural and self-evidently virtuous destination.

Despite proposing to repair the domestic sphere through the salvation of Danny and Maggie's relationship, *The Boxer* forgoes a wholly optimistic conclusion. It alludes to some of the potentially uncomfortable choices that might lie ahead for republicans, namely policing dissent within their own ranks, by violent means if necessary. *Divorcing Jack*, on the other hand, offers a more upbeat ending, but even its romantic conclusion is dependent upon an act of violence, in the shape of Brinn and Keegan's mutual double-cross, leaving both men dead. Conveniently, however, neither Dan Starkey nor Danny is morally compromised by having anything to do with the violence that underwrites the recuperation of their private lives and homes.

Bamako

Where *The Boxer* and *Divorcing Jack* strive to detach their domesticated protagonists from the world of politics, *Bamako* presents the everyday lives of the residents as inseparable from the political and economic issues being thrashed out in the court proceedings in their yard. Actual figures from African civil society are called upon to present evidence before the court. For instance, writer and political activist, Aminata Dramane Traoré, rejects the popular notion that Africa's key characteristic is its poverty. Rather, she says, Africa is a victim of its riches and has been subject to a process of 'pauperization'; a deliberate strategy rather than a natural state of affairs. The apparently unscripted nature of such testimonies adds to their persuasive power and the film's documentary aesthetic.

Likewise, humdrum aspects of domestic and working life in the backyard are presented in a way that is relatively free of the linear causality associated with narrative cinema, giving it the appearance of 'a slice of life'. Such apparently inconsequential goings-on are sometimes entwined with the weighty matters under discussion in the court proceedings: a mother with an infant in her arms walks into the frame, winds her way through the lawyers and witnesses and out of shot. Sometimes the effect of combining the trial with everyday life is humorous and can acknowledge the spectator's desire for relief and distraction from the intense political discourse of the court: for instance, one witness's fervent contribution on the topic of textile production is intercut with a shot of a toddler. As the witness concludes, the camera follows the infant walking before the judge's bench, each unsteady step accompanied by a shrill squeak coming from the toy-soles on his shoes. On another occasion, a woman suddenly interjects during the proceedings and angrily scolds the African members of the IMF and World Bank's defence team for their perceived treachery. But otherwise, many of the residents take little notice of the court: a cloth dyer carries on working despite poor health; a marriage takes place in the yard; a couple goes through the process of breaking up; and a man lies dying in bed. But whatever they are doing and no matter the level of the residents' interest, Sissako's locating of the trial in the backyard makes the point that the political arguments and counter-arguments are, at a literal and metaphorical level, the continual background noise to the residents' lives. The closest the film comes to providing a narrative arc is the separation of Chaka, an unemployed man, and Mélé, his wife, who provides for them by singing in a nightclub.

Chaka cuts a desperate figure. He is in the process of losing his wife and has no means by which to provide for his daughter. The full extent of his hopelessness is illustrated by his tragic-comic attempt to find work, teaching himself Hebrew, so that should the Israelis ever open an embassy in Mali, he will be well placed for the position of guard.

In the end, he shoots himself by the roadside with a gun, stolen from a sleeping policeman during the hearings. His death then is quite explicitly connected to the trial. It gives him the opportunity to steal the gun with which he kills himself, and it is clear that we are being invited to consider how the system being indicted during the court's proceedings is responsible for his despair and eventual death. In *Bamako*, unlike its Belfast counterparts, there is no romantic transcending of the political and social world. In fact, Sissako seems more concerned with the way many Africans are excluded from political discourse. Indeed the question of who will listen, who gets to speak and how, lies at the heart of *Bamako*.

Before he shoots himself, Chaka gives an interview to a journalist who asks his opinion on the SAPs but his comments are accidentally erased from the cassette tape. Asked to repeat them, he declines, saying no one will listen anyway. Chaka is already aware that language empowers, indicated by his learning Hebrew, but the language of the court is French, a legacy of colonialism, which instantly discriminates against some witnesses, among them an elderly farmer, Zégué Bamba. Unfamiliar with the court's formalities, he speaks out of turn and is made to sit down. When he comes forward a second time, again uninvited, he berates the court with an impassioned chant in his native language. No subtitles are provided, in what is perhaps a deliberate decision to provoke European and North American audiences into thinking about their own privileged position with regard to political discourse. The scene is made all the more poignant as it comes after the appearance of a former schoolteacher, Samba Diakité. He gives the court his name and profession but then stands in silence for some time before he turns and leaves the yard. At first, his speechlessness might appear a form of protest, but it becomes clear it is a measure of his despair when later he confides in a friend about having a recurring dream about a sack full of severed heads belonging to various heads of state. His friend advises him never to speak of it again.

Bamako then is more than a political polemic. It invites us to think about the problem of political representation and communication in a world of asymmetrical social relations, perhaps recalling Gayatri Chakravorty Spivak's (1988) enquiry into whether the subaltern can speak. Its residents are the subjects of political and economic forces but they are simultaneously excluded from the very public discourse that defines and gives shape to those forces. Conversely, Belfast's virtuous residents are depicted as determinedly self-excluding from politics, which is taken as a sign of Northern Ireland's emergence, at last, from an atavistic nightmare to the 'real' world where capitalism is so omnipresent and natural that it does not bear commenting upon.

The ideological comfort of home

Michael Ryan and Douglas Kellner make the point that:

> The political stakes of film are [...] very high because film is part of a broader system of cultural representation which operates to create psychological dispositions that result in a particular construction of social reality, a commonly held sense of what the world is and ought to be that sustains social institutions.
>
> (1990: 14)

In this respect, *The Boxer* and *Divorcing Jack* provide almost unconscious ideological cover for Northern Ireland's entry into the global free market. Their politically disinterested, thoroughly domesticated protagonists are the ideal and seemingly willing subjects of free-market capitalism. Transcending history and politics, their neutral, benign version of 'home' appears natural, universal and inalienable. In their disavowal of the political, they reveal themselves as deeply ideological films. As Slavoj Žižek explains: 'The contemporary era constantly proclaims itself as post-ideological, but this denial of ideology only provides the ultimate proof that we are more than ever embedded in ideology' (2009: 36).

Of course, stories of romantic restoration and de-politicized domesticity also provide a degree of ideological comfort in a society like Northern Ireland where public space and territory still have the potential to provide violent sectarian flashpoints. Indeed, the notion of 'home' as a politically neutral sign offers respite in an environment where all of the other signifiers are spoken for by one sectarian designation or the other (see Butler, 1995: 135). However, we should not make the mistake of seeing the demarcation of unproblematic domestic, romantic intimacy from troublesome politics as somehow normal or inevitable.

In Irish cinema, there have been occasions when films have employed romantic and domestic relations as metaphors through which questions of national identity and belonging could be explored. For instance, Pat Murphy's *Maeve* (1982), Joe Comerford's *Reefer and the Model* (1987) and *High Boot Benny* (1993), and Thaddeus O'Sullivan's *December Bride* (1990) radically re-imagined personal relationships and challenged conservative notions of community and nationhood. The renegades and misfits that come together as 'family' in Comerford's films are provocative alternatives to traditional versions of Irish nationalism, while Thaddeus O'Sullivan's *ménage à trois* in *December Bride* offers an affront to patriarchy and religious, communal conformity. Similarly, *Maeve* challenges and questions the patriarchal assumptions of Irish republicanism, using a radical visual style and disruptive narrative. In the film, Maeve's relationships with her father, mother, sister and boyfriend provide the context for an often very intense dialogue about the history and myths of national belonging and gender. Martin McLoone argues that these films were typical of 'a cinema of national questioning' (1994: 168).

It is hard to detect any such qualities in 'ceasefire cinema'. *The Boxer* and *Divorcing Jack* can only recommend 'home' as an anodyne sanctuary from political challenge and their vision of domesticated citizenship provides a rite of passage into the global free market. Conversely, *Bamako* refuses the banal assumptions of its Belfast counterparts in order to offer an indictment of the oppressive economics being imposed upon Africa. This is tempered by a pessimism that acknowledges there may be little that Africans can say, let alone do, that will elevate their circumstances. Chaka's words are erased; Zégué Bamba speaks out of turn; Samba Diakité is speechless, warned to keep his violent dreams to himself. Even Sissako's central conceit of bringing the IMF and World Bank to trial is such an audacious contrivance that it reminds us just how fanciful an idea it is. Nevertheless, in its explicitly political content, its willingness to expose and question power, and its formal self-consciousness with regard to the asymmetry of cultural representation, *Bamako* refuses to take for granted the economic and political status quo. If it fails to imagine something beyond the persecuting logic of neo-liberalism and the inequities of capitalism, it does at least open up the possibility of a discussion about what that future might be.

Notes

1. 'Ceasefire cinema' is so-called because of its coincidence with the period of the loyalist and republican ceasefires and the peace process.
2. A full discussion of these different media and cultural forms' responses to the new dispensation in Northern Ireland can be found in our book, *The Propaganda of Peace: The Role of Culture and Media in the Northern Ireland Peace Process* (McLaughlin & Baker, 2010).
3. John Hill offers a historical account of this trope in *Cinema and Ireland* (Rockett et al., 1987: 147–93).

10
'Many Sides, Many Truths': Collaborative Filmmaking in Transitional Northern Ireland

Laura Aguiar

This chapter examines some of the challenges of making documentary films in Northern Ireland's current transitional period from violence to peace. I offer a reflection of my experience as editor and co-director of the 60-minute documentary film *We Were There* (Aguiar & McLaughlin, 2014) about the women's experiences as visitors and workers of the Maze and Long Kesh Prison.[1] The film was made in collaboration with the Prisons Memory Archive (PMA) and its participants.[2]

Although filmmaking is, by nature, collaborative, and it is almost impossible to make a film about other people completely on your own, I use the term 'collaborative' here to refer to a process that allows participants to have some degree of control over the production, editing and dissemination, and that this attempts to transform them from passive objects of the film gaze into agents in the meaning-making process. In this model, both filmmaker and participants invest in, and are rewarded by, the film project (Pink, 2007: 57).

Collaborative filmmaking has precursors and is commonly traced back to Robert Flaherty's early works, such as *Nanook of the North* (1922), during the making of which the director worked closely with his Inuit participants. This model of filmmaking received more attention in the 1960s as a result of technological developments and the new affordability of lightweight cameras and portable synchronous sound equipment. The National Film Board of Canada's programme *Challenge for Change* (Low et al., 1960–80), set on Fogo Island, gave the islanders an opportunity to edit out parts they were not comfortable with and actively participate in decisions on screening possibilities (Barbash & Taylor, 1997: 88). Since the 1980s, various filmmakers have expanded the

Challenge for Change framework and adapted it to their personal projects' needs and contexts (for example, see Turner, 1992; Elder, 1995; Miller, Luchs & Jalea, 2011; Mairs, 2013).

I will begin this chapter by providing an examination of Northern Ireland's transitional political and social scenario and of the challenges faced by any film project dealing with its troubled past. I then hope to demonstrate how *We Were There* was edited in collaboration with participants, before finishing by setting out the lessons that were learnt during this process and the role of the filmmaking practice in politically sensitive societies.

Northern Ireland today

The conflict in Northern Ireland, known by the designation 'the Troubles', left over 3,500 people dead and over 40,000 injured (McKittrick & McVea, 2001) over more than three decades. This is a considerable number given its 1.5 million population and the major psychological scars that it has left: one in five people has suffered multiple experiences relating to the Troubles, including post-traumatic stress disorder (Muldoon, Schmid, Downes, Kremer & Trew, 2005: 87–8); at least 100,000 people have been directly affected by imprisonment (Coulter, cited in Sullivan, 1999: 11); and over 99 'peace walls',[3] street murals and flags have continued to mark symbolically the deep division within loyalist and nationalist areas (McDonald, 2013).

Various paradigms have been used to interpret the conflict, with the 'two warring tribes' narrative – republicans/nationalists (mostly Catholics) versus unionists/loyalists (mostly Protestants) – being the one often used by governments and the media (McKeown, 2001; Dawson, 2007). However, the conflict had more protagonists and could be better characterized by 'systematic and sustained abuses of human rights by the British State, and a systematic blurring, by all protagonists of violence, of the categories of armed combatants and unarmed civilians' (Dawson, 2007: 9).

Although the level of violence has diminished considerably with the signing of the Good Friday Agreement in 1998, some of it has remained frequent, with sporadic occurrences continuing to this day. Dissident republican groups who have publically expressed resistance to the peace process have targeted and killed security staff,[4] leading to an average of more than one security alert per day in 2012 alone (Kilpatrick, 2013). Loyalist groups have taken to the streets to protest, in some cases through violence, against decisions to restrict the flying of the union flag over Belfast's City Hall to designated days, and also against proposed restrictions of marching routes during the 12th of July parades.[5] In 2013, a six-month inter-party negotiation failed to reach an agreement on issues of flags, parading and other questions with historically embedded significance (McDonald, 2013) and, up to the time of writing, no agreement has been reached on any of these issues.

Some have proposed that the conflict has been maintained 'consciously through other means, including contestation over housing, education, delivery of services and disparate interpretations of the past' (Shirlow & McEvoy, 2008: 3). Hence, it could be argued that Northern Ireland has yet to pass the 'post' of the term 'post-conflict', and that instead it finds itself in a transitional period from violence to peace. As one person's 'victim' may be another's 'perpetrator' and a hierarchy of victims remains debatable (Dawson, 2007; Shirlow & McEvoy, 2008; Mairs, 2013), it is not surprising that there is what McGarry and O'Leary have termed a 'meta-conflict'; a verbal conflict about what the primary conflict is about and how it might be addressed (cited in Moloney, 2014: 13). Given a situation in which such a meta-conflict might exist, it is inevitable that film production in Northern Ireland is more than a mere economic or purely cultural matter. Indeed, for the last 40 years, the Troubles have been a distinct feature of fiction and non-fiction films about Northern Ireland, making it difficult to set a film there 'that does not deal with the impact of the conflict in some way' (Hill, 2006: 242). The sensitivity around dealing with the past requires that filmmakers think thoroughly about 'each political and physic circumstance of community, group and individual' (Mairs & McLaughlin, 2012: 41).

Making *We Were There*

It is against this historical context and contemporary background that *We Were There* was made with the PMA and its participants. My collaboration with them began in the post-production phase, four years after the participants' interviews (which lasted for three years, from 2011 to 2014) were recorded and digitized. The PMA recorded a wide range of narrated experiences, from prisoners to prison staff, and relatives who were recorded inside the empty building sites. Participants were filmed by a single camera operator who followed them while they walked and talked. The focus was on the participants' engagement with the site and on their memories of it. Deliberately, therefore, leading questions were rarely asked. In this manner, participants acted as co-authors, as they had control over the content of the interviews. Co-ownership of the recordings and the right to veto or withdraw statements were also granted to all of the recorded subjects.

Motivated by the near absence of women's diverse lived experiences in cinematic depictions of the Maze and Long Kesh Prison (Bergquist, 1996; Farley, 1999; Sullivan, 1999), I selected ten interviews from the recorded material that featured 15 female participants. Since prisons in Northern Ireland have become 'masculinised places which have in ways re-entrenched the feminisation of the home' (Dowler, 1998: 160), the idea was to tell the story of this prison from a female perspective and to help foster a consciousness about women's plural experiences and agency inside and outside the prison walls during the conflict.

Throughout the editing process, I regularly met Cahal McLaughlin, the PMA's director and the film's co-director, and carried out four meetings with each participant. During these conversations, we discussed the rough cuts of the film, and made collaborative decisions on the inclusion and exclusion of parts of the recordings and on the addition of images of the prison, various selections for the soundtrack and options for the on-screen text that would be included. Hence, consent was 'an on-going process of negotiation, not a single request at the beginning or end of a project' (Mairs, 2013: 176); something ensuring that the participants' earlier role as co-authors was maintained throughout the editing phase.

This collective filmmaking group held the view that *We Were There* should transcend differences of political, social or religious affiliation, and privilege the human story over the historical context. We prioritized recordings that offered a wide range of female experiences as workers and visitors, and labelled them according to their various relationships to the prison. This involved a careful approach to our choice of words to describe interviewees, in one case selecting the phrase 'Mother of *former* prisoner' over 'Mother of *loyalist* prisoner'. We also agreed to let participants narrate their own stories and to use visuals of the prison, text and soundtrack minimally as a way of supporting, rather than directing meanings behind, the women's own voices. We favoured the contemporary imagery recorded by the PMA and eschewed adding other archival material, such as readily available BBC newsreel footage or published newspaper photographs. Text was used only to offer basic details on events, dates and location. We also agreed that the music should not be too intrusive or too ideologically leading, and collaborated with sound designer Liz Greene, who produced a soundtrack that enhanced the ambient sound of the recordings, without intruding upon the women's testimonies or guiding the audience's emotions.

When the film was completed, participants were invited to attend the screenings and to take part in panel discussions; something that gave them the opportunity to see how their stories impacted upon viewers, as screenings were followed by audience-led conversations. We organized a private première and an informal reception for participants and their guests at the art-house cinema Queen's Film Theatre (QFT) in Belfast, before going on more general release. This closed screening enabled them to see their stories emerge from the private to the public domain gradually, to get accustomed to audiences and to meet each other for the first time. Following this, we set up a public première during the Belfast Film Festival, including a panel discussion with all of those involved in its production before an audience of approximately 250 spectators. Afterwards, the film was brought to various places across Northern Ireland and abroad, including community groups, art-house cinemas and universities. All of the proposed venues for exhibition were discussed and agreed with participants and they were invited to take part in post-screening discussions in as many cases as was feasible.

Collaborative filmmaking: Lessons

Co-authorship

Sharing authorship with participants in the filming and editing processes offers a bottom-up approach to representation that is more likely to satisfy their perception of how they have been portrayed in the film, regardless of whether or not their stories are narrated intercut with others that present contrasting life experiences. In assessing their experiences of the filming and editing processes, participants shared the sense of being in control of them. One prisoner's relative, for instance, found that it 'made a massive difference', as she knew that 'nobody would try to hijack it or depict one side or another, demonize anyone, just to tell stories' (interview with participant, June 2014).[6]

However, it would be naïve to assume that sharing authorship automatically means that 'all the perspectives of various contributors can be combined into a kind of composite conglomerate' (Barbash & Taylor, 1997: 89). Filmmakers and participants belong to specific socio-economic classes, have certain predispositions and views, and mere open collaboration cannot automatically negate these variables. For example, when negotiating the representation of the republican hunger-strike period,[7] our different points of view were evident: while republican participants believed that the event deserved a long section in the film because of its importance in Irish history, other participants believed that this was just a small fraction of what took place in the prison site and were happy with a brief nod in its direction. As the director of the PMA, McLaughlin was particularly concerned with the possibility of the film over-emphasizing the republican narrative if a perceptibly imbalanced screen time was devoted to it. I was less inclined to dwell upon this specific story angle, because the recordings did not offer much material on how the strikes affected women on a human level (the key focus of my thematic search). Ultimately, with dialogue, we were able to reach an agreement and include a brief section that pleased all of the collaborators. This one case highlights how crucial it was to acknowledge that sharing authorship 'does not require agreement on all things, but a mutual commitment to talk things through, to reach a common understanding, and to respect considered differences' (Rouverol, quoted in Zembrzycki, 2009: 225).

It is equally important to be aware that sharing authorship does not necessarily guarantee equal sharing of tasks and that people will have different roles throughout the filmmaking process that carry different weight responsibilities. In this case, participants expressed a certain confidence that my motivations and aspirations as a filmmaker aligned with theirs and, as a result, that there was a greater sense of trust in relation to the editing process. As one of the prison workers put it, 'Of course you had the bigger picture in your head in terms of how it is going to work but I felt that you actually listened and talked about things, even if something may not have worked' (interview with participant, June 2014). This shows that having the 'expert' filmmaker in charge of the process does not undermine the attempt to share authorship, as long as there is an expressed commitment to engaging in dialogue and negotiation with transparency and willingness to listen to participants' concerns. If there is no such commitment, then there is always the danger that the filmmaker remains as 'the real author, with the participants being simply brought in to legitimate a collaborative rubber stamp' (Barbash & Taylor, 1997: 89). This commitment is instrumental when working with people who have often been over-researched and misrepresented in the media, or who have been segregated from one another and have been getting accustomed to working alongside those who have for so long been perceived as the 'Other'.

Individual meetings versus groups

Meeting participants individually, as opposed to in a group, proved to be an important tool to build a trusting and transparent relationship. While group dynamics can trigger unique exchanges of experiences and ideas, it can also lead to the muting of '[t]he voices of the less confident, the poorer and the powerless' (Slim, Thompson, Bennett & Cross, 2006: 147). Therefore, working individually with them enabled my attentive listening to their concerns and to my being more sensitive when it came to selecting sections from their recordings. This was particularly valued by participants. One of the educational workers, for example, took issue with a particular story in the first rough cut and was pleased to see that it had been removed in the following: 'the lack of context made me unhappy about it and you kindly changed it [...] you did a brilliant job of listening. You were very generous and you weren't precious about your time' (interview with participant, June 2014).

Moreover, our individual encounters enabled participants to develop a sense of the group in a natural and organic way. They first became familiar with each other's journeys during the process of viewing rough cuts, so by the time of the full screenings, they felt comfortable participating in panel discussions together and, by then, perceived themselves as part of a group. Thus, it could be suggested that when working with sensitive stories and with participants from different, and sometimes opposing, backgrounds, the slow building of a sense of group identification may be more effective in minimizing the risks of participant withdrawal and of re-traumatization.

Public validation

Participants found that recording their stories and taking part in the editing and screening of the film publicly validated the importance of their life experiences. For example, one of the probation workers noted that '[I]t was historically a very interesting and important time and the whole peace process was born there and we were part of it. So it's been part of history; you know, it's a very affirming thing to see yourself' (interview with participant, January 2014). However, while first-hand storytelling can offer this sense of validation, it also requires special attention to the boundaries between the public and private. As Sarah Pink reminds us, 'people express some things in one context that they would not say in another; and in the apparent intimacy of a video interview an informant may make comments that he or she would not make elsewhere' (Pink, 2007: 56). Hence, filmmakers should be aware that some experiences may be too personal to be shared and can lead to embarrassment, harassment, re-traumatization and, in some cases, even real or perceived life-threatening situations for participants.

There is no guarantee that stories will always receive a welcome reception, especially in a situation such as that of Northern Ireland, where people's attitudes and view of themselves and of the 'Others' are volatile (Mairs, 2013: 177). Although *We Were There* has received mostly positive feedback, in one particular occasion during the festival première, we experienced a tense situation when one member of the audience angrily expressed his disappointment with how prisoners had so often been portrayed positively while prison officers had often been depicted negatively in films. Reactions such as this highlight the unavoidable risk of publicly invalidating or dismissing an individual's story which may, as a consequence, add to his/her existing exasperation.

Learning process

Collaborative filmmaking offers an invaluable learning opportunity for both filmmakers and participants. My close relationships with all involved enabled me not only to learn how to represent individual stories better, but also to gain more insight into the women's experiences of the conflict and prisons. For the participants, it offered the opportunity to develop a critical awareness of media, in particular, of how representations are constructed in films. One participant stated that it opened her eyes in relation to 'all of those stages that you have to go through' (interview with participant, June 2014), while another believed that it has changed the way she watches documentaries, as she is now more interested in 'how people actually select out different interpretations of things and do them differently' (interview with participant, June 2014).

For individuals who have previously experienced misrepresentation, this media awareness may help to restore their trust in the media, inasmuch as they see that filmmaking can be ethical and beneficial. This is paramount in Northern Ireland where the main task remains 'to find ways to encourage storytelling so that those who tell the stories can do so in safety and those who listen are mobilized into dealing with the legacy of past violence and working together to prevent future violence' (Hackett & Rolston, 2009: 372).

Opening spaces

Collaborative filmmaking can potentially offer safe spaces for unheard and under-represented stories to be remembered and shared publicly. This is more likely to happen when they are used in tandem with strategies that privilege human stories over historical context, as they can help to reduce, rather than reinforce, the sense of othering (Mairs, 2013: 142). For *We Were There*, the strategy used was to intercut the stories that united interviewees (experiences of the prison site), rather than separate them (their contrasting political or religious affiliations).

Narratives based on first-hand humanized accounts are more likely to create 'coexistence in plurality' and can potentially contribute to 'shared commemorative practices that allow for reparative remembering' (Jackson, quoted in Mairs, 2013: 142). If they are adopted in tandem with a dissemination plan developed together with participants, they can possibly 'provide truly unique openings for individuals to have a voice and claim space in venues that may have been previously off-limits' (Miller & Smith, 2012: 345). This is very much needed in Northern Ireland where cultural memorial practices have often fostered division (Roger, Leydesdorff & Dawson, 2004: 22).

Conclusion

I have argued in this chapter that the adoption of a collaborative framework has had more strengths than limitations when making *We Were There*. The filmmaker benefited from the participants' creative ideas and was able to create a film that contained an adequate representation of their stories. Working closely with participants enhanced the trusting nature of the relationship and helped minimize risks of misrepresentations, misunderstandings and de-contextualization.

For participants, taking part in the production, post-production and dissemination processes helped to validate their past experiences, and offered the opportunity for them to frame their own interviews and to learn from/about each other and about filmmaking processes. Although none experienced re-traumatization or any sort of disappointment throughout this project, one has to be careful if one thinks that collaborative filmmaking will always be unproblematic. Even if the filmmaking process is ethical and transparent, one can never predict how audiences will react to the stories once the film is brought to the public.

This chapter has demonstrated that when people have the opportunity to frame their own stories through a multi-layered collaborative media project, the gap between media representations and people's diverse experiences is more easily addressed. Therefore, I have proposed that films in the operational vein of *We Were There* can contribute to mobilizing people into dealing with the complexity of the past, into understanding and acknowledging the diversity of people's experiences and into working together to create a future away from violence. As one of the participants pointed out, Northern Ireland needs discussions in 'a more multi-faceted way, not one side or the other, but many sides, many truths, many journeys, many stories' (interview with participant, June 2014).

Notes

1. The Maze and Long Kesh Prison housed mostly male paramilitary prisoners from 1971 to 2000. Some of the major events of the conflict were transformed by the prison, and because of its contested symbolism, there have been difficulties in deciding what to do with the empty prison site since its closure. Armagh Gaol served as Northern Ireland's only female prison during the conflict until its closure in 1986. For more details, see McCafferty (1981), Murray (1998), Corcoran (2006) and Alison (2009).

2. The PMA holds 175 interviews of people connected to the Maze and Long Kesh Prison and Armagh Gaol and the aim is to make it available through an interactive exhibition platform. While the PMA seeks funding to create this exhibition, it has brought PhD students to work with some of the material at the post-production stage. Jolene Mairs (2013) was the first student and worked with the Armagh Gaol material, while I was the second and focused on the Maze and Long Kesh recordings.

3. The 'peace walls' separate interface areas with the purpose of minimizing inter-communal violence between nationalists and loyalists.

4. The Catholic police officer Ronan Kerr died after a booby-trap bomb exploded in his car in 2011, and a year later, prison officer David Black was murdered on his way to work. In the run-up to Christmas of 2013, there were 18 bombing incidents in seven weeks, with many of these attacks being against police officers. Luckily, none of the incidents caused injuries (*Belfast Telegraph*, 2013).

5. The 12th of July yearly marches celebrate the victory of Protestant King William of Orange over Catholic King James II at the Battle of the Boyne (1690). These marches have led to conflicts in interface areas between nationalist and loyalist communities, as the former sees them as triumphalist and intimidating, while the latter sees the marches as a celebration of their culture.

6. I have opted to anonymize the participants' responses primarily because of the small sample size and also because their visible identity in the film could compromise confidentiality. Hence, in order to differentiate between them, I refer to them by their prison role as workers or relatives of prisoners and prison staff.

7. The removal of political status for paramilitary prisoners in 1976 led to protests by loyalist and republican prisoners. After years of 'blanket' and 'no wash' protests, when republican prisoners wrapped themselves naked in blankets and defecated within their own cells, they went on two hunger strikes, in 1980 and 1981. The last ended with the death of ten republican prisoners (for more details, see Ryder, 2000; McKeown, 2001; McKittrick & McVea, 2001).

11
The Suffering Male Body in Steve McQueen's *Hunger*

Raita Merivirta

Hunger (2008), British filmmaker Steve McQueen's début feature, co-written by McQueen and Irish playwright Enda Walsh, deals with the Irish republican prisoners' 'dirty protest' in the Maze Prison/Long Kesh and its escalation into a hunger strike in 1981. The 'dirty protest' and hunger strike were a continuation of the 'blanket protest' begun by IRA prisoners in Long Kesh in September 1976 against the criminalization policy and withdrawal of the Special Category status by the British government's Northern Ireland Office, which denied the IRA and other paramilitary groups any acknowledgement of political motivation. IRA prisoners in Long Kesh started campaigning for political-prisoner status and refused to carry out prison work as was expected of 'ordinary decent criminals', or to wear prison uniforms, wrapping themselves in blankets instead. This insubordination was penalized by the prison administration: the inmates were kept locked in their cells except to go to the toilets, showers, Sunday mass and to receive visitors once a month. Access to the toilets was controlled by guards and it could be delayed or denied. The naked prisoners were also vulnerable to beatings and body searches by the guards on their way to the toilets and showers.

In 1978, the prisoners embarked upon a 'no wash' campaign that soon escalated into a 'dirty protest'. Prisoners refused to leave their cells, to wash or to empty their chamber pots, disposing of the waste through windows and door peepholes until these were boarded up by the guards. Finally, prisoners started smearing their excreta on their cell walls. The prison authorities responded by forcibly moving the inmates to other wings in order to steam-clean the cells. They later subjected the prisoners to forced baths and haircuts. Resistance was met with beatings by the guards and cell and body searches were frequent. Some of the prisoners decided to escalate the protest by going on a hunger strike in 1980 and again in 1981. Bobby Sands was the first of ten hunger strikers to die. He passed away on 5 May 1981, having been elected MP on the 40th day of his hunger strike.

Interestingly, the history and politics of the protest and strike are not the main themes of *Hunger*. The opening titles of the film give a few pointers of the situation in the prison and some hard-line statements by Prime Minister Margaret Thatcher are heard in voice-over during the course of the film, but neither Bobby Sands' politics nor the historical context of the strike is scrutinized in great detail. McQueen in fact describes his film as non-political and essentially humanist: 'People say, "Oh, it's a political film", but, for me, it's essentially about what we, as humans, are capable of, morally, physically, psychologically. What we will inflict and what we can endure' (cited in O'Hagan, 2008). Of the four films – Terry George's *Some Mother's Son* (1996), Maeve Murphy's *Silent Grace* (2001), Les Blair's *H3* (2001) and *Hunger* – that have been made about the dirty protest and hunger strikes, *Hunger* 'is', as Emilie Pine notes, 'the only film to fully depict the process of the strike and the wasting of the striker's body, and because of this focus it is also the film which least contextualizes the hunger strike as a historical event' (2011: 106). While George chose the perspective of two mothers of republican male prisoners 'as a lens through which to investigate the complexities of the hunger strike; something hitherto portrayed as a narrative of Irish male sacrifice' (Pettitt, 2000: 260–1), *Silent Grace* portrays republican women prisoners who took part in the 'dirty protest' and hunger strike in Armagh Jail. The focus of *H3* and *Hunger* is again more traditionally on the Irish male sacrifice; that is, on the IRA male prisoners in the Maze Prison/Long Kesh. While *H3* depicts the progress of the protest, contextualizes the hunger strike and allows its characters to express their political views, *Hunger* focuses on 'the body politics' of the protest. In this film, the body of Bobby Sands, 'not his politics, is the object of cinematic scrutiny' (Pine, 2011: 116). In this chapter, I focus on the representation of the suffering male body in *Hunger*. I also explore the visual links McQueen establishes between the sacrificial body of Christ and the body of Bobby Sands.

The fighting body

In the first half of the film, *Hunger* depicts the inmates' life in the prison during the 'dirty protest' in harrowingly realistic detail. The camera lingers on the excrement on the walls, the rotting food and crawling maggots in the corners of the cells, and shows the prisoners' urine spilling from under the cell doors into the corridor. The protesters, with long hair and beards and dirt under their fingernails, look appropriately scraggy and unwashed, much more so than the naked and half-naked inmates in *H3*, who, despite their untidy hair, always look surprisingly clean, even in their dirty cells. For the (excessively) realistic visual look of *Hunger*, McQueen drew from interviews of ex-prisoners and prison officers as well as from existing documentary footage. McQueen has, however, pointed out in interviews that 'there's only 90 seconds of footage shot of that period within the prison' (Chan, 2009; see also Wigon, 2009; Huston, 2009). He has explained that what he 'wanted to do was construct that time again on film, a time that wasn't ever seen by an audience in clear detail. It's like going back and trying to put a jig-saw puzzle back together' (Chan, 2009). He notes that his 'job in some ways was to document what actually happened physically in those cells' (Huston, 2009).

Les Blair's fictional film *H3* had shown similar images – of inmates smearing excrement on the wall and hiding 'comms' and other things, such as radios, in the orifices of their body, maggots crawling on cell floors, guards beating the prisoners and subjecting them to humiliating mirror searches – but none of these images was as (excessively) realistic or harrowing as in *Hunger*. *H3* is a more conventional narrative film, more character-driven than *Hunger*, with a focus on a group of inmates, their politics, psychology, decisions and the consequences of those decisions. *H3* is not as 'bodily' or materially, sensorially, an oriented film as *Hunger*. In McQueen's film, the focus is on the suffering male body, on the physical reality, the material conditions of the situation in the prison, and on the physical and sensory experiences of the inmates.

Also, spectators are immersed in the reality of the prison with its sights, sounds and smells. Even the pain of the beatings, the humiliation of the body searches and finally the pain of hunger seem oddly visceral, as within the sensory grasp of the audience. Spectators cringe as the film vividly illustrates invasions of the bodies of the inmates, such as the loathed mirror searches, described below by an IRA ex-prisoner:

> They made you squat on the floor on your haunches. You wouldn't do that so they beat you, they sat over you and probed your back passage, and then with the same finger some would search your mouth,

your nose, your hair, your beard, every part of your body, there was nothing private about your body.

(Cited in Aretxaga, 1995: 127)

In *Hunger*, the prison guard searching the inmate uses rubber gloves – not the medical kind of disposable gloves but the thicker kind used to do gardening or cleaning bathrooms – which in all its probable realism further emphasizes the inhumanity of the situation and the deliberate humiliation of the prisoners. As an ex-prison officer (Cages and the H-Blocks) described the practices in the prison: 'Humiliation was a big weapon' (cited in Feldman, 1991: 192). 'Among the staff it was understood that it was government policy to lower the status of political inmates. [...] The instructions to break the prisoners came from the highest levels of government because the policy was criminalization to be implemented by prison staffs' (ex-Prison Welfare Officer, Cages and the H-Blocks, in Feldman, 1991: 191). Despite the humiliating practices and the dirty cells, the inmates are shown to keep their dignity and pride, and the guards seem to be by-and-large unable to break their resolve. For most of the time, the prisoners display extraordinary steadfastness and bodily control as they turn to masochistic practices by refusing to wash, smearing their excreta on the wall, leaving food to rot in cell corners, bearing invasions on their (bodily) privacy, enduring beatings and finally, refusing food. In the first third of *Hunger*, the half-naked male bodies are shown in action, actively protesting and using their bodies as the means of that protest. McQueen has said that he wanted to show how the protesters used 'their body as a weapon [...] That was interesting for me to show, visually, because it had never actually been filmed' (cited in Wigon, 2009). *Hunger* does not depict the birth and escalation of the 'blanket' and 'dirty protests', but starts at a point when the naked male body is already used as a powerful weapon against the hated regime. The film is essentially a spectacle of the suffering male body, an examination of the use of the (naked) male body as a highly controlled and disciplined weapon.

Kent L. Brintnall suggests that '[a] suffering male body can potentially signify vulnerability, limitation, and lack, in contrast to dominant cultural myths about masculine identity' (2011: 30). Interestingly, in *Hunger* the vulnerability of the naked male bodies is turned into a strength, partly because the men turn their naked bodies into organic weapons, but also because the spectacle of suffering seen on screen invites the sympathy of the audience. The immediacy and materiality of what we as viewers see before our eyes takes over, almost as a physical reaction, and leaves little room for historical contemplation or contextualization. When Bobby Sands is first seen 25 minutes into the film, he seems to be just one of the inmates, or even one of the victims of the prison system as it has started to seem. The audience realizes only later that he is the historical Sands and OC (Officer Commanding). Nothing is told about his background or activities before being imprisoned, nor has what he has been sentenced for been divulged; the viewers see him merely as one of the republican prisoners on the protest. Watching the blanketmen in *Hunger*, it is possible to forget that the protesting inmates 'viewed the 1981 Hunger Strike as a military campaign and organized it as such. For them, it was a modality of insurrectionary violence in which they deployed their bodies as weapons. They fully expected a coupling of this act of self-directed violence with mass insurrectionary violence outside the prison' (Feldman, 1991: 220).

Although *Hunger* also strives to show the other side of the conflict, and what happened outside of the prison, demonstrably when, at the beginning of the film, one of the guards has to check under his car for bombs before going to work. In a later scene, the same officer is cold-bloodedly shot in the head in front of his old mother in a nursing home. Viewers' positions, therefore, are not clear-cut, as they are not only likely to sympathize with Sands and the other inmates who live in the inhumane prison conditions. The guards are now also seen equally as victims of the same violent prison regime as the inmates, and as disconnected from the politics of the outside violence as those interred are. This is especially the case with Sands when the audience sees him for the first time, struggling against a number of guards who are forcibly taking him to a bathroom where his hair and beard are brutally sheared and he is viciously scrubbed in a bathtub. Bleeding and bruised, he is then carried back to his cell. Therefore the audience, deprived of simplified details of Sands' background, is likely to relate to Sands merely as a victim; a victim of the guards' brutality and the regime that has forced them to protest in this inhumane way. He is ultimately a victim of the British state, which is represented here not only by the guards, but by the unsympathetic and, in the context of the corporeal focus here, significantly disembodied voice of Prime Minister Thatcher.

The fact that the naked and thus vulnerable Sands is outnumbered and badly beaten by the guards – and yet does not rescind on his position of protest – endows him with heroic quality. In his article about masochism and the sexy male body in Mel Gibson films, Jeffrey

A. Brown writes that battering and bruising make action stars' characters more rather than less attractive:

> The cuts and scrapes displayed so proudly on the suffering hero's body function as visible proof of the character's toughness and mark him as worthy of audience sympathy. Viewers are encouraged to both admire and feel sorry for him. The hero's strength of character is evidenced through his strength of body.
>
> (2002: 139)

I would argue that this is true of Sands' character as well. As he is treated brutally by the guards, he is marked 'as worthy of audience sympathy'. The naked, suffering men appear manly and victorious rather than passive and weak. They may appear to be victims of a brutal regime, but they are framed as victims who, due to their resilience and strength, deserve audience sympathy rather than pity. The protesting prisoners, and especially Sands, appear at once both as active agents in this battle of power and as victims of a brutal system. Michael Fassbender's performance as Bobby Sands further emphasizes the mental strength of the main character and raises the point of moral superiority, even if the film otherwise puts great emphasis on material things.

The sacrificial body

Richard Hamilton's painting *The Citizen* (1981–3), which depicts a prisoner on a blanket in a dirty cell in the Maze Prison, is one of the iconic images of the 'dirty protest'. According to Hamilton, 'the main source of the imagery' for the painting was the aforementioned TV footage (quoted in Riggs, 1998). Those 90 seconds of film of the blanketmen show 'two prisoners, bedraggled and Christ-like, wrapped in dirty blankets, shouting out their demands from a filthy, excrement encrusted cell' (O'Hagan, 2008). Hamilton wrote in his catalogue text that accompanied the 1983 exhibition *A Cellular Maze*:

> The picture presented, first by Granada Television and later by the BBC, was shocking less for its scatological content than for its potency. An oft declared British view of the IRA as thugs and hooligans did not match the materialization of Christian martyrdom so profoundly contained on film. One became acutely aware of the religious conflict that had resulted in the civil inequalities that gave

a platform for IRA activity. The symbols of Christ's agony were there, not only the crucifix on the neck of the prisoners and the rosary which confirmed the monastic austerity but the self inflicted suffering which has marked Christianity from the earliest times.

(Quoted in Riggs, 1998)

The Christian martyrdom and self-inflicted suffering that Hamilton mentions, as well as his mobilization of Christian iconography, have all had a strong influence on portrayals of the blanketmen, including cinematic ones. As Pine points out, 'Christ-like images of protesting male prisoners, with heavy beards and long hair, wearing only a blanket' (2011: 109) have dominated the remembrance of the hunger strikes.

In *Some Mother's Son*, the first fiction film about the IRA prisoners on the 'dirty protest', the glimpses of the blanketmen which the audience gets to see reproduce the familiar, now iconic, images of the protesters. As one of the characters says in *Some Mother's Son*, Bobby Sands (John Lynch) looks like Jesus Christ in his long dark hair and beard and grey blanket. Sands maintains this look throughout the film, both when he is participating in the 'dirty protest' and when he is on hunger strike. Terry George, who was 'criticised for mythologizing Bobby Sands' in the film, defended himself by saying: 'that was the reality of the situation. We've all seen the photographs, and they looked like that' (quoted in Linehan, 1996: 11). Les Blair's film *H3* offers images of both Christ-like blanketmen as well as of prisoners who have agreed to shower and cut their hair. Sands, however, is portrayed in very much the same way in *H3* as in *Some Mother's Son* – with pale face and long dark hair and beard – unchanging throughout the film. The first images of the blanketmen in *Hunger* fall into the same familiar category. In the first third or half of the film, the audience sees a protesting republican prisoner who is very much like the blanketmen in the previous films, reproducing the image of the iconic blanketman with long hair and beard, wearing only a blanket or a towel, as well as images of the cells as they are seen in the existing documentary footage of the protest. But when the focus shifts from the prisoners as a collective, to the individual – focusing on Bobby Sands – we see a different-looking blanketman, as McQueen, committed to historical visual accuracy and not content to reproduce familiar images, develops the depiction of the hunger strikers further than George had in *Some Mother's Son* or even as Blair had in *H3*.

In *Hunger*, Sands is first seen when he is taken naked for a forced haircut and bath by the guards. Through the rest of the film he has short, ginger hair and he is more often seen either naked or wearing clothes (for example, in trousers when he receives visitors, or in striped pyjamas in the hospital) than wrapped only in a blanket. I have argued elsewhere that *Hunger*'s excessive realism and the actual emaciated body of the actor Michael Fassbender – who in fact fasted for ten weeks under medical supervision before shooting the third part of the film and lost more than 23 kilograms altogether – served to 'disrupt the sanitised, iconic image of the hunger strikers' (Merivirta, 2013: 252). In this, I was proposing that the images of long-bearded and long-haired men in blankets were manifestly reminiscent of many cinematic and sanitized portrayals of (the suffering) Christ: even prior to Mel Gibson's *The Passion of the Christ* (2004), which was much discussed for its exceptionally realistic or unsanitized portrayal of the suffering of Christ. When Sands goes on hunger strike in *Hunger*, he looks distinctly different from the usual images of the Christ-like blanketmen.

However, although *Hunger* moves away from the usual image of the bearded blanketman, there are some visual links between McQueen's Sands and portrayals of the sacrificial body of Christ. Some critics see them as very pronounced. Dennis Lim has written in the *New York Times*:

> It is hard to miss the overtones of Christian art and iconography in 'Hunger', especially in the Passion-like final act, but Mr. McQueen, without exactly disavowing the religious associations, shrugs them off. 'It's a naked skinny guy dying – sort of unavoidable,' he said. 'People mythologize it because that's easier to digest.' (2009)

It can be argued that Sands' hunger strike registers as extreme masochism and, as Tim Edwards suggests, 'the most fundamental of all images of male masochism comes from Christianity in relation to the sufferings of Christ' (2008: 167). Therefore, associations of Christ-like suffering are perhaps unavoidable, as McQueen has said himself. Yet some visual links between the body of Sands and the body of the suffering Christ in *Hunger* seem quite intentional, and their purpose and effect can be duly discussed.

After his forced haircut and bath, the naked and bleeding Sands is carried back to his cell by two guards in a position not unlike that associated with Christ on the cross. This reference to crucifixion seems intentional. Writing about male bodies in films, Richard Dyer has argued that 'the recourse to crucifixion can be a key moment in establishing the moral superiority of not specifically Christian characters' (1997: 150). I would argue that this scene has a similar effect. Sands, who has

just been introduced to the audience, is of course a Christian character, but he has not been portrayed as especially religious and, although
his Catholicism comes up in the following discussion with a priest, his
faith does not seem to be steadfast, or even a strong, motivating factor informing his decision to embark on his hunger strike. Therefore,
I would argue that Sands' crucifixion-like position between the guards
signals Sands' moral superiority and determination more than it likens
him to Christ as a spiritual leader. This case might be all the more
strongly made as Sands is carried in this position immediately after
he has been shorn of his Christ-like appearance. Sands' expression in
this scene is noteworthy and the 'crucifixion' moment seems to signal a
point of decision for Sands: he soon informs the priest of his decision to
go on hunger strike. Leon Hunt has discussed the representation of the
male body in crucifixion scenes in epic films, noting the contradictions
involved:

> passivity offset by control, humiliation offset by nobility of sacrifice,
> eroticism offset by religious connotations of transcendence. If the
> gladiator is unwilling to die, the epic hero embraces crucifixion with
> some degree of acceptance/willingness; it is the moment where he
> demonstrates his control over his own body through his ability to
> give it up.
>
> (1993: 73)

In the 'crucifixion' scene, Sands' expression exudes control that offsets
the passivity and humiliation of his being carried by guards. The eroti-
cism of the candidly portrayed naked male body is offset not only by
the excessively realistic light in which his beaten body is shown, but
also by religious – though, I would argue, not necessarily or exclusively,
Christian – connotations of transcendence once he begins his hunger
strike. Most importantly, Sands seems to come up at this point with the
ultimate solution of demonstrating 'his control over his body through
his ability to give it up', which he does in the last third of the film.

Maud Ellman writes thus about the hunger strikers: 'It was not by
hungering as such, but by making theatre of their own starvation, that
the prisoners brought shame on their oppressors and captured the sym-
pathies of their co-religionists' (1993: 72). In *Hunger*, McQueen shows
the spectacle, or theatre, of the dirty cells and bearded, naked inmates
as well as the starving body of Bobby Sands, and makes a contemporary
point about the suffering of the men. As the images remind viewers of
Abu Ghraib, Guantánamo Bay and other contemporary prisoner abuses,

the film raises questions around the rectitude and shame on the abusers, and the governments that allow such treatment of prisoners. Thus, the film becomes less historically specific and local, and more universal in its tone. As Debbie Ging notes, '*Hunger* is a distinctly postmodern and transnational meditation on the nature of (male) suffering derived from the context of Irish history, in which this form of protest is not understood as an atavistic legacy of the fanatical Celtic soul but as the last refuge of the oppressed' (2013: 148). It could be argued that McQueen has drawn from a larger pool of images depicting sacrifice and suffering than merely those associable with Christian iconography. In the third part of the film, Sands' frail frame and striped pyjamas can be interpreted as referring to Holocaust victims and concentration camps, as well as to the suffering Christ. This again suggests that Sands' character can be read as that of a universal suffering prisoner and a victim of a brutal regime as well as a self-sacrificing martyr dying for a cause.

12
Mickybo and Me: A Cinematographic Adaptation for an International Audience

Brigitte Bastiat

Mickybo and Me, directed by the Northern Irish Terry Loane in 2004, falls into the category of initiatory tales that reveal a society in crisis. It is a rite-of-passage film that takes place during the 'Troubles'. The script presents two eight-year-old Protestant and Catholic boys from Belfast in the 1970s, who become and remain friends, despite bigotry and violence. Notwithstanding the progressive contemporaneity of the original scenario and its attempts to render characterizations in a nuanced way, my contention here is that the representations of the Protestant and Catholic communities, as well as the representation of the so-called innocent childhood, are rather safely stereotyped in the film. I will propose that this is perhaps most evident where the scripted language is concerned. In fact, it is clear that the dialogue in the film, an adaptation of a play by Owen McCafferty first published in 1998, has sometimes been toned down, thus rendering the stereotypification all the more simplistic in its legibility; something that is all the more marked in the French subtitles, although perhaps surprisingly less so in the dubbed version. Subtitling and dubbing films are very difficult tasks and are subject to certain constraints; with general concessions, namely, that a line of subtitles should not exceed 32 alphabetical characters for legibility on a television screen and that they should not be sustained for more than four or five seconds (Bellos, 2012: 149). Where dubbing is concerned, the synchronization of the words spoken by the indigenous actors and the lip movements of the original performers add significantly to this difficulty. Of course, these technical requirements determine the choice of words, but I would like to foreground in this chapter how the language used is also crucially influenced by the target culture.

In his book, *Film Adaptation*, James Naremore draws attention to how academic and journalistic critics often consider popular contemporary adaptations as 'belated, middlebrow or culturally inferior' (2000: 6). This severe condemnation of the exercise is fairly common when dealing with film adaptation. However, it seems that some theorists have upgraded this appreciation. Thus, Linda Hutcheon, Professor of English and Comparative Literature at the University of Toronto, published a book in 2006 in which she attempts to identify various aspects of adaptation and give it a more positive outlook. In order to overcome the notion of faithfulness to the original work against which it is often judged, she provides the following triple definition of adaptation, which gives it a life of its own as 'a formal entity or product', 'a process of creation' and 'a process of reception' (Hutcheon, 2006: 7–8). *Mickybo and Me* is certainly 'a formal entity or product' with a 'life of its own': that is to say, the transposition of a piece of work from one type of medium – here, a theatre play – to another independent manifestation – in this case, a film. Notwithstanding the adaptation process, the thematic objectives and context are the same in that both the play and the film speak of friendship, violence and the construction of masculine identities in Belfast in the early 1970s. However, the methods of characterization and communication differ in the sense that the playwright, Owen McCafferty, uses the presence of the play's narrator on stage to take us inside the minds of the young Protestant and Catholic boys from Belfast, with their humour, fears, imagination and violence – affected or real – whereas film director Terry Loane concentrates more on their actions, in spite of an attempt at introspection using the cinematic technique of the voice-over. In addition, for experimental and economic reasons, the play tries something that is theatrically less easily transposed to the cinema: as a two-hander, both players play all of the 17 male and female roles on stage.

The language of the characters (especially that of the children) which was transformed by the screenwriters of the film adaptation is one aspect of the process of creation and reception mentioned by Linda Hutcheon, and in this instance, it is deeply interwoven with the construction of character and the process of thematic exploration. The play is written in Belfast slang and is pervaded by a sense of humour that is imbued with local references, culturally and linguistically. The boys' speech is rarely linear or rational, and consists of 'jump-cuts' in ideas, sometimes absurd, sometimes coarse, but always imaginative. There is no clear and inviolable boundary between their real and imaginary worlds. Moreover, there are other characters, such as Mickybo's mother, who use humour and imagination to make the family's life more bearable. An example of this can be seen with the latter character in the way that she nicknames her husband, whom she loves, despite his flaws: 'The man that I love header and all as he is...' (McCafferty, 1998: 23). This example (and so many others like it) brings a specific tonal quality to the piece that places it in a very precise spatial and temporal context: we are in 1970 at the beginning of the Troubles, which will cost the lives of thousands of people. The most important thing for the two young protagonists, who are not fully aware of the conflict, is not the daily violence, but the world that they are building to make their lives more interesting and in which they play a considerable heroic part. According to Owen McCafferty, the play is not really about ideology,[1] but about the absurdity of sectarianism. In fact, the conflict is no more than a backdrop because the play revolves mainly around the budding friendship between two young boys and the influence of another major event that summer; the release of the film *Butch Cassidy and the Sundance Kid* (Hill, 1969). We have a *mise en abyme* – a story within the story – in both the original and adaptation, but it is more effective in the film version because this medium can integrate visual intertextual qualities of the Western genre more directly, and can subtly lead the viewer from one image to another and from representations of the 'real' world of the children to the virtual world of Butch and Sundance. This exemplifies the idea mentioned here: that the worlds of reality and fiction are not entirely separate for the children, who can, like the film's spectator, move easily from one visual and ontological dimension to another. Significantly, this fluidity also works acoustically through language, as the kids sometimes speak like their heroes, imitating their American accents. Problematically, of course, this is impossible to express in written subtitles. In the dubbed version, however, while the young actors might have been directed to imitate an American accent in French, this option was not taken.

In the play, the boys are called Mojo and Mickybo; nicknames that matter more to the children than their real names, which would more readily reveal the fact that they belong to different districts of the divided city of Belfast. In Ireland and Britain, one can also often guess the social origin and religion of a person when hearing his/her full name and accent. It should be noted that in the film, Mojo's name is changed for the more modern, 'Jonjo', and that this version also sounds more American. Yet, this removes to some extent the mirror image aspect that the children play with at the beginning of the play when they say, 'mojo mickybo mojo – sounds like a gang' (McCafferty, 1998: 12).

The impression that we get is that the two names go well together and could even be swapped. There are two boys, at least as defined by name, but it is suggested that they have a common identity, a point that is of central importance given the political context. Other names are also significantly changed in the adaptation: 'Fuckface' in the play becomes 'Fartface' in the film, and the nickname 'Fartface' also appears in the French subtitles – which does not mean anything to a French audience and could have been easily and literally translated by *'Face de pet'*; a phrase that allows additional amusement. In the dubbed version, it becomes *'Face de fion'* (Arse Face), which sounds appropriately ridiculous. 'Gank the Wank' in the play is reduced simply to 'Gank' in the film, both in English and in French, while 'Barney Rip the Balls' in the play is just plain 'Barney'. These changes were certainly made to avoid offending the sensibilities of the public and to limit the use of offensive language, which may seem surprising in a contemporary film. These alterations nonetheless show how market realities and formal classification are inevitably mutually informing. Taking into account the sensibilities of wider audiences, it is possible that the use of certain terms by little boys may have been regarded as too racy. In any case, the tone and the language in the film is watered down from the original play and only the occasional expletive 'fuck' has survived. Most of these have been replaced by 'friggin', a slang word rarely translated in the French subtitles. In the dubbed version, the word *'putain'* is sometimes used as a substitute. The slang used in Belfast is replaced by words that can be understood by the British and American public. Thus, words such as 'geg' (*marrant*), 'catmalogion' (*nul*) and 'weeker' (*extra*) are replaced by the more modern word 'beezer', subtitled in the film by *'balèze'* – a French slang word meaning both very strong and clever – and in the dubbed version by *'putain de Dieu'* – literally 'whore of God' – whose strangeness and foreign-sounding oddity further marks the linguistic and cultural diversities that become framed and muted in the French translation. In the last scene of the film, one may notice a mistake in the French subtitles. While we can hear Jonjo's voice saying, 'If you're ever down under give me a call' translated by *'si tu as le cafard, appelle-moi'* ('If you feel down, call me'), it is likely that the translators did not know that the expression 'down under' meant 'Australia'. In the dubbed version, however, it has been more accurately translated as *'si tu descends par chez nous, appelle-moi'* ('If you come down our way, call me'). Another typical Australian expression – 'G'day, G'day, G'day' – was also left out by the translators of the subtitles, although in the dubbed version there was an attempt to translate it when Mickybo's father says *'allez, allez, allez'* ('go, go, go'). When translating the play with Frank Healy, we decided to replace this expression with French stereotypes about Australia, and the father says, *'Sidney Koala Skippy le kangourou.'*[2]

The Belfast accents of the characters were retained in the English version of the film as a result of strategic casting. In the dubbed version, the characters speak with a standard French accent and use common slang. Nowadays in France, there is no such thing as local slang and Mojo and Mickybo could not have spoken in any local slang. Even if big cities like Lyon, Marseille or Lille have had their own slang, according to Denise François-Geiger, French slang originally comes from relatively homogeneous nomadic groups, such as harvesters, chimneysweepers or, more recently, mobsters. However, she dates the development of a common French slang to the beginning of the 20th century (François-Geiger, 1991: 8).

In terms of translation, on the whole, the dubbed version is evidently more daring in its choice and use of slang words than the subtitled one. While this might seem counter-intuitive, it may be due to the fact that the eye has less time to read the cues than the actors have to speak their lines. Additionally, when spectators are distracted momentarily from the full frame as they read the subtitles, they are likely to miss the plenitude and semiotic totality of the cinematographic language of the images. All of this would tend to indicate that – contrary to the widespread notion that there are evident advantages to watching films in both the original version and their dubbed versions – these assumptions can only be held when translating and acting are well accomplished.

In the film, the public is immediately aware of the political context of the story and of which characters are Protestant and Catholic. In the play, by contrast, the fact of not knowing is important because the playwright uses the ambiguity in order to explain his point that boys live in a world of their own and are only secondarily subjected to the absurdity of the sectarian attitudes of adults. Nevertheless, this dramatic technique might also have been better applied in the film to explain the situation to an international audience, who might be less familiar with the social, political and historical contexts of Northern Ireland. Actually, having watched the play in French at the University of La Rochelle in November 2014, some members of the audience said that they could not make out who was Catholic or Protestant. Even at the end of the play when Mickybo shouts 'Orange bastards' (translated as *'connards d'orangistes'*) to insult his former friend Mojo, the expression did not make sense to some members of the French audience, who were not familiar with the term *'orangistes'* as being associated with Protestants. However, as translators, we had chosen to use the word '*orangistes*' instead of 'Protestants' because it rooted the play in a Northern Irish linguistic and cultural context, and also because it did not really matter who was who. This decision further underscored the central point of the play wherein the two boys and both communities were interchangeable, as both were subjected to the absurdity and cruelty of sectarianism. In November 2014, some French students who saw both the play and the film thought that the film was more explicit and they confessed it had helped them to grasp the tensions of the Northern Irish divided society better, perhaps explaining Terry Loane's alterations in the cinematic version.

Whereas violence is omnipresent in the movie adaptation, it is not as often diegetically presented in the play. The first scene differs from the opening of the play and sets the tone by showing the explosion of a bomb in a shoe store; a sequence accompanied by the upbeat soundtrack song 'I'll Tell My Ma'. There are often very shocking scenes in the film, such as the one in which Mickybo waves aloft a finger that he has found on the site of an explosion;[3] the stabbing of Jonjo by Mickybo at the end; and the sequence in which the eight-year-old Mickybo holds a real gun and shoots at other boys. Holding an ideologically consistent position, this kind of violence is acceptable to producers, something broadly representative of the time, and notably different to attitudes to performed swear words, many of which were more readily censored. (A noteworthy example was Ken Loach's *Sweet Sixteen* [2002], a film that was censored in Britain in 2002 due to violent and bad language.) That the style of some of the dialogue in the play has been softened in the film version problematically relegates the swearing as a marker of identity. Notwithstanding these linguistic alterations, it is clear that the director has kept the spirit of the play, appropriating it by creating new humorous scenes.

To make the story more accessible to a wider British and North American audience, the film adaptation (a co-production of US studio Universal and British Working Title Films) has muted almost every political and historical Belfast specificity, in both language (as mentioned here) and in socio-cultural situations and sequences. The presence of tanks and British soldiers and the Northern Irish accent immediately, unambiguously, situates the action in a definite time and space. Overall, however, the film could just as easily be telling the story of two small children in Northern England or Scotland, somewhat reminiscent of examples of Ken Loach's work or Anglo-Irish comedies such as *The Commitments* (Alan Parker, 1991), *The Snapper* (1993) and *The Van*

(1996), both directed by Stephen Frears. In the film, Mickybo is a lively, dirty and coarse redhead scoundrel who raises hell and is constantly up to mischief. He represents the modern version of the long tradition of naughty English boys like 'William' from the *Just William* series of books by Richmal Crompton. This series of books portrays a confident and strong-willed 11-year-old boy who does not care about his physical appearance and whose imagination and love of adventure always get him into trouble. His social background is middle class like Jonjo's, and William's best friend, Ginger, has red hair like Mickybo; perhaps offering another shorthand stereotypical personality reference. Mickybo's family is also a good example of stereotypical English eccentricity, notably including the requisite twin sisters who say the same thing at the same time, a recurring trope evident in twin characters going as far back as the characters of Tweedledum and Tweedledee from Lewis Carroll's *Alice in Wonderland*. These references and narrative elements are examples of the quality of 'palimpsestuous intertextuality' which characterizes any adaptation, according to Linda Hutcheon (2006: 21).

To be considered successful in its 'process of reception', an adaptation must satisfy both its informed public, which predictably has some expectations, and a public that does not necessarily know the social and historical context of the represented narrative. In this instance, for clarity, I will offer some examples in proposing how the cinematographic adaptation was changed specifically in order to meet some requirements in the search for a balance between producers' judgement of the tastes of the target audience and the profits that they hoped to make from the film. For instance, in one of the scenes from the play, Mojo and Mickybo are caught in an Orange parade that they pretend is some kind of carnival which they proceed to mock.[4] The sequence was removed from the film and replaced by a scene in an amusement park, in an alteration likely made to avoid provoking strong criticism from the Protestant community. Also, the hilarious monologue in the play, when Mickybo's mother tells Mojo how she was forced to sell her son to the gypsies for a few pennies in order to pay the gas bill, was considerably shortened in the film. The director has stated that he made this choice 'to move the story forward more quickly'.[5] It may also be because the monologue in the play provides a good example of regionally specific Belfast humour and may sound too local, or be too incomprehensible, to an international audience. Notwithstanding the omission – which provides a certain damping down of cultural specificity – designed for the purpose of plot progression, the French version of this monologue has anecdotally always been a great success in Francophone theatres so far.[6] In fact, it is often the case that the local can reflect a greater universality and that it may be better to avoid over-processing the adaptation in an attempt to reincarnate the script into what may seem a more internationally accepted and understood version. Owen McCafferty once confided that Terry Loane had made certain choices to appeal to a wider audience in order to compete with other 'child narrative' films, such as *Stand by Me* (Reiner, 1986). Nevertheless, this competitive comparison might have been a moot point if only because of the predictable marketing potency of the Hollywood machinery and, unsurprisingly, *Mickybo and Me* was not as successful at the box office as *Stand by Me* in the United States.[7]

Many of the sectarian and gendered visual stereotypes – in relation to both Catholics and Protestants, and men and women – have been maintained. Jonjo, therefore, represents the Protestant who is neat and tidy, who hardly swears and lives with his parents in a middle-class suburb; Mickybo, on the other hand, lives in a very poor Catholic neighbourhood and his clothes and demeanour reflect this. In the film, Mickybo was given a large family, clearly a cliché of Catholic families that Terry Loane chose to integrate into his script, whereas in the play, Mickybo's siblings are not introduced.

The final scene in the movie gives a universal message of reconciliation between the two communities. In it, Jonjo and Mickybo are shown as adults many years after the main events of the story. Jonjo has immigrated to Australia where he has started a family. Terry Loane seems to suggest here that emigration was a potential way out of the conflict in Northern Ireland; a fact that might be corroborated by the photograph that Jonjo sends to Mickybo, in which we see a man who has succeeded in life and looks radiant. Mickybo, however, is sitting at the bar at the place where his father was murdered, and Loane offers the atavistic notion that he has been unable to escape the city and his poor working-class condition. Nevertheless, the friendship remains and Jonjo's gesture of camaraderie is sincere; a positive image acceptable and affirmative for a popular audience. By contrast, in the play, the two former friends, now adults, pass each other one day on a Belfast street and ignore each other. The very end of the play shows Mojo and Mickybo as kids playing in the park, a scene that may imply that kids are stronger than war. However, their voices become gradually covered by the sounds of rifle shots; a powerful defying of easy loose-end resolution and a much less optimistic message. This is the moment when the mirroring of the two previously inseparable characters – each at one time being the reflection of the other – finally breaks, and we are concretely, symbolically shown the logical continuation of the political context of the time. One can also assume that the film, released in 2004, has an ending that differs from the tragic end of the play, because the play was published in 1998, just before the start of the peace process. On 10 April 1998, the Good Friday Agreement was signed by Tony Blair, the prime minister of Great Britain, and Bertie Ahern, the Taoiseach of the Republic of Ireland, supported by David Trimble of the Ulster Unionist Party, John Hume from the Social Democratic and Labour Party, and Gerry Adams from Sinn Féin. It put an end to all claims of the Republic of Ireland on Northern Ireland (as listed in the Irish Constitution), established the foundations for the future government and launched a programme of disarmament and release of prisoners.[8]

Despite the added and deleted scenes and other changes inherent to adaptation, the film will always potentially reach a wider audience than the play, and can thus make – or be required to make – its themes even more universal. In fact, when stories travel, as is the case with adaptations, they eventually relate what Edward Said calls a different 'process of representation and institutionalization' (1983: 226). While the exported texts start within a specific context, ideas inevitably change and become transformed, facing acceptance or resistance by new audiences. In this way, the local particularities are transplanted into new territories and the result becomes a hybrid and new work. This 'new entity' exists thanks to the liberties that screenwriters and film directors take, and they are part of the 'creation process' of adaptation as defined by Linda Hutcheon and, as she says: 'Like jazz variations, adaptations point to individual creative decisions and actions, yet little of the respect accorded to the jazz improvisers is given to most adapters' (2006: 86).

Notes

1. From informal discussions with Owen McCafferty between 2010 and 2012.
2. Frank Healy, with whom I co-translated the theatrical script, is a colleague from the University of La Rochelle.
3. The finger still has a ring on, but Mickybo throws it away and prefers to keep the cut-off finger as a war treasure.
4. The Orange parades are held in the summer, especially on the 12th of July, which is the day when Northern Irish Orangemen parade the most to commemorate the Battle of the Boyne (1690), which saw the victory of the Protestant William of Orange over the English Catholic King James II, who had taken refuge in Ireland after having been overthrown during the 'Glorious Revolution'.
5. Bonus interview of Terry Loane in the DVD *Mickybo and Me*.

6. This remark is based on my own experience as a member of the audience during about a dozen performances in Tours, La Rochelle and Paris between 2012 and 2014.
7. From an informal conversation with Owen McCafferty in Belfast, November 2014.
8. On 22 May, two referenda (one in the North and one in the South) validated this agreement: 71.1% voted yes in the North, 94.4% in the Republic. Half of the Protestant population and 10% of Catholics voted against. Access Research Knowledge (ARK), www.ark.ac.uk.

Part IV
Overseas Perspectives

13
Singing in the Rain: The Irish-Themed Film Musical and *Schlager*'s Hibernian Moment

Fergal Lenehan

Genre has not played a very extensive role within Irish film studies, with to date just one edited volume (McIlroy, 2007) dedicated to the topic of genre and Irish cinema. However, as McIlroy's book makes clear, an orientation towards genre allows for the study of cinema beyond a narrowly constituted canon. It also enables scholars to view cinematic texts as interrelated *groups* of texts that build upon and correlate with one another rather than simply as single, stand-alone representational artefacts with which to indulge one's hermeneutic musings. An emphasis upon genre also illuminates two of cinema's naturally opposing elements in relation to form: its often quasi-universal generic structure and its extensive and organic cultural hybridity that allows for cultural borrowings.

The topic of this chapter is the film musical genre and a wide, industry-oriented definition of the musical is used here. Musicals are seen simply as movies with music created and communicated *within* the reality of the film. More specifically, here, I will deal with the Irish-themed film musical. Indeed film musicals from Hollywood and the British film industry with Irish thematic elements are actually relatively large in number, especially from the 1930s through to the 1950s, the golden age of the film musical. It is perhaps surprising, thus, that the Irish-themed film musical has been rarely dealt with, at least within specific generic terms rather than simply glossed over within overview historical studies of Irish cinema.[1]

Rick Altman (2005), in an essay originally published in 1984, has proffered what he terms the semantic/syntactic theoretical approach to film genre. For Altman (2005: 31), generic semantics are the 'building blocks' of a movie, the 'common traits, attitudes, characters, shots, locations, [and] sets', while the generic syntax is the overarching structure into which these semantics are arranged. Altman (2005: 33) believes that the syntax becomes the 'specific meaning-bearing structures', while 'generic meaning comes into being only through the repeated deployment of substantially the same syntactic strategies'. Thus, for Altman (2005: 39), within the Hollywood musical, making music often retains the semantics of making a living – particularly for musicals set within an entertainment or vaudeville milieu – while making music within this genre often retains a very different *syntax*, a lovemaking that often climaxes with romantic duets. Altman does not mean for his theory to be viewed in an essentialist manner however; his semantic and syntactic categorizations must be seen as fluid and flexible. The use of Altman's genre theory allows us, however, to view Irish-themed musicals collectively, as interrelated generic texts, and enables us to chart developments and changes within this filmic text type.

It is here argued that the Irish-themed musical retains three common and recurring sets of semantics based on setting, filmic imagery, character and the specifics of 'Irishness' communicated within the film texts. These semantic sets may be seen as migration semantics: primarily Irish-American and Irish-British situations, rural, non-'modern' semantics, often dominated visually by a type of 'matte painting pastoralism' (not unusual for the period of their making) and urban-Dublin 'modern' semantics. The semantic development also charts, one may at least contend, the changing contours and dominating 'landscape' of perceptions of 'Irishness'. The syntax, the often-recurring meaning-giving structure, it is argued, may frequently be seen in relation to music-making, dancing and singing as a form of *bonding*. This bonding is often (but not always) based upon an ambivalent sense of common 'Irishness'. The musical elements within these movies also communicate certain kinds of 'Irishness' to highly specific temporally and culturally diverse intended audiences.

Irish-themed musicals with migration semantics are by far the largest in number. The influence of vaudeville is here unmistakeable and, indeed, many of the Irish-American and Irish-British semantic situations are explicitly set within the vaudeville milieu. There are quite a few biopics of the composers of sentimental Irish songs for the American diaspora, most notably James Cagney as George M. Cohan in *Yankee Doodle Dandy* (Curtiz, 1942), but also of the composer Chauncey Olcott (whose sentimental song 'When Irish Eyes Are Smiling' is ubiquitous within American migration musical films). There is also a large number of British-produced musicals with Irish migration semantics. The musical syntax is marked by a sentimental, nostalgic sense of 'Irishness' – unsurprising perhaps given the theme of migration, while some of the intended audience was also, of course, the wider Irish diaspora. This is communicated via the use of 'traditional' songs – such as 'Molly Malone' and 'The Mountains of Mourne', and Irish-American songs, such as Olcott's 'Mother Machree' and 'Wild Irish Rose' – as well as the figure of the Irish tenor, the use of (pseudo) Hiberno-English, (pseudo) Gaelic and (pseudo) Irish dancing. How such elements are used as a source of bonding in relation to a sense of common 'Irishness' is seen superbly in *Little Nelly Kelly* (Taurog, 1940), as Nelly (Judy Garland) marches with a crowd of people during the New York St Patrick's Day parade. She begins to sing the song 'It's a Great Day for the Irish', with its 'begorrah, begosh' repeated lines and its line detailing how the 'sidewalks of New York are thick with blarney', as her father glares at her disapprovingly. Eventually, after Nelly has detailed all of the Irish families marching in the parade and also engaged in some Irish dancing, the scene culminates with all of the Irish-American marchers singing in unison with Nelly. The scene undoubtedly communicates greatly a sense of Irish-American community; a common feeling of 'Irishness' that acts as a bonding agent between various individuals that, otherwise, would probably have little to do with one another.[2] In a scene from the Oscar-winning *Going My Way* (McCarey, 1944), Bing Crosby's young Irish-American priest, Father O'Malley, bonds with Barry Fitzgerald's older Irish-born priest, Father Fitzgibbon, as Father O'Malley sings 'Too-Ra-Loo-Ra-Loo-Ra (An Irish Lullaby)'. Father Fitzgibbon, becoming nostalgic although sometimes hostile to O'Malley, tells the younger priest that his mother used to sing this song for him. Thus, an Irish and an Irish-American priest connect because of their sense of common 'Irishness', at least as expressed in this sentimental Irish-American song. In the concluding scene of Francis Ford Coppola's *Finian's Rainbow* (1968), the chorus sings the song 'How Are Things in Glocca Morra?' as Fred Astaire's Finian McLonergan says goodbye to his daughter Sharon. Hence, at a time of sorrow, Irish father and daughter, in a new American homeland, are united indirectly via their nostalgic sense of 'Irishness', encapsulated by their shared longing for their lost village, in their lost Irish homeland; a village of which only they, within this scene, have direct experience.[3]

Irish-themed musicals with rural Irish, non-'modern' semantics are fewer in number and come also largely from the golden age of musicals: the 1930s to the late 1950s. If transatlantic movement takes place within these movies, it is usually in the opposite direction, from North America to Ireland. The semantics here are often marked by what may be called a matte painting pastoralism that dominates the filmic imagery and provides a sense of an Irish pastoral landscape that does not, however, quite escape its actual origins within the confines of a film studio, even if interspersed with some original landscape footage. So, for example, *Darby O'Gill and the Little People* (Stevenson, 1959) – famously filmed on Walt Disney's range in Burbank, California – ends with Darby, his daughter and (probably) future son-in-law driving a horse and cart towards a green Irish landscape that is very obviously a studio matte painting. The John McCormack vehicle *Song o' My Heart* (Borzage, 1930) begins with scene-setting images of sheep and stone walls, while the later John McCormack musical (in which the tenor plays himself), *Wings of the Morning* (Schuster, 1937), contains the song 'Killarney', sung to images of the Kerry lakes. The sense of 'Irishness' that is communicated is similar to musical films with migration semantics; a sentimental nostalgic sense of 'Irishness' largely intended, probably, for an American audience. Thus, for example, Henry Fonda, playing a Canadian character, sings the Irish-American song 'Mother Machree' in the predominantly Irish-island set *Wings of the Morning* (Schuster, 1937). In *Top o' the Morning* (Miller, 1949), the Irish-American Joe Mulqueen is fully accepted into a small village near Blarney in county Cork when he shows himself capable of singing a verse of 'The Donovans' in the local public house. Soon all of the revellers in the bar, beer glasses in hand, are collectively singing about the (presumably fictional) Donovans and how they are 'as Irish as they come again'. Crosby, while his character was still in New York, had even earlier sung 'When Irish Eyes Are Smiling'. In *Darby O'Gill and the Little People*, the bonding is of a definite romantic (if explicitly Hibernicized) nature, as the shy flirtation of Séan Connery's Michael and Janet Munro's Katie eventually culminates in a short duet on the song 'Pretty Irish Girl', following their own individual versions of this song.[4]

The late 1950s marked the end of the golden period of musical film, and musicals from then on featured far less within the cinema programme. Consequently, this period also marks the end of the earlier quite common Irish-themed musical, which had enjoyed its heyday in the 1940s. The year 1991, however, saw the return of an Irish-themed musical, *The Commitments* (Parker), with radically different semantics, those of an urban-Dublin 'modernity'. *The Commitments*, with its social realist aesthetic, depicts a less sentimental Ireland, an urban working-class Dublin marked by a hopelessness punctured only by the creation of a band. This band now engages in a globalized, American idiom with a Hibernicized tint, soul music with a distinctive Dublin working-class accent. Making music is also here a form of bonding (at least initially). This is evident in the scene on the Dart suburban railway as one of the band members begins to sing the soul song 'Destination Anywhere'. The rest of the band gradually joins in, until the singing reaches a collective crescendo, the band members united in their longing to go on a 'journey', away from the hopelessness and meagre employment prospects of their daily lives. The more recent musical *Once* (Carney, 2006) also retains an urban-Dublin 'modern' semantics; Dublin is now a globalized space inhabited by Eastern European immigrants, cleaning the houses of the Dublin bourgeoisie and watching the soap opera *Fair City* (Agnew et al., 1988) with a view to improving their English. The film is also, of course, an Irish-Czech love story based explicitly upon the act of shared music-making; actually a very traditional type of filmic musical syntax, even if now in a more realist mode and via a globalized musical idiom. The music of the movie is dominated by the figure of the singer-songwriter, a form that, according to McLaughlin and McLoone (2012: 317), has become synonymous with Irish music. While 'Irishness' in the earlier musical films was often very explicitly and consciously *performed* within the musical syntax, it here retains an undoubted secondary position, the intended audience being of a global nature not necessarily very familiar with Ireland.

Ruth Barton, in her history of Irish national cinema, sees the Irish 'national film text' as consisting of part of a 'creative bricolage' and proposes that one of the principle tasks of Irish film scholars is 'to see how an image of Ireland on screen emerged out of the national industries of other countries' (2004: 4). 'Other countries' has generally been seen by scholars to mean the Anglo-American context, perhaps understandably so, as world cinema has been so thoroughly dominated by Hollywood. Yet, if scholars are to avoid falling into the trap of Anglocentric provincialism, researchers dealing with Irish film studies must also investigate the national cinemas of non-anglophone countries for their representations of Ireland, as I have argued elsewhere (Lenehan, 2012). Indeed, the need to avoid an anglophone-only view is also true of wider Irish cultural history, not least in relation to Irish-language sources.[5] To this end, the West German produced musical... *nur der Wind (Only the Wind)* (Umgelter, 1961) will now be discussed in terms of Irish-themed musicals.

... *nur der Wind* is a German *Schlager* film. McLaughlin and McLoone (2012: 305), in their otherwise paradigm-creating monograph on Irish popular music, mistakenly see *Schlager* in an overly romantic light as the 'European musical theatre (*Schlager*) tradition associated with Weimar Germany in the 1920s and 1930s'. In fact, *Schlager* are *any* popular songs sung in German at *any* time, not just the Weimar period. The *Schlager* movies of the 1950s and early 1960s were star vehicles with popular music sung in German, based upon the structure and form of the Elvis Pressley movies (Hake, 2008: 120). Dismissed or ignored by film critics, these musical films were immensely popular with the young people of the time (Schildt & Siegfried, 2009: 237). ... *nur der Wind* was a star vehicle for the Hamburg-based Austrian singer Freddy Quinn, who had cultivated a seaman's image that intermingled cosmopolitan elements and a corresponding sailor's poignant homesickness. Part of Quinn's cosmopolitanism stemmed from his partly Irish background, his father being an Irish merchant. The authenticity of this widely communicated biographical fact has since been questioned, however.[6]

Filmed extensively on the Aran Islands and in Dublin, ... *nur der Wind* has, indeed, a very conventional plotline. The fishermen on the island of Dun are suffering economically and have sent Tim O'Connor to Dublin with money to buy a new modern trawler. The naïve Tim spends the money among Dublin's 'high society' and comes under the influence of gangsters who force him to rob the rich Mrs Collins. He does this, injures a security guard, stashes the loot in a locker in Westland Row railway station and sends the key to his home address on the island of Dun (when he panics as he thinks the Gardaí are following him). He elicits the help of Dun islander Mike O'Brien, played by Freddy Quinn, who is living in Dublin and working as a boat builder. Having been led to believe by the gangsters that he has killed the security guard, he shoots himself. O'Brien, without knowing this, takes the 'mail boat' from Dublin to Dun to retrieve the key and is followed by the gangsters who also want the key. Eventually, the truth becomes clear and the whole island comes together to support Mike O'Brien and fight the Dublin gangsters in a limestone field on Dun. The very last scene shows Freddy Quinn's character on a new and modern fishing trawler, heading out to sea while singing the poignant title song *nur der Wind* and smiling at the Dun islander Eileen who is standing at the pier (with whom he has also fallen in love during the duration of the film).

While the plot of ... *nur der Wind* is decidedly formulaic, the depiction of Ireland within the movie is actually quite multifaceted. Indeed, three distinct Irish spaces are to be seen: a rural proletarian space based upon sea fishing on the island of Dun (filmed on the Aran Islands and Dalkey pier); an urban proletarian Dublin space based around boat building (shot mainly at the Quays and the Customs House); and an urban upper-middle class 'hip' Dublin space dominated by images of yachting (filmed at Dún Laoghaire). It is also interesting that all three sets of Irish-themed musical semantics are present. Migration semantics are represented, highly unusually, by Irish rural to urban migration; a type of migration that rarely features within representational cultural texts or within scholarly literature, due probably to the lack of a distinct driving group dynamic.[7] Rural, non-'modern' semantics are present in the scenes that are shot on the Aran Islands, while urban-Dublin 'modern' semantics also feature prominently, as Dublin is represented in a manner that is reminiscent of scenes of 1960s 'swinging London'. Indeed, film scholars often see *The Courier* (Deasy & Lee, 1988) as the first 'Dublin movie', yet here we have a film from 1961, albeit a German film largely unseen by Irish audiences, that makes excellent use of numerous Dublin locations. The musical syntax of ... *nur der Wind* (Umgelter, 1961) is less obviously Irish and represents the longing of the Freddy Quinn character for love rather than bonding as such, as is manifestly represented by the title song. This song, recurring throughout the movie, with its chorus *'nur der Wind, weiß wie einsam wir sind'*/'only the wind knows, how lonely we are', emphasizes images of wind, sea and water, as well as the 'emptiness' of the Irish landscape. This song undoubtedly communicates a nature-oriented romantic German idea of 'Irishness' and Ireland (Holfter, 2011: 85).

The movie may also point us towards a way of analysing cultural hybridity and reciprocity of influence with regard to form within cultural products. McLaughlin and McLoone make the very valid point that the 'post-colonial debate often appears merely to celebrate hybridity as an end in itself' and they have looked to 'the process rather than the products of hybridity' (2012: 7). A perspective that analyses cultural hybridity within cultural products may help to unravel the deeply entangled layers of agency and narrative elements within film texts, and indeed other cultural texts in the widest sense. It may also lead to a better understanding of the products themselves, while also enhancing the study of genre as it examines the interaction of generic forms and their local, culturally specific deployment. Thus, ... *nur der Wind* is an Irish film because of its setting, locations, imagery and plot. It is also a German movie, as it features an Austrian star, numerous German actors, and because it was made by a German film company and shown only to a German-speaking audience. It is also an American film as it is a rock musical, inspired by the contemporaneous Elvis Pressley movies. Indeed, as Altman (1987: 127) notes in his history of the American film musical, the exoticism of what he terms the American 'fairy tale musical' – based upon the premise of being in 'another place', such as the majority of the Elvis movies – has its origins in Central European operetta and originally often retained Habsburg-Austrian semantics. Cultural hybridity and the intermingling of cultural elements come full circle here, thus, in an American-inspired rock musical featuring an Austrian singing star.

Notes

1. An exception is the article by Séan Griffin. See: Griffin, 'The Wearing of the Green: Performing Irishness in the Fox Wartime Musical', in: Diane Negra (ed.) (2006) *The Irish in US: Irishness, Performativity and Popular Culture*. Durham, NC: Duke University, pp. 64–83.
2. For the historical importance of the New York St Patrick's Day parade, in its actual and mediated form, in relation to the creation of Irish identity in the USA see: Kenneth Moss, (1995) 'St. Patrick's Day Celebrations and the Formation of Irish-American Identity, 1845–1875'. *Journal of Social History*. 29(1), pp. 125–14.
3. For further examples of American productions of Irish-themed migration musicals see: *Smiling Irish Eyes* (Seiter, 1929), *Lillian Russell* (Cummings, 1940), *Doughboys in Ireland* (Landers, 1943), *Sweet Rosie O'Grady* (Cummings, 1943), *Irish Eyes Are Smiling* (Ratoff, 1944) and the Olcott biopic *My Wild Irish Rose* (Butler, 1947). For examples of British-produced Irish-themed musicals with migration semantics see: *Irish for Luck* (Woods, 1936), the Richard Hayward film *Irish and Proud of It* (Pedelty, 1936), *Kathleen Mavourneen* (Lee, 1937), the Sydney Morgan directed *The Minstrel Boy* (1937), *Let's Be Famous* (Forde, 1939) starring Jimmy O'Dea, *Danny Boy* (Mitchell, 1940) and *The Hills of Donegal* (Argyle, 1947).
4. For other Irish-themed musicals with rural, non-'modern' semantics, see here also: *The Londonderry Air* (Bryce, 1938), the Richard Hayward movie *Devil's Rock* (Burger, 1938) and *Shamrock Hill* (Dreifuss, 1949).
5. For the importance of cultural historians writing about Ireland over extensive periods of time to have an ability to read Irish-language sources, see: Michael Cronin (2013) 'Half the Picture'. *Dublin Review of Books*, 11 March. Available at: www.drb.ie/ESSAYS/half-the-picture [Accessed 2 October 2014] and Brian Earls (2013) 'Oscar Wilde and the Irish'. *Dublin Review of Books*, 11 February. Available at: www.drb.ie/ESSAYS/oscar-wilde-and-the-irish [Accessed 2 October 2014]. In relation to screen culture and Irish-German links see also: Lenehan (2014) '"I'm Aware You Don't Speak German – Yet." Depicting Germans on Irish Television', in Hofmeister, F. and Böhnke, D. (eds) *Kulturkontakte – Cultures in Contact*. Leipzig: Hamouda, pp. 133–44 and Lenehan (2014) 'Irish-German Interconnections in Popular Culture: Rock and Popular Music and Michael Fassbender's German-Irish Celebrity', in O'Reilly, C. and O'Regan, V. (eds) *Ireland and the Irish in Germany – Rece ption and Perception*. Baden-Baden: Nomos, pp. 181–200.

6. The general narrative of Quinn's life, including that of his Irish father, which has been in circulation for many years, has run so: Born in Vienna, his father was an Irish merchant who left the family when Quinn was seven years old, his mother marrying consequently the wonderfully named Baron Rudolf Anatol von Petz, who also legally adopted her son. Quinn left school early, went to sea and eventually settled in Hamburg, where he began to sing at the famous Reeperbahn. In 1953, he legally acquired his biological father's name of Quinn and discarded the name von Petz. See here for example: Bardong, M., Demmler, H. and Pfarr, C. (eds) (1993) *Das Lexikon des deutschen Schlagers*. Munich and Mainz: Schott. The journalist Elmar Kraushaar, in a recent book, suggests that Quinn's biography is largely fictional and was a marketing tool used to communicate a specific image expressed also in his music. Kraushaar could not, however, locate any conclusive evidence regarding the identity of Quinn's biological father and failed to either prove or disprove the idea that he was an 'Irish merchant'. See: Kraushaar, E. (2011) *Freddy Quinn: Ein unwahrscheinliches Leben*. Zürich: Atrium Verlag. Quinn, although he has admitted that his management imposed the sailor image (he apparently ran away to the circus rather than to sea!), has maintained that his biological father was indeed Irish and that he died in an accident in the United States in 1943, while he has openly spoken of his great love for his Irish father. See Quinn's last print interview conducted in 1999, titled intriguingly 'My Life Sounds Like an Invention': Ankowitsch, C. (1999) 'Mein Leben hört sich wie eine Erfindung', *Die Zeit*, 9 September. Whether true or not, Quinn's 'Irish' background has remained a fairly constant feature and, for example, appeared in numerous celebratory articles upon his 80th birthday in September 2011. See: Nyary, J. (2011) 'Freddy Quinn zum 80. Geburtstag'. *Berliner Zeitung*. 26 September. Available at: www.bz-berlin.de/kultur/fernsehen/freddy-quinn-zum-80-geburtstag-article1281863.html (22 April 2011); Weber, M. (2011) 'Freddy Quinn wird 80 – Schulze kriegte den Blues'. *Stuttgarter Zeitung*, 26 September. Available at: www.stuttgarter-zeitung.de/inhalt.freddy-quinn-wird-80-schulze-kriegte-den-blues (22 April 2013); and (2011) 'Der singende Seemann feiert seinen 80. Geburtstag'. *Berliner Morgenpost*. September 27. Available at: www.morgenpost.de/vermischtes/article1776897/der-singende-seemann-feiert-seinen-80-geburtstag.html (22 April 2013).

7. An exception is the article by Barry Sheppard regarding the quasi-racist reception of the group of Irish-speaking colonists from Connemara at Rathcairn, County Meath in the 1930s, in the artificial creation of a Meath Gaeltacht. See: Sheppard, B. (2012), ' "It Was Not the El Dorado That They Thought It Would Be": Opposition to the Meath Gaeltacht Colonies in the 1930s'. *Scoláire Staire*. 2(3), pp. 12–18. Available at: issuu.com/scolairestaire/docs/vol2iss3issuu [Accessed 2 October 2014].

14
Irish Cinema: A French Perspective

Isabelle Le Corff

Ireland has been celebrated in France for its music, its literature and its poetry for decades, but when it comes to cinema, the country is hardly identifiable. Of course, Ireland is an English-speaking country and, as it is geographically part of the British Isles, Irish cinema may easily be included in the larger concept of British cinema. A filmmaker or an actor may come from one part of the British Isles and work in another: Ken Loach (British) made an Irish film in Ireland with an Irish cast (*The Wind That Shakes the Barley* [2006]), while Damien O'Donnell (Irish) made a British film (*East Is East* [1999]) in Great Britain with a British and Indian cast. On numerous occasions, the Irish have proved that they can be part of the wider global marketplace and they have found influential positions in American cinema. They have also attested that they are profoundly hybridized in many aspects of their culture. Why should the paradigm of 'national cinema' still pervade in such circumstances? Dudley Andrew reports:

> We still parse the world by nations. Film festivals identify entries by country; college courses are labelled 'Japanese Cinema', 'French Film' and textbooks are coming off the presses with titles such as 'Screening Ireland', 'Screening China', 'Italian National Cinema' and so on.
>
> (2006: 26)

The concept of 'nation' is one of the possible identifiers, but not the only one. The idea of an authentic culture is one that has been present in many recent debates about post-colonial cultural production. As a consequence of the country's difficult past, Irish cinema has only developed in the last two decades of the 20th century.

Martin McLoone notes: 'As a small national cinema [Irish cinema] exists in the space between the local and the global, between the national and the transnational, between its own national cultural traditions (whether historical or "invented") and the influences of external global forces' (2009: 22). He insists: 'an Irish national cinema is as much a process of national questioning and exploration as it is of celebration' (McLoone, 2009: 21).

Ireland remained a colony of the British Empire until the 20th century, and the constructed boundaries between peoples, nations and cultures have developed through the English language. 'The idea of the border is clearly crucial to post-colonial studies' (Ashcroft et al., 2007: 25), and one of the reasons why Ireland's identification remains problematic from a French perspective may be the fact that the border does not correspond to the geographical island; Northern Ireland still being part of the United Kingdom. A lot of films, discernible as Irish films, also involve the Troubles and have therefore become part of the United Kingdom's political dimension.

The centre-periphery model that prevails in ex-colonial France reinforces a tendency to incorporate as belonging to the ex-empire a culture that it surveyed and invaded. Does this tendency apply to the neighbouring ex-British Empire?

The legitimacy of Irish cinema in France

Looking for criteria for the legitimacy of Irish cinema in France, one is struck by the lack of interest in Irish films in the academic field. None of the books on Irish cinema or Irish filmmakers has so far been translated into French. Estelle Épinoux and I held the first conference on Irish cinema in Limoges in 2007, and then edited *Cinemas of Ireland* (Le Corff & Épinoux, 2009), but this opus only added to the list of books in English.

A second indicator might be the LUMIÈRE database. Launched in November 2000, it collects data on films distributed in Europe since 1996 and provides precise figures to measure a film's commercial success. However, Ireland has a very poor coverage rate (between 0.1% and 7%), due to lack of information.[1] The LUMIÈRE database reminds the readers that 'There are no widely accepted international or even European definitions of the criteria to be used to determine the country of origin of a film' (www.lumiere.obs.coe.int/web/sources/astuces.html). The pragmatic approach adopted in this instance indicates the country that has provided the majority of financial investment in the production in the first place.[2] The database proves unable to produce the figures of admissions in Ireland for most Irish films, as these figures are included in the larger scale of British admissions.

The festival circuit has also become crucial in terms of defining national cinemas and the Cannes Film Festival has been highly significant in terms of opening national cinemas to a wider public. As Thomas Elsaesser has noted: 'Since its inception, Cannes has remained the king-maker of the festival circuit and a site which has retained the auteur as the king pin at the centre of the system.' (2005: 83). He also suggests that film festivals do not represent a neutral mapping of world cinema; they have an agenda-setting function, constructing a canon of 'quality cinema', where, often, 'one author is a "discovery", two are the auspicious signs that announce a "new wave", and three new authors from the same country amount to a new "national cinema"' (Wimmer, 2009: 214).

If Cannes is an essential public site in terms of discursive value and for the production of critical perceptions, a close look at the reception of Irish films there proves extremely disappointing. Indeed the maps of all the countries recompensed by the Palme d'Or unfortunately show that no Irish filmmaker to date has received that reward. Of course *The Wind That Shakes the Barley* (which won the Palme d'Or at the 2006 Film Festival) was British Filmmaker Ken Loach's success, and one cannot ignore the very high degree of admiration that France holds for Ken Loach, no matter what film he makes.[3]

Adding the Jury Prize (*prix du jury*) to the Palme d'Or, one realizes that the number of European countries that never got one or the other reward decreases, but Ireland remains among the unfortunate. The two major Irish filmmakers of the 1990s, Jim Sheridan and Neil Jordan, were rewarded significantly in other European countries. Jim Sheridan won the Golden Bear in Berlin for *In the Name of the Father* in 1994. Neil Jordan won the Golden Lion in Venice in 1996 for *Michael Collins* and the Silver Berlin Bear for Best Director at the Berlin Film Festival in 1998 for *The Butcher Boy* (1997). The comparison with our neighbours highlights a difference that is difficult to understand, coming from a country renamed for its 'cinephile' culture and for the large amount of critical attention usually devoted to small-scale national cinemas.

It would be unfair not to mention that some Irish films have won prestigious awards at the Cannes Film Festival over the years. In 1984, *Cal* by Pat O'Connor was awarded the prize for Best Actress for British actress Helen Mirren. *Mona Lisa* by Neil Jordan won the prize for Best Actor for British actor Bob Hoskins in 1986. The Jury Prize was given to British Director Ken Loach for *Hidden Agenda* in 1990 and British Filmmaker John Boorman won the Best Director prize for his Irish film *The General* in 1997.

That Jim Sheridan bought a house on the French Riviera or that Neil Jordan shot a remake of *Bob Le Flambeur* (*The Good Thief* [2002]) on location did not help to change the situation. Neither director ever got major consideration in Cannes, or even more generally in France. French cinephilia, characterized by the very influential French critique, is also instrumental through the production of discursive value in terms of critical perceptions of a national cinema. The researcher Le ila Wimmer notes:

> At the turn of the 21st century, *Cahiers du Cinéma* and *Positif* can be said to represent the last bastions of the 'classical era' of cinephilia, as French cinephilia has become increasingly diversified in as many cinephilias as there are audiences.
>
> (2009: 206)

Examining the two magazines closely, we observe that very little attention has been paid to Irish cinema over the years. *Positif* published a small folder on Jim Sheridan in 1994 and Irish films have at best benefited from short reviews on their release dates in France.

Written by Camille Nevers in *Les Cahiers du Cinéma*, May 1992, on *Hush-a-Bye-Baby* (Harkin, 1990), one of these short reviews proves truly fascinating: 'Not easy for a young girl to become a woman, no sooner in love than pregnant, in the ultra-Catholic Ireland under British Control of the 1980s.' The reviewer resumes: 'trying to catch up with History, Margo Harkin slips into pathetic minor history that aims at giving information (abortion is forbidden in Ireland) rather than pure emotion.'[4] She concludes: 'cinema does not go along with politics.' Camille Nevers obviously mixes up Éire and Ulster and has very imprecise knowledge of the political situation in Ireland at the time. But this deficiency does not prevent her from writing highly prejudiced comments. To her, the story is awkward and self-conscious, the Irish get drunk, the story lines are clumsy and the film lacks pure emotion.

Irish researchers have been down that path before. Martin McLoone identified two dominant trends in the tradition of representation of the Irish in British and American cinema:

> On one hand, Ireland has been represented as a kind of rural utopia, bathed in a romantic sensibility that ignored the urban centres [...]. On the other hand, Ireland was also presented as a society torn asunder by violence and internecine strife, where a proclivity to violence was seen as a tragic flaw of the Irish themselves.
>
> (2000: 34)

It is likely that such representations have permeated internationally. Leila Wimmer considers that 'The daily press such as *Le Monde* and news magazines such as *Le Nouvel Observateur* and *Le Point* also offer highly influential regular sections on cinema and exhaustive film reviews' (2009: 209).

In order to substantiate the prejudiced reception of Irish film in France, I analysed 35 reviews of Neil Jordan and Jim Sheridan's films in the daily press and weekly magazines, and archives of the French cinémathèque covering the years 1986 to 2006. The reviews came from varied newspapers and magazines[5] and I endeavoured to search three different criteria:

• Ireland being perceived as a British colony or belonging to Great Britain;
• Ireland being peopled with violent, boorish peasants;
• Ireland being perceived as a rural utopia, with beautiful landscapes, red-haired people and folkloric legends.

This study was published in *Les Images en Question* (Le Corff, 2011: 229–41), and I will only make a concise account of the first two criteria here. In the methodology that I engaged with, the words used could either relate to the film, to the characters, to the story, to the filmmaker, or to the actors. A film review could also be categorized twice if it contained two different references to my criteria. In those 35 short articles, I collected 98 references to one of the three previously listed criteria.

Ireland being perceived as 'British' was found in 26 articles.[6] I must make it clear that in a lot of instances it was not meant as injurious. In *Télérama* for example Neil Jordan was qualified as 'an extremely gifted British filmmaker' (August 1986). Daniel Toscan du Plantier in *Le Figaro-Magazine* (January 1993) reported that 'two perfectly English films remind us that the English language is not only spoken in Hollywood but also in a country that has much contributed to the history of cinema with such talented filmmakers as Chaplin and Hitchcock'. The 'two perfectly English films' by Jordan and Sheridan were *The Crying Game* (1992) and *In the Name of the Father*.

In *Libération*, the journalist blames the appalling state of British cinema to justify that he felt like ripping the camera out of Jordan's hands (May 1986). Jim Sheridan does make an attempt at explaining the particular situation of Ireland in an interview published in *Libération* (14 March 1994): 'We are the only White Europeans to know what "being colonised" really means. It is very difficult to have people understand the situation without giving the impression that we are eternal victims.' A total waste of time! Jim's interviewer calls him 'British' in the very same article. It is also alleged that Sheridan's work takes after that of Ken Loach for its realism (*Le Quotidien de Paris*, September 1990; *La Croix*, March 1994), but no journalist ever mentions a new wave of Irish cinema. The repetition of the words 'English' and 'British' suggests that Ireland is still perceived as a small anglophone culture firmly embedded within the hegemony of Britain. Its difficult past as a colony is completely ignored.

When Ireland is mentioned, it is rarely for the best, and the second criterion shows 38 instances in a total of 35 reviews. People are often deemed as backward country peasants. *The Field* (Sheridan, 1990) provides many such comments, but *The Butcher Boy* also gives way to despising words, sometimes even too offensive to be translated.[7] In *Pariscope*, Bull McCabe – the principal character in *The Field* (Sheridan, 1990) – is described as being 'as primitive and violent as his wild land' (May 1991). Jean-Michel Frodon in *Le Monde* comments that the film 'gets stuck in the mud' (July 1993) and a journalist from *7 à Paris* replicates a country swearword to make fun of the film (May 1991).[8] The word 'bumpkin' is repeated on numerous occasions. The Parisian critic Gerard Lefort probably writes the most injurious comments on *The Crying Game* in *Libération*, using words that are exceedingly vulgar and offensive – *'blaireau irlandais, chierie, crac damned, pataquès politico-irlandais'* – in order to qualify the characters and the story lines. He ends up with a pitiful pun on words, playing on the similarity of 'crying' and 'crier' to assert that the film is so bad that one feels like screaming murder: *'A nouveau, The Crying Game dérape dans le mauvais décor du début: cris, sang, hystérie. Alors là, oui, il y a de quoi crying au meurtre'* (January 1993). It is all too clear from the various comments that long-established stereotypes of the Irish have permeated the Parisian public opinion and tend to sustain a sense of cultural inferiority that plays a role in the reception of Irish cinema. In brief, the fact that Ireland is perceived as a backward country corresponds to the thinking that Irish filmmakers have not had access to the subtleties of film art and that is why they produce excessively retrograde films. Sheridan and Jordan are held to make 'cottage films': craft rather than art (*L'événement du Jeudi*, March 1994). In *In the Name of the Father*, 'Jim Sheridan lacks Preminger's directing talent and Loach's attention to details' (*L'Humanité*, March 1994). *Télérama* (March 1994) adds that Sheridan should leave the complexity of political analysis to Ken Loach and to his excellent *Hidden Agenda* (1990). Even though each review is meant to be singular and reads separately, the repetition of such qualifiers as 'clumsy' and 'awkward' from one review to the next is all the more striking, as the papers these reviews emanate from endorse different political lines. These clichés are rarely supplemented by cultural references. Most of the time Ireland is cited as Joyce's country, but *The Hostage* by Brendan Behan or *Guests of The Nation* by Frank O'Connor are never referred to in reviews of *The Crying Game*.

The 2009 study not only proved how little attention was paid to Irish cinema, it also brought to light the large number of negative comments. The different indicators led to the same conclusion that, as an ex-colony, Ireland was still prejudiced. France was reluctant to acknowledge that Ireland was part of a modern economy in terms of cinema.

The reception of Irish film in France since *The Wind That Shakes the Barley*

As mentioned above, Ken Loach won the Palme d'Or in 2006 with an Irish film that dealt with the Irish Civil War. *The Wind That Shakes the Barley* was acclaimed in France, scoring 934,013 entries when *Michael Collins* by Neil Jordan had recorded 298,569 admissions in 1996. The following year, Irish filmmaker Lenny Abrahamson won the CICAE Art and Essai Cinema Prize at the Cannes Film Festival. '*Art et Essai*' is important in France and it immediately positions the director as an author. Even though *Garage* (2007) was not part of the prestigious Official Competition, Abrahamson was the first Irish filmmaker ever to win this prize at the Cannes Film Festival. Did that help construct a canon of quality cinema as advocated by Thomas Elsaesser?

In order to update my study, I analysed a sample of reviews taken from the French daily press and weekly magazines on five Irish films released in France between 2007 and 2011. The reviews analysed are archives of the French cinémathèque. They cover the following films:

Garage (Lenny Abrahamson, 2007): 14 reviews;
Once (John Carney, 2007): 10 reviews;
In Bruges (Martin McDonagh, 2008): 16 reviews;
Ondine (Neil Jordan, 2010): 12 reviews;
The Guard (John Michael McDonagh, 2011): 10 reviews.

In my analysis, I focused on the nationalities mentioned and on the stereotypes at work in the previous sample. When reading the selected reviews on *Garage*, the first striking feature is that the film undoubtedly identifies as Irish, the words 'Ireland' or 'Irish' being used in 13 reviews out of 14. 'Irish ballad' is repeated several times, but for the first time ever, an Irish actor is almost unanimously praised. *Le Monde* (May 2007) declares that the quality of the film is mainly due to Pat Shortt's performance. Pat Shortt is also cited in *La Croix* (January 2008), *Le Figaro* (May 2007), *Le Figaro Magazine* (January 2008), *France Soir* (January 2008) and *Les Inrockuptibles* (December 2007). He became the most famous Irish actor in France almost overnight. The film is acclaimed in most papers, but the left-wing daily paper *L'Humanité* expresses a negative opinion of it. *Garage* is said to be deprived of interest and boring (*L'Humanité*, May 2007). The prestigious *Cahiers du Cinéma* does not praise *Garage* in unison either. They do identify the story as taking place in Ireland, but they castigate the film for its 'usual British morbid paraphernalia – tea bags, biscuits, oil containers' (*Cahiers du Cinéma*, February 2008).

Also released in 2007, *Once* (Carney, 2007) did reasonably well in France with 77,085 admissions. In the reviews, it is described as 'an Irish romance' (*Le Figaro*, November 2007), 'a simple and charming story' (*Le Figaroscope*, November 2007), 'an Irish ballad' (*France Soir*, November 2007) and 'an Irish romantic comedy' (*Le Nouvel Observateur*, November 2007), but above all, it is a simple, modest film. Shot on an extremely tight budget (noted in *Le Nouvel Observateur*, November 2007),[9] it fits the expected representation that French reviewers have of Ireland, or at least of Irish cinema, and no one consequently resents the aesthetics of a 'small film'. It was summed up thus, in *France Soir*: '*Once*, a small Irish film shot in two weeks with a DV camera, relies on the universal axiom of girls being charmed by a musician' (November 2007). 2007 was a good year for Irish cinema in France, in the way that the two films helped each other in the process of identification of a small-scale national cinema. That both films were relatively modest helped the French critique accept a cinema that fitted its representation of the country.

Commenting upon *Garage*, the newspaper *L'Humanité* praised a national cinema that had so far been famous for only two filmmakers, Neil Jordan and Jim Sheridan (January 2008). This comment is all the more surprising, as both directors were scarcely acknowledged as Irish in the previous decades. It seemed that time had done its job after all. Irish cinema, however, is still implicitly part of British cinema, even though it might be expressed more subtly. Indeed, all the major Irish film directors exist within the realm of 'social realism' and thus take after their master Ken Loach. The fact that Ken Loach won the Palme d'Or with an Irish subject probably reinforced the connection between the two. As a result, Lenny Abrahamson 'copies' Ken Loach's *Raining Stones* (1993) and *My Name Is Joe* (1998) (*La Croix*, January 2008). He tells a 'Loachian tale', according to *Cahiers du Cinéma* (February 2008). Jean-Baptiste Thoret also points at Ken Loach concerning Neil Jordan's *Ondine* in *Charlie Hebdo* (June 2010), and Brendan Gleeson is a British actor seen in Frears and Loach's films for *Le Point* (June 2008). Disapproving of *Ondine*, the magazine *Les Inrockuptibles* gives a brief account of Irish cinema that reads as follows:

> In the wake of the new wave music of the 80's [*sic*], a handful of filmmakers formed a neo-new British wave for a while. Neil Jordan was one of the leaders (*The Company of Wolves, The Crying Game*). After a detour to Hollywood (*Interview with the Vampire*), he returned to his Irish home, demonstrating unwillingly that British cinema, undermined by the brain drain (example: Christopher Nolan), had sunk body and soul.
>
> (June 2010)[10]

As regards Neil Jordan, Gérard Lefort's review in *Libération* is also enlightening. While one may recall his '*il y a de quoi crying au meurtre*' (quoted above in reference to *The Crying Game*), he had obviously forgotten his acerbic interpretations when he later remarked:

> Neil Jordan had seduced with *The Company of Wolves* [...] we were moved to tears by *The Crying Game*, a politico-sexual imbroglio taking place in the context of Irish terrorism [...] Since then it is the well-known seesaw career.
>
> (August 2010)[11]

The film he condemned in 1993 is now remembered to have moved him to tears. Such commentaries endorse my assumption that perceptions are slowly being displaced. Neil Jordan's *The Crying Game* got bad reviews in France when it was released, but the success of the film abroad has reverberated and gradually transformed the perception that the critics had of the film and of the filmmaker.

With *In Bruges* (2008) and *The Guard* (2011), the McDonagh brothers have given rise to new confusion owing to their Anglo-Irish origins.

They have alternately been identified as 'Irish', 'from Irish parents' or as '100% English'. These misunderstandings also pertain to the setting of *In Bruges*. According to *Figaro Madame*, the film relates the story of 'two English killers on the run' (July 2008). *L'Humanité-Dimanche* mentions 'a Belgian story with English custard cream' and *Les Inrockuptibles* enjoyed a 'subtle British thriller' (July 2008). Like many others, *Journal du Dimanche* also reviewed *In Bruges* as a British thriller, and the film was classified as Irish in only seven papers out of 16, Colin Farrell being revealed as a major Irish actor on three occasions. The French title *'L'Irlandais'* helped the critics identify *The Guard* (McDonagh, 2011) as Irish. It was reviewed as a 'Connemara Western' in *Le Monde* (December 2011), while in the same month, *Le Nouvel Observateur* found the thriller as exhilarating as a pint of stout. *Télérama* mentioned the famous Irish Guinness (December 2011) and *Le Figaro* (December 2011) sensed a taste of turf in the film. Even though such Irish stereotypes as the green island (*Le Figaro Magazine*, December 2011) and the desolate and sublime landscapes (*Le Monde*, December 2011) were still operating, the film's humour was almost unanimously celebrated. Gleeson's dark ironic sense of law was qualified as 'politically incorrect' in five reviews out of ten. The Irish sense of humour was defined as 'gruff' in *Le Figaro* (December 2011) but none of the reviews mentioned the Irish accents (Le Corff, 2013). They did not point to Irish people's ways of making fun of their own flaws, as for example in the casual criticisms of Dublin or in Boyle's racial insults being part of his culture: 'I thought that Black people couldn't ski...or is that swimming?' 'Aren't all drug dealers black?' 'I'm Irish. Racism is part of my culture.'[12] It did not occur to the French reviewers that there was something specifically Irish about that sense of humour. *Le Point* even qualified the humour as being typically British (December 2011).

In conclusion, a close analysis of the daily press and weekly or monthly magazine reviews reveals that the perceptions of Irish cinema in France have altered considerably since 1986. The reviewers have acknowledged the existence of an Irish cinema and some Irish cultural markers have become obvious (actors' performances, humour, settings), while more subtle markers like Irish accents remain undetectable from a French perspective. Low-budget Irish films have proved excellent tools for branding the nation. The next step will hopefully bring the French critique to acknowledge that Irish cinema aesthetically combines an international outline with national constituents, giving Ireland unique prestige in the world.

Notes

1. It has information concerning non-national European films distributed in Ireland and information submitted by distributors to the MEDIA Programme.
2. http://lumiere.obs.coe.int/web/search/ country of origin of the film: defining the nationality of a film is a complex task. There are no widely accepted international or even European definitions of the criteria to be used in order to determine the country of 'origin' of a film. This is both a legal and a statistical problem. It is enlightening to compare the lists provided by the different national sources that I use: countries involved in a joint production are not always indicated (even when the main co-producer is from another country). Different national records – and the statistics on which they are based – can show the same film as having a whole range of nationalities. In a general pan-European database such as LUMIÈRE, I have had to adopt a pragmatic approach. I try to list all co-producing countries in the database in a standard way, and attempt to classify them in order of importance (whether known or assumed), with the country having provided the majority financial investment in the production in the first place.
3. Also see: *Ken Loach: Une dramaturgie de l'engagement* (Nice: Cinémathèque de Nice, 2001), Francis Rousselet, *Ken Loach: Un Rebelle* (Paris: Editions du Cerf, 2002), Erika Thomas, *L'univers de Ken Loach: misères de l'identité profession-nelle* (Paris: l'Harmattan, 2005), *Ken Loach: un regard cinématographique sur l'aliénation familiale* (Paris: l'Harmattan, 2006), *Ken Loach: Cinéma et société* (Paris: l'Harmattan, 2008).
4. *'Pas facile pour une jeune fille de se découvrir femme, bientôt amoureuse et sitôt enceinte quand on vit dans l'Irlande ultra catholique et sous contrôle britannique des années 80. C'est en substance, le message que nous transmet, un peu maladroitement, le film de Margo Harkin. Quand elle cherche à rattraper l'histoire ... elle dérape dans la petite histoire lourde et pathétique, et communique davantage d'information stricte (le droit à l'avortement est interdit en Irlande) que d'émotion pure ... Ce n'est plus seulement la jeunesse irlandaise qui se grise pour oublier les soldats anglais postés à chaque coin de rue, mais des jeunes gens qu'intimide l'autre et qui, le temps d'une danse, s'y frottent sans plus penser à rien ... Quant au reste, il n'y avait pas de quoi en faire un plat: le cinéma se marie mal à la sauce politique'* (Cahiers du cinéma, May 1992).
5. *Les Echos, Libération, Le Quotidien de Paris, Le Monde, Le Figaro Magazine, Le Figaroscope, Le Canard Enchaîné, Le Nouvel Observateur, Les Inrokuptibles, 7 à Paris, Télérama, France Soir, Le Point, La Croix, L'Humanité, L'Express, Pariscope.*
6. According to Wikipedia, *est britannique ce qui a trait au Royaume Uni* (http://fr.wikipedia.org/wiki/Britannique), and *'Le Royaume-Uni [...] est un État membre de l'Union européenne situé en Europe de l'Ouest, composé de la Grande-Bretagne (l'Angleterre, l'Écosse et le pays de Galles) et de l'Irlande du Nord'* (http://fr.wikipedia.org/wiki/Royaume-Uni).
7. In *Libération*, 6 May 1998, in relation to *The Butcher Boy*: *'Les sabots du film pèsent des tonnes et la gigue irlandaise nous brise les tibias et le reste.'*
8. *'L'Irlande des années 30. Le souvenir de la grande famine est encore dans tous les estomacs. Le sacré vinduiou de champ!'*

9. ' ... *tourné avec trois francs six sous ... comédie irlandaise romantique bricolée par un réalisateur inconnu et des acteurs non professionnels'.*

10. *'Dans le sillage de la new wave musicale des 80s, une poignée de cinéastes constituèrent pendant quelques lustres une néo-nouvelle vague britannique. Neil Jordan en était l'un des chefs de file (La Compagnie des Loups, The Crying Game). Après un détour obligé par Hollywood (Entretien avec un vampire), il est retourné à ses pénates irlandais, démontrant à son corps défendant que le cinéma british, miné par la fuite des cerveaux (exemple: Christopher Nolan), avait sombré corps et âme.'*

11. *'Neil Jordan avait autrement séduit avec La compagnie des Loups ... on mouilla des mouchoirs à la vue de The Crying Game, imbroglio politico sexuel sur fond de terrorisme irlandais ... depuis, c'est le zigzag bien connu sous le nom de carrière en dents de scie'* (*Libération*, 25 August 2010; http://next.liberation.fr/cinema/2010/08/25/a-la-queue-l-eau-l-eau_674111).

12. Quoted from the film.

15
Is Adaptation an Act of Transformation? J. B. Keane's *The Field* on Screen

Noélia Borges

'The authentic . . . is never obvious and is forever in need of the supplement of commentary.' Cultural production and reproduction is an instrumental manifestation of this supplement of commentary.

(Graham, quoted in Monahan, 2009b: 1–2)

This chapter presents an analysis of the adaptation of J. B. Keane's play *The Field* into its cinematic version, by considering the developments that took place in the transition from stage to screen. Thus, the purpose of this work is to examine how playwright and filmmaker construct their own texts in order to frame differences and similarities between the source text and the target one.

Initially, it is worth considering that the boost in the film adaptation of literary works has grown tremendously and reached increasing popularity in all of its various media forms. Throughout the decades, we have seen that literature has been the main source from which many films from different countries have been drawn. It is not surprising that the contemporary Irish cinema has also been interested in putting onto screen many pieces of recent literary productions. A large and significant body of Irish literary adaptations to screen evince the impetus for a consideration of this mechanism and the list is not restricted to ideologically separated categories of 'high-' or 'low-brow' texts. Roddy Doyle's *The Commitments* (1991) and *The Woman Who Walked into Doors* (1996), Frank McCourt's *Angela's Ashes* (1996) and Cecelia Ahern's *P.S. I Love You* (2004) fit neatly with the work of many canonical writers like James Joyce's *Ulysses* (1986), Samuel Beckett's *Waiting for Godot* (1994) and Oscar Wilde's *The Picture of Dorian Gray* (1997) in this regard. Family, frustration, sin, dreams of escape, social affairs and Catholic morality in conflict with sexuality – the most common themes of their work – are preserved in the process of film adaptation, despite the alterations the screenwriters take when they transfer the stories from page to screen.

If we go through concepts and debates on adaptation, we will bring together a vast range of theoretical ideas in the field. Robert Stam and Alessandra Raengo, Linda Hutcheon, Thomas Leitch, Dudley Andrew, Gérard Genette and many others have been concerned with how the meaning of a given text is caught and transformed in its cinematic counterpart (Andrew, 2010). So, if we think of defining adaptation, we will have a crowded list of concepts and profuse suggestive metaphors for the process of adapting one medium into another. The tropes are largely suffused with denigrated ideas of adaptation for they happen to deploy against it accusations involving language such as 'parasite' or 'split personality', or they carry a profoundly moralist charge, as the terms 'infidelity', 'betrayal' and 'violation' inevitably do. My goal here, then, is not to evaluate adaptation in terms of its status; that is, to propose the superiority of one medium over the other. Such an assumption would be based on prejudice or hostility to the visual arts and might happen only to prove the validity of one's own faith or subjective critical acumen. Initially, the idea is to highlight a set of tropes and concepts about adaptation as a way to understand Jim Sheridan's adaptational reading of J. B. Keane's play.

It is interesting to note that words such as 'fidelity', 'faithful' and 'original', so much considered taboos or aberrations, are used by some theorists and filmmakers (even in brackets) in their work. For instance, Linda Hutcheon is more inclined to accept the term 'adapted text' instead of 'original' or 'source', while many do not assume any prejudice in using them. Also, considering that the most recent theorists on adaptation have attacked the fidelity discourse sponsored by George Bluestone – the pioneer in adaptation studies – preferring to embrace Bakhtinian intertextuality, the term nevertheless still prevails in the studies of Denise Faithful, Thomas Leitch and Hutcheon herself, among others. Indeed, the persistence of humanist values on adaptations and their originals is an evaluative impulse which film scholars and critics share, whether to agree or disagree with them. Some insist that fidelity to the original model is an unquestionable touchstone of value for their adaptations; others consider this notion based on competing models in the marketplace. Apart from theorists who consistently use the question of fidelity as something of a fetish with which to evaluate adaptations, there are those who are concerned with how the meanings of a given text are caught and transformed within the film's text (Andrew, 2010) or see adaptations as intertextual or trans-textual operations (Genette, 1982: 1–2). The distinctions among modes or types of adaptation have not masked the fact that the field is still being haunted by the notion that adaptations ought to be faithful to their ostensible putative texts. Thus, the diversity in beliefs about fidelity, together with the constellation of aesthetic evaluation, has justified and allowed the development of further adaptation studies.

Still in this discussion on adaptation, Dudley Andrew states that 'the making of a film out of a previous written text is virtually as old as the machinery of cinema itself' (2000: 29). He also claims that the act of adapting a film from a novel is a question of a personal interpretation, which may differ from reader to reader. Thus, it is fair to understand that any given adaptation may reflect the filmmaker's particular point of view of the source text, and, consequently, every adaptation may favour certain aesthetic resources and foreclose others.

What I want to highlight here is that, no different from novels, plays and films also share basic elements: dialogue, plot, story, characters, theme, setting, scenery, point of view and time. They help to create the illusion of life in its instability and conflict together with the readjustment of forces to settle a new kind of stability. In short, they help to interpret life and human values in terms of what is good or bad in human nature and attitudes.

In this paper, I focus on the adaptation of J. B. Keane's play *The Field* (1965) for the screen, and propose the question: is adaptation an act of transformation? The immediate answer is that the film retains most of the relevant elements of the play, mainly its themes, such as the importance of the land, the question of religion, the hatred of the acquisitive colonial 'Other', the poverty of the people and many other related aspects. However, in the move from telling to showing, the adapter – in this particular case, the filmmaker – seems to take into account not only the formal aspect of the new medium, but also the target audience (in terms of distribution and reception). In this view, the filmed version of *The Field* (Sheridan, 1990) undergoes alterations/transformations to attend to both the new medium as well as the cultural context of the export market where it will be received. Moreover, as the film adaptation was directed by Jim Sheridan, an Irish director, with a keenly experienced sensibility to foreign audiences' taste and knowledge, as well as an acute knowledge of the marketplace, it is fair to assume that he was inevitably influenced by the specifications and hegemony of the values of the global dominant culture. That is to say, the filmed version as a form of representation comes to be a mere fabrication with political and ideological effects according to the symbolic system of transnational capitalism.

Let us first consider that, as drama, text is structured in a dialogue-heavy format; a fact that does not mean that plot in drama is much simpler to grasp than that of the novel. To understand plot, one has to identify all the events as specifically chronologically arranged in the play; something that can be done by examining scenario details as they have been constructed by the playwright. The scenario events are generally dramatically arranged in such an order that they may come to have the most effective and considerable impact on an audience. The distinction and the relation between plot and setting are very significant in the understanding of film adaptations based on plays. Although the dramatic text has its own settings and plots, film devices and techniques (in conjunction with other dialectical aesthetic actions) can create a thoroughly new perspective within a dramatic text. For instance, different cinematic angles of action can gain a distinct quality and emphasis by specific use of the camera. The skilful application of long shots, close-ups, edits, lighting, photography and soundtrack – techniques very particular to film aesthetics – are elements that can enrich the source text in terms of visual resources. Moreover, film versions of literary works or any other aesthetic artefact may inevitably suffer physical alterations to attend to both the different media and cultural contexts in the export markets.

There is no doubt that J. B. Keane's *The Field* is an excellent choice to examine the transposition of the theatrical work to film. What can be seen of this discussion around cinematic adaptation is that when the adapter makes use of cinematic resources to give a realistic quality to the images, language and events of the written text, he/she may consequently reproduce the ideological position of the source material, or facilitate a more revisionist approach in its reframing of the same.

We should also consider, here, that to represent a country or an individual performance (or even to reproduce images of objects, places, people or events) is to appropriate certain particular points of view and circumstances in the construction of a narrative with alternative perspectives and value judgments. Representation is an act of appropriation and adaptation. Thus, to adapt means to translate, to transcode, to paraphrase (Bluestone, 1957: 62) and to transfer a constructed representational identity rather than a simply transparent 'reflection' or reproduction of a pre-existing reality. In terms of film and stage adaptation, both filmmakers and theatre directors often have their own formulae to deal with representation. Here, I will discuss how setting, theme, characters, narrative, language, style and point of view are constructed and *re*-presented in the production of the adaptation of *The Field* to screen.

The Field was written by Keane in 1965 and adapted for the screen by the Irish director Jim Sheridan in 1990. The story takes place at a specific historical time, and in a particular place in the south-west of Ireland. The beautiful rugged environment that shapes Keane's art is translated into film by Sheridan with the facility of technical effects and technological innovations. A simulacrum of real and authentic topography seems to be used to highlight Hollywood generic product and gain commercial success, rather than to promote a touristic landscape as the primary concern. The viewers are effectively drawn into the spatial aesthetic of the film with its dramatic topography and mythic spaces mimetically tied to images of Ireland, and, particularly, to the content of the story; utopian mythic images difficult to sustain within the values of a materialistic society. Cliffs and valleys, the rough sea, as well as deep wells are a combination of natural and built elements identified with Irish landscapes. They are used in the film adaptation because they carry out wider symbolic meanings related to violence and therefore come to play a dramatic role in the story. By comparing the play with the film, we see that the opening scenes differ both formally and in content. Whereas Jim Sheridan concentrates on the evocation of nature by presenting the stark contrasting shots – the beauty of the landscape and the death of a donkey flung into a lake (which foreshadows the death of the Yank) – J. B. Keane privileges indoor scenes in a pub to instigate his story. In the film, external scenes through visual and audio sources are used to connote the atmosphere of hardship lived by McCabe's family. From the beginning, natural and modern worlds come together to show their conflicting influence on the lives of the human beings that are being represented.

Considering Sheridan's screenplay, it is impossible to watch it and not recognize a conventional ideological text that its ancestral narrative refuses to provide. That is to say, by confronting the two narratives and using our skills in looking, attention, perception and background knowledge, we inevitably end up seeing that Sheridan's film allows viewers the possibility of seeing how national imagery can be explored and processed by the film industry through a fixed repertoire of familiar traditionally 'backward' images and gestures associated with Irish identities. Again, in an important sense, in its narrative construction, Sheridan's film is especially concerned with the generalizing modernity/tradition binary opposition as a means of understanding Irish culture – the central appeal that we can observe in capitalist ideology.

Both the play and film deal with the question of land: an aspect of Irish history deeply connected to narratives of dispossession, famine, restriction, oppression and, consequently, violence. Those familiar with Irish history know that the Irish were dispossessed of their land by the Normans and later by the English. Added to this historical narrative was the dramatic experience of the Famine (1845–52), which killed millions and forced mass emigration. Thus, narratives of ownership and dispossession of land are frequently replayed in the Irish cultural memory. *The Field* then tells the story of 'Bull' McCabe and his strong link to the land that he and his family have farmed for generations; a tradition that is threatened the day that the widow who owns the field decides to auction it publically. As McCabe has sacrificed himself endlessly for the sake of the plot of land, he believes that he has rightful possession of it. But while no one in the village would dare to enter the competition bidding against him, an English resident, William Dee (altered to an American character, played by Tom Berenger, in the filmed version), with Irish ancestors, decides to purchase the field in order to build a highway. Both Bull and his son try to convince the affluent man to give up the bidding on the field, but he refuses to heed their pleadings. Their eventual threatening of Dee ultimately leads to drastic consequences. McCabe's obsession with the land that he claims predictably leads to disastrous results both for him and his whole family, and also for the prospective owner. In spite of his attempts to reason with those who are against him – predominantly the American and his ally, the local parish priest –, Bull tries to justify his right to buy the field by mentioning how much love, labour and sacrifice he and his family have invested in it. He explains the hard times that his family has endured to remain in Ireland after the Famine. When his arguments do not convince the priest and the 'Yank', Bull decides to take the law into his own hands. Bull and his son Tadhg beat the Yank to death for his determination to purchase the contested piece of land.

Characters as constructions may be usefully ideologically read in their significance for the message and values that they convey. Thus, considering the cast in *The Field*, we can already see that Jim Sheridan makes changes by suppressing certain ones (such as the bishop and Michael Flanagan's children), by adding others (the gypsy), by altering names, nationalities and characters' attitudes; all developments which may be considered as not having affected the core meaning of the source text. Richard Harris as Bull McCabe – positioned as a prototypical symbol of Ireland's manhood – brings a certain gendered weight to the role; that is, one more aggressively present as an on-screen entity in terms of negative actions. In the film, Sean Bean as Tadgh, Bull's son, is seen clandestinely harassing the owner of the field, Mrs Butler. Tadgh is worthless and less potent as he does not share his father's dream. He is unable to confront his father, who wants to see him married and settling down to take care of the field as his ancestors have done. Tadgh is torn between his desire to get rid of the repressive situation that his father creates and the desire to respond to his father's affection. Sheridan's version differs from the source text in that there he decides to leave his home and marry the Tinker gypsy girl and live a nomadic life; a symbolic attempt at breaking ties with his father and the land. However, his marriage is considered abhorrent for his father, as the gypsy represents everything that his father despises; notions of a displaced people who he believes do not care about stability, love of their land, ownership or 'settled' family tradition. Brenda Fricker, as Bull's wife Maggie, is mentioned but does not appear in the play. In the film, she is evidently contained and oppressed in the domestic environment, and she is unable to deal with her husband's ferocious temper and uncontrolled ambition. Only in the end is she touched by her husband's madness when it is too late. Bull thus represents the system of patriarchy in which men possessed the power and control over women. Jim Sheridan gives a different justification for the lack of communication between husband and wife. Whereas in the film adaptation Bull's wife has not spoken a single word since the suicide of her other son 20 years earlier, in the play, his wife's stoic silence is due to years of her husband's mistreatment of her. John Hurt, as Bird O'Donnell, is a spectral and foolishly comical figure among the main characters. Despite his manifestly powerless position in the story, he is able to manipulate individuals and events, as well as subtly instigate mischievous acts: a characteristic made much more obvious in the film's narrative construction. He accompanies Bull most of the time and advises him to change his mind. Later, he behaves as an informer when he betrays Bull. By embracing the attitude of an informer, Bird renounces his Irishness to act as 'the other'; the traditionally historical outsider in similar Irish land-themed narratives (whether English or American).

The town priest, played by Sean McGinley, receives an expanded role as Father Liam McDermott in the film. His threatening discourse of divine punishment, which he addresses to the Christian parish community during the Sunday mass, reveals the power of religion in its strategy of intervening in the human mind and its concerted weakening of free will. His authoritative discourse happens to be the way in which the filmmaker changes the end of the story. We may suggest that Bull's search for his own death echoes Sophocles' Oedipus's self-punishment, when he discovers his own corruption and tears out his eyes. A cursory examination of the English resident William Dee – replaced in the film by the more sympathetic Irish-American, Peter (now situated as the predominant conflict character of the story) – shows that he clearly represents the threatening power of capitalism. In the play, he states that Ireland is the right place for the recovery of his wife's health after her nervous breakdown and that the field is the right spot for his business as a concrete block supplier. In contrast with the play, Peter just wants to use the land for a highway. The roles of the auctioneer Michael Flanagan and his wife are considerably reduced in the filmed adaptation. In the play, they are constantly present in the story. We are able to see how Mick is mendacious and sly in his attempts to help Bull to secure the field and how Mammie is flirtatious and charming. Despite the strained relationship that she keeps with her husband, Mammie helps him in his business and shows the strength of her relationship with her eldest son, Leamy.

In the filmed version, Sheridan gives Keane's play a fatalist treatment by punishing the main character with madness and, eventually, death. The filmmaker charts the psychological turmoil of an ambitious character guided by primitive impulses and personal despair. He confirms the pathology not only of the character himself, but also of the political system of colonization moved by violence and condemned for its lack of positive social values. Sheridan, therefore, seems to aspire to fuse traditional Irish life with its contemporary counterpart.

The filmmaker has thus structured the screenplay in a linear three-act narrative; that is, he has plotted it in a linear arrangement of related incidents, episodes and events that lead to a specific dramatic resolution: the death of the Yank on the bank of a river near the field, lit by the highlights of his car. It labours upon Bull's obsession and how it drives him to madness, Tadgh's being accidentally driven over the cliff in a cattle stampede and Bull's final moments in the raging sea. The original play does not follow a similar structure. Bull's slavish devotion to tradition instigates his violence over the dispute about the land and over the silence of the local community that hides the culpable ones who are not represented. Although McCabe and Tadgh do not purge their crime with their deaths, it seems that the sense of justice prevails and Bull will be punished by his own conscience. In short, we are granted a set-up that introduces the main characters and establishes the location, clearly establishing an idea of the main theme. Later, an incident motivates the protagonist to act, and this becomes the turning point. From then on, his world is changed significantly. Obstacles and opportunity force the action towards the inevitable climax. It is there that all the various threads of the dramatic narrative come together in a conflict that places the protagonist under the most severe strain.

In *The Field*, we see the representations of Ireland's agrarian past and the dramatic psychological effects of the system of colonization on the self and the community. Sheridan's *The Field* challenges viewers to recognize the inevitability of the past and its ongoing influence on the present. The journey that McCabe undertakes serves as an example of the painful individual struggle to adapt to modern life, as well as displaying the nature of violence, whether personal or political. The hero's lonely degeneration into madness in the final scenes is one of the key changes that Sheridan makes to Keane's text. He highlights fate not only to emphasize the tension between tradition and modernity, but also to demonstrate the impact of colonization on the individual and community. The hero's insanity in his futile attempt to beat back the waves with his stick, wading ever more deeply into the ocean only eventually to be drowned, comes to configure a kind of religious ritual of cleansing, purity and return. The end of the film is clearly an intertextual retelling of the Cuchulainn myth. Bull McCabe, like Cuchulainn, is unable to fight and change his destiny. Similar to the God-like hero in the Celtic myth of the Ulster circle, he inadvertently kills his own son and is trapped by his fate.

Like written language, films have their particular resources to communicate meanings denotatively and connotatively. Icons, indexes and symbols work to differentiate these two levels in films. Likewise, metaphors, metonymy, synecdoche and other terms used in literary studies are also forms to convey connotative meaning within the artistic and imagistic discourse of film. *The Field* is loaded with such linguistic treatment of the source text from the beginning up to the end. We can enumerate just some examples, such as the symbol of the dead donkey at the beginning of the film as an indexical foreshadowing of someone's death later on. Bull's stick becomes an objective correlative of the law and the silence of his wife acts as a symbol of her unhappy married life. Most evidently, the 'field' becomes a microcosm for the country, a synecdoche of its colonially contested history.

In short, both the play and film adaptation show the dangers of internalizing the dominant group stereotypes, the complexities of breaking from established traditions and adapting to modern life, and the tragic nature of political and personal violence. Alterations in the filmed text help to intensify the dramatic tension of the play, and facilitate options for the filmmaker in terms of embracing, or modulating, its verisimilitude and finding alternative visual methods for challenging the audience's expectations. The original text is often used for the purpose of anchorage: the filmmaker's interest was not in the text 'as it is' but as in 'how it might be'. The look of the production allows a critical perspective that moves away from the sense of fidelity to the primary text in order to embrace broader criticism of specific contexts, such as those values associated with the value of tradition.

To conclude, adaptations must also be considered in the light of the post-celluloid world of the new media. It means that, together with the series of innovations in film technology – sound, colour, 3D, digital editing – the revolution brought by the Internet, electronic games, CD Roms and DVDs needs to be considered. These developments have also changed the production and consumption of films radically, and, consequently, the very requirements of how we might approach and apply adaptation theory. New digital media coupled with more traditional media have not only helped to change the idea of purity, originality or images' 'fidelity', but they have also complicated notions of reproducibility within an interactive circuit. The possibilities of hyper-textual collaging and digital re-editing share some characteristics with film adaptations facilitating entirely different compositions and versions of any story. Any number of filmmakers might be subjects of interest in this respect. In Jim Sheridan's adaptation of J. B. Keane's play, the extra-verbal aspects of the discourse in the opening scene of the film (the impact of the astonishing images of the field and landscapes – Connemara, County Galway – combined with the death of a drunk thrown in the river, which is underscored with appropriately dramatic music) render the film with a multiplicity of visual signifiers through which that medium works uniquely. The playwright's well-designed symbolic language was carried over onto the screen, bringing the play to 'life' in a visually nuanced way. Sheridan's Ireland, unlike Keane's, is transformed into a new version of modernity entirely in keeping with functions of the archetypal mechanism and apparatus of the modern period: the cinema. The filmmaker replaces the local, the historical and the culturally specific meanings of the literary text with universal and ahistorical meanings; an action that ends up reflecting the ideological force of a US-dominated transnational capitalism. Keane's text comes to serve merely as an inspiration to reinforce the idea of cinema as painting in motion. Accordingly, the transformation of the source text at the level of narrative together with the reshaping of characters seems to illustrate the hybridity of the contemporary Irish identity and how it is subsumed into such a transnational symbolic order. It implies that modern Irish culture is a site of challenge and resistance, and open to a plurality of influences beyond differences of space and time. Significantly, the question is not whether the film was 'unfaithful' to the source text or not; the question is how images of Ireland can be reduced to the level of commodity and cultural hybridity, as they might be generically transformed into a format inherently recognizable as a by-product of global capitalism.

16
Irish Cinema in Italy: The Roma Irish Film Festa

Ciara Chambers and Barry Monahan

Susanna Pellis is the creative mind behind, and artistic director of, the Rome Irish Film Festa, the only annual (non-Irish) European festival of its kind that is entirely dedicated to celebrating Irish cinema. Established in 2007, and now going into its 8th season, this unique event was not only designed with a wholly inclusive approach to every aspect of Irish indigenous production – combining screenings of features and shorts, involving guest artists, authors, actors, producers and directors, and incorporating workshops, masterclasses and public interviews – but it has also been an instrumental cultural event in providing connections between participants and other home-based festivals and their organizers.

Since its inception, Pellis has attracted some of the most important protagonists working in Irish film, and the intimacy that the Festa offers to audiences and filmmakers has proven to be one of its strongest points. It has consistently facilitated a public forum for the discussion of the cultural significance of a peripheral and minor cinema within broader national, international and transnational contexts. Increasing tendencies towards co-financed productions across (often three or more) European states may ensure a relatively stable continuation of cinematic output, but do little to foster, develop or strengthen individual national cinematic cultures with any degree of independent expression. Even as we might acknowledge the history of aesthetic contribution by European filmmakers to the mainstream Hollywood apparatus, we frequently perceive the history of Europe's cinematic production on a national scale diachronically, as a series of 'movements' – each one replacing the last in an ephemeral way – rather than as an integral, continuous phase in the evolution of indigenous cinemas. So it happens, more often than not, in academic and other critical discourses, that German Expressionism, Italian NeoRealism, the French Nouvelle Vague, British Social Realism or the Dogme95 Project in Denmark are mentioned in ways that relegate the national aspect of the movements, or fall more broadly under a titular European umbrella. Even within the global hegemonic system, where Hollywood continues to dominate the English-speaking market, and in spite of American mechanisms such as the Sundance Festival and the earlier incarnation of the Weinsteins' Miramax – both of which were instrumental in the promotion of indie and European cinema in the USA from the 1980s – it is still rare for a smaller nation's film from this continent to be recognized as anything other than 'European' on that side of the Atlantic. Furthermore, there is increasing potential for national cinemas to become almost completely eclipsed by the forces of cultural imperialism. Against this backdrop, the need for champions of local cinema is all the more acute and Pellis' role as an enthusiastic ambassador for Irish film, offering both exposure and discourse, cannot be overstated.

Having seized upon the opportunity to connect with a number of Irish cultural bodies, and use Rome as the setting for the Rome Irish Film Festa, Pellis has designed an event that works as a worthwhile platform for the dissemination of significant elements of Irish cinema. By offering a multi-dimensional platform for practitioners and enthusiasts in the field, the festival manages to allow a singularity of voice and a coherence of expression that are not in any way essentialist or nationally reductive. But the occasion is no less politically engaged or pioneering in its polemical opinions or challenges to any financial, aesthetic, or policy-driven status quo. In this respect, the festival has facilitated some critical discussions and debates about the current state of Irish film and raised questions about the indigenous funding and policy-making bodies that are responsible for designing the contemporary and future shape of this visual culture.

Outstanding among them have been a number of important public deliberations on the significance of the cinematic medium as critical cultural expression in the 21st century: including conversations with Bob Quinn on the vital nature of film for a healthy society; with Lelia Doolan on film's integral address to authorized and unofficial state histories; with Stephen Rea on allowing a (literal and metaphorical) accent to emerge from a smaller nation onto an international stage; and with Patrick O'Neill on the functioning of the Irish Film Board.

Recognizing, furthermore, the benefits of hearing directly from the creative voices on both sides of the camera, Pellis has regularly invited highly critically acclaimed guests to share their philosophies on the nature of the medium and the potential of its unique aesthetic capacities. Visiting artists – with whom Roman audiences have been asked to enter into discussion – have included actors Eileen Walsh, Stuart Graham, Ciarán McMenamin and Fionnula Flanagan; directors Declan Recks, Juanita Wilson, Terry McMahon and Gerard Hurley; and screenwriters Mark O'Halloran and Eugene O'Brien. In tandem with these features, Pellis runs presentations and interview-based forums with invited experts and university representatives who have offered ruminations into subjects as far-reaching as representations of Northern Ireland and the 'Troubles', development in Irish television and the creative possibilities that new technologies open for a new generation of film practitioners.

The Rome Irish Film Festa has been structured by Pellis in a way that also simultaneously respects the work of established filmmakers and screenwriters such as Neil Jordan, Jim Sheridan and Terry George as much as it promotes the creative work of up-and-coming directors like Terence White, Graham Cantwell and Brian Deane, as well as many others whose short productions are screened in competition every year.

We have had the opportunity to discuss this important annual contribution to Irish film culture – and specifically the fact that it is an overseas look at the contemporary condition of Ireland's indigenous cinema – with Susanna Pellis. The interview published here does not claim to be exhaustive in its consideration, nor does it purport to offer irrefutable conclusions on the state of current European cinema: its financial situation, policies and strategies, or its mechanisms for production support and distribution. It will be valuable, we hope, in its offering a personal reflection by the artistic director of the highly successful Rome Irish Film Festa into how and why she decided to embark on the yearly event, and on what her own relationship has come to be with the whole apparatus of Irish film production and backing, as well as its broader cultural merit.

Authors: When did you first have the idea of running a film festival in Rome?

Pellis: I never really had the idea directly. I used to attend festivals here in Italy: trans-European ones, but very nice festivals that excited me, and maybe I had some inkling already. I liked them because they were small and there was always the possibility to meet people, and to talk with the directors and the actors. That was really the format of a festival that I really liked. So it probably all started gradually over time.

Authors: That's really interesting because the intimate format is a large part of what you do every year with the Roma Ireland Festa.

Pellis: Yes, and, for example, I have never been to the bigger festivals...I don't care for that kind of festival: Cannes and others just don't interest me. Although there are interesting people there, you don't have the opportunity to interact with them, the contact that I like.

Authors: How long did it take, from the first year, to get to where it is? Did it immediately fill the capacity that you wanted, or did take a couple of years to build up to that?

Pellis: Yes, it took about two years. At the beginning we only had – not only, but mostly – members of the Irish community here in Rome attending. It took at least that time to get the Italian public involved and actually looking for the festival. That's something that's very important because otherwise it remains 'small' in the worst sense of the word.

Authors: What were the first steps that you took to get it off the ground? Who did you contact, for example?

Pellis: Interestingly, I *was called*! The Irish Film Institute was looking for someone to organize an Irish film festival for one year. I think that it was through the university that they found me. To me, it was immediately clear that I could organize an annual festival, and not just one showcase. That, really, was the very beginning.

Authors: And what about the kind of functions that you had to perform on the Italian side: the sources of sponsorship, and establishing a relationship with the Casa Del Cinema, and so on...

Pellis: Yes...the Italian side was very difficult. Apart from the Casa Del Cinema, where things are very well organized, and it's easy to get access to the management. So as soon as I began to initiate the festival operation, there were three different directors [from the Casa Del Cinema] and I met with all of them. It was definitely the best part on the Italian side of things. The others were very difficult to get on to. This is one of the big differences between Ireland and Italy. Here, the directors and presidents don't get back to you, I've found personally.

Authors: So, at what stage did the Irish Embassy come on board, or at what point did you contact them?

Pellis: They were involved from the second year. They were so helpful and dedicated to the event. From this side they gave us any money that was available, and they were supportive generally, and told me recently that this festival was the most important Irish cultural event in Italy. The Irish Film Institute had already read the first book that I'd written and they saw that I really felt confident that I could do it.

Authors: And so, why Irish cinema?

Pellis: Well I had focused on Irish cinema during my studies in film which I'd completed, and my thesis was about Irish cinema, and my first book was on that subject too. And it had really become my passion: so, I thought, 'why not?' It was just normal for me. My first idea was to write my thesis on Nanni Moretti, the Italian director. But when I saw *In the Name of the Father* – I didn't necessarily think that it was a fantastic film, not one of the best that Irish cinema had to offer – the story made me realize that there was something powerful about it, something very real to it. My thesis was about a certain section of Irish cinema, and films about the struggle for Irish independence, and I chose four films that depicted this history in different ways: *In the Name of the Father, Michael Collins, Anne Devlin* and *Some Mother's Son*. My interest started from there, and also because I loved the work of some of the established Irish actors, there was something very special that drew me to them.

Authors: So what about Irish cinema do you see as having any kind of particular, recognizable qualities or themes? Do you see any strands that connect many of the films from Ireland that have attracted you?

Pellis: Well Irish cinema at its best is something between a European art cinema and American movies. It takes on aspects of the best of both. I think that some of the best films going right back were based on Irish history: they were challenges to finding ways of telling the real story of Ireland. They managed their stories of the past in an interesting way, which always seemed to rise above the difficulties that some Irish filmmakers might have had with the structuring of fictional scripts. It was strange that a country so full of great literature and theatre and fiction, seemed to struggle with that narrative form of expression. What I believed early on was that the Irish cinematic culture had mostly strength in its actors – forced to work abroad, of course – but what I saw increasingly was a balance between a strong visual style, very solid narratives and exceptional acting.

Authors: We've always been very impressed by Irish actors on the stage and, as you've said, we have a very solid theatrical, literary tradition. Do you think that that filters into film, or that Irish film is a little more theatrical stylistically than most?

Pellis: No. I think that maybe only after several years do Irish actors become capable of acting in a special way for the screen, which is something very different to the theatre. I remember Brendan Gleeson explaining that it was difficult to realize that when the camera was focused on your face, you were forced to act in a different way. I'm convinced that now they have become more adept at changing acting styles depending on this focus.

Authors: Since you began the festival in 2007, how do you feel that it has served Irish cinema at home and in Europe?

Pellis: There has been a palpable effect in Rome for sure, because nobody knew anything about Irish cinema. Irish films get relatively little exposure in Italy and when they do, they're perceived as either English or American. Very few people considered it, or really knew of the existence of an Irish cinema. In this sense, the festival has helped a lot. In Europe – or in Ireland – maybe, as James Fair noted, the festival gave Irish filmmakers another opportunity to meet and to form a little network. And I was very pleased to hear this because it was really something that I wanted the festival to do. That it was not just about screening films.

Authors: We can answer the 'at home' part of the question a little bit for you because even having been to Rome ourselves, we have been able to invite guests to our own home universities to meet our students, and that provides a great opportunity for them.

Pellis: I am very glad to hear that, and I must say that I have benefitted from the connections made too within the Irish filmmaking network. I like the idea that the consequences go way beyond the event itself as a kind of cultural exchange.

Authors: How would you like to continue to develop the festival in the short and medium terms? You've already said that you like it at its current size in terms of audience turnouts, but if anything, is there an aspect that you've not cultivated yet?

Pellis: You want to hear some of my ideas?

Authors: Yes...your dreams!

Pellis: Well I would like the festival to have broader recognition around Italy, possibly even with Cinemobile: that would be my biggest aspiration. Then I'd like to start a little distribution of Irish films in Italy that would be perennially available on demand, maybe assisting with facilitating getting Italian subtitles, or maybe even arranging online releases. I would also very much like to keep the acting masterclasses. It would be great, for example, to hold a masterclass led together by an Italian and an Irish actor: perhaps not at

every annual festival but a special occasional event, or something
like that. I would also like to see greater collaborations with universities, and also tour some theatrical pieces from Ireland around Italy.
Of course, this is not cinema but, you know, there is no reason – as
we're interested in the performance side of things – that we should
remain 'just cinema'. And it would be useful to organize something
besides the cinematic event.

Authors: The festival has had many strands already, cultural off-
shoots, that haven't always related directly to Irish film, per se, so
you've had interventions into Irish literature and music, for example... Why did you decide to do that? Does it relate at all to the
bigger cultural possibility that you've mentioned when you speak
of Irish theatre?

Pellis: Yes. I think that I have a very realistic view of the festival,
and even when I studied Irish cinema; I started by looking at Irish
history. Because it was immediately clear to me that it would be
impossible to understand an Irish film without knowing something
of the historical context behind it. I couldn't separate the subject
matter that I love from the narratives designed around it, and also
because this context provides such an important understanding of
the motivations behind directors like Lenny Abrahamson and Neil
Jordan – even if, or especially if, Jordan might be considered a better
screenwriter than director – and Lenny's films are full of rich references (maybe to Beckett in *Adam and Paul* and *Garage*), and some
are now based on books. Then, as far as music is concerned, I really
don't think that you can separate that form of cultural expression
through film from the films themselves.

Authors: So, you're not a purist? You wouldn't feel that you had
lost anything if you moved out beyond the typical perimeters of
a uniquely 'film' festival?

Pellis: I will certainly continue to concentrate mainly on film because
it's my competence and it's my passion: I wouldn't feel able to speak
about music, for example, in the same way because I don't know
anything about it. But I would happily invite someone to the festival to talk about that area, if I felt that it would work in the context.
It's certainly the way that I see it and I feel that it could work in the
future to accommodate that kind of development. It's something
that I might feel at the right time could help to explain film better.

Authors: How successfully do you think that the different elements of
the festival have worked? It's had many strands (workshops, readings, question and answer sessions, interviews with the artists and

so on) before screenings and after screenings: they've all been a big part of the bigger picture, so how successful do you think that all of that has been?

Pellis: I think that's probably the best part of the festival. If you hear a director explaining how certain decisions have been made, you'll probably understand the film better. It's a bit like the extras on a DVD! And there's always the possibility of making the experience more 'real': especially with actors where it's interesting to discover the person behind the character. I feel that we can understand another level of the performance by watching him or her, having discussed the motivations and processes. I wouldn't design a festival with screenings alone.

Authors: This is a more technical question, but has it been difficult to acquire prints of the films that you've wanted to show? You obviously attend festivals in Ireland before making your final decisions, so you have some idea of the films that you'd like to get, but has it ever been a problem to get them?

Pellis: Occasionally it has been very difficult, and at other times, it hasn't been a problem. Generally speaking, when I meet directors or producers in person in advance, I have no difficulty whatsoever. When there is an agent attached to a film, or a distributor, then it can be difficult if not impossible. This is a considerable problem: the films are either expensive, and agents ask for a fee that is very high, simply too much for a small festival. But generally – and this is a bit of a paradox – it's easier to get a film from Ireland than it is from Italy. If a film, for example, already has an Italian distributor and it's already in Rome, let's say at a film society here, or the company is based in Rome, it is often impossible to get a print.

Authors: You've had some of the big players in Irish cinema as guests. Could you mention a few who you would consider to have been highlights?

Pellis: Well, I can say immediately that my favourite has been Stuart Graham! He was such a fantastic guest and he's a wonderful performer. But we have had many greats: Stephen Rea, Fionnula Flanagan, Eileen Walsh...They were fantastic because they were so enthusiastic about coming. That was really the surprise for me. It was surprising for me to see that such important and well-known actors and artists were willing to be here. But as the question was about the highlights, I think that I should mention one relevant to this. Maybe the most emotional moment at the festival was when Laurence McKeown was here for the first time in Rome and we screened *H3*, and after that he was talking about Bobby Sands and then, out of the blue, he stopped silent. I couldn't understand why: I looked at him, and could see that he seemed upset, that he was on the brink of crying. That was really an incredible moment.

Authors: The festival is not an awards festival, although you have presented a few prizes – Stuart Graham has won, and Peter McDonald has won, for example – so why did you decide to set it up in that way?

Pellis: Without prizes?

Authors: Yes, specifically not as an awards festival.

Pellis: Well I think that it's a very complex thing, and it's not at all easy to compare films and ultimately say that one is 'better' than another. With shorts [the only category in which prizes are given] there is a difference, perhaps. I decided to put on the shorter screenings to underline the fact that Irish short films are very well structured, that there are so many supportive schemes and initiatives, and they're of such a high quality. So I think that maybe for the shorts it was a good idea to have a small competition to acknowledge this. With the features, I really didn't see that there was any point.

Authors: It's interesting all right, because we saw *Volkswagen Joe* for the first time in Rome and then it was presented at the Schull Film Festival, and one of its honours – as mentioned at Schull – was the fact that it had won the award in Rome, and that's an amazing thing for an early career director [like Brian Deane, director of *Volkswagen Joe*] to be able to bring back to his or her home country. The fact that it has had recognition 1,500 miles away turns out to be a very worthy tribute for filmmakers back in Ireland.

Pellis: Well this is, of course, wonderful to hear!

Authors: It's actually interesting to see that it has been so successful among Roman audiences. Why do you think that this has been the case?

Pellis: The truth is that there is really now a high demand for original artistic-quality European cinema, because we only get the blockbusters here, for the most part, in the approximately 300 screens in Rome. I think that the festival responds precisely to this.

Authors: Do you have a general philosophy of the festival: what it is and what it does, or might do?

Pellis: Well, it's not supposed to be a big celebrity event: no red carpets, no cocktails, and no big sponsors, and I would not like that kind of development to reduce my control over what it becomes.

And I like the fact that this festival is like me... easy-going! This is, I think, the philosophy behind it!

Authors: What are the different Irish cultural bodies that have supported the festival and how have you found their response to your work?

Pellis: Well, as you know, we are backed by the Irish Embassy, by Culture Ireland, by the Irish Film Institute, the Irish Film Board and the Arts Council. And, to mention one of these, Culture Ireland has been extremely positive about what we've done. The Irish Film Institute helps out in very practical ways and is affirmative about the project.

Authors: Do you have any hopes for the kind of cultural contact that two or more European countries might have around this kind of event? What could you imagine in this respect, from your own experience?

Pellis: In Italy, there are other examples of national festivals which are supported by embassies, but they are more showcases than real selections or festivals. So, I don't know. I could answer in a different way, maybe, that by organizing this kind of festival and by starting by thinking about this kind of cultural connection, you might just be able to avoid certain tendencies towards poor quality co-productions. I don't like co-productions which are made solely on the grounds of attracting funding from both countries. When the stories are forced to go in an unintended direction or the characters are designed to accommodate the other country: I find that the result can be very 'unnatural'. I don't think that something that might grow out of the Irish Film Festa would be so unnatural. Such a collaboration, evolving organically, could be something very important: I believe that it's a more genuine way of facilitating artistic partnership.

Authors: It's interesting to hear you speak of the process from the point of view of 'purity', and the idea that you might lose something 'natural' that comes from a place with an inappropriate approach to financially motivated transnational co-operation.

Pellis: You miss out something important in the story... something generated on the ground...

Authors: ...and then you do get some interesting examples of how that can work differently, with some success, like *Once*, then, which is a completely 'Irish' film, but it does have the other European character at the heart of the story.

Pellis: Yes, and another good example is *Nothing Personal*...

Authors: Finally, to wrap up: do you feel that there are ample mechanisms in place (in Europe) to encourage and facilitate the development of film festivals like this one?

Pellis: No, I don't think so. There may be more openness to, or facilitation of, festivals that connect many European countries at the same time. So there is no support for small festivals between two nations...none!

Authors: But, wouldn't it be logical to imagine that the way forward might be at first to connect two countries, and then perhaps three, and then more on the back of that?

Pellis: And, yet I think that what's most interesting is the smaller kind of festival that connects fewer and not many nations. What we have already seen for years are the bigger international festivals. But what I would find more interesting is an arrangement where there could be smaller festivals of French cinema, or Danish cinema, or Irish cinema. Then we can allow the films to ask other questions about the idea of the nation – in the Irish context, about an 'all-Ireland' cinema – and about being a nation and having national cinema in Europe today.

This interview was conducted with Susanna Pellis on 15 February 2015.

Bibliography

20th Century Fox/Sky Pictures (2000) *'When the Sky Falls'* Press Kit.

Access Research Knowledge (Ark) [Online] Available at: www.ark.ac.uk.

Ahern, C. (2004) *P.S. I Love You.* London: HarperCollins.

Alba, R. D. (1990) *Ethnic Identity: The Transformation of White America.* New Haven, Conn./London: Yale University Press.

Alison, M. H. (2009) *Women and Political Violence: Female Combatants in Ethno-National Conflict.* London: Routledge.

Allen, K. (2000) *The Celtic Tiger: The Myth of Social Partnership in Ireland.* Manchester: Manchester University Press.

Altman, R. (1987) *The American Film Musical.* Bloomington and Indianapolis, Ind.: Indiana University Press.

Altman, R. (2005) 'A Semantic/Syntactic Approach to Film Genre', in Grant, B. K. (ed) *Film Genre Reader III.* Austin: University of Texas Press, pp. 27–41.

Anderson, J. (14 December 2007) *'P.S. I Love You* Review', *Variety*, [Online] Available at: http://www.variety.com [Accessed 17 October 2014].

Andrew, D. (1984) *Concepts in Film Theory.* Oxford and New York: Oxford University Press.

Andrew, D. (2006) 'An Atlas of World Cinema', in Stephanie Dennison, S. and Hwee Lim, S. (eds) *Remapping World Cinema: Identity, Culture and Politics in Film.* London: Wallflower Press, pp. 19–29.

Andrew, D. (2010) *What Cinema Is.* Oxford: Wiley-Blackwell.

Anthias, F and Yuval-Davis, N. (1993) *Racialised Boundaries.* London: Routledge.

Aretxaga, B. (1995) 'Dirty Protest: Symbolic Overdetermination and Gender in Northern Ireland Ethnic Violence'. *Ethos.* 23(2), pp. 123–48.

Ashcroft B., Griffiths, G. and Tiffin, H. (2007) *Postcolonial Studies: The Key Concepts.* London: Routledge.

Augé, M. (2009) *Non-Places: Introduction to an Anthropology of Supermodernity.* London: Verso. Available at: http://www.movies.ie/interviews/snap__carmel__winters_talks_about_the_highly_rated_irish_movie [Accessed 5 November 2014].

Bachelard, G. (1994) *The Poetics of Space.* Boston: Beacon Press.

Barbash, I. and Taylor, L. (1997) *Cross-Cultural Filmmaking: A Handbook for Documentary and Ethnographic Films and Videos.* Los Angeles: University of California.

Barton, R. (2004) *Irish National Cinema.* New York and London: Routledge.

Barton, R. (2006) *Acting Irish in Hollywood: From Fitzgerald to Farrell.* Dublin: Irish Academic Press.

Barton, R. (ed) (2009) *Screening Irish America.* Dublin: Irish Academic Press.

Beckett, S. (1994) *Waiting for Godot.* New York: Grove Press.

Behan, B. (2014) *The Hostage.* New York and London: Bloomsbury.

Belfast Telegraph (2013) 'Fire Bomb Attack part of "Upsurge"', *Belfast Telegraph*, [Online] Available at: http://www.belfasttelegraph.co.uk/news/local-national/

northern-ireland/fire-bomb-attack-part-of-upsurge-29845512.html   [Accessed 20 October 2013].

Bell, D. (2004) 'Telling Tales: Narrative, Evidence and Memory in Contemporary Documentary Film Practice', in Barton, R. and O'Brien, H. (eds) *Keeping It Reel. Irish Film and Television.* London: Wallflower Press, pp. 88–99.

Bellos, D. (2012) *Le poisson et le bananier.* Flammarion: Paris.

Bennett, J. (26 July 2010) BBC Vision. 'Putting Programmes on the Map', BBC.co.uk., [Online] Available at: http://www.bbc.co.uk/mediacentre/speeches/2010/bennet_jana_cardiff.html [Accessed 28 November 2014].

Bergquist, M. I. (1996) *Mother Ireland and the Gun: Representations of Women and Violence in the Films of Northern Ireland.* Masters Thesis, Queen's University Belfast.

Bluestone, G. (1957) *Novels into Films.* Berkeley and Los Angeles: University of California Press.

Bourdieu, P. (1984) *Distinction.* Cambridge, MA: Harvard University Press.

Box Office Mojo (2014) *P.S. I Love You,* [Online] Available at: http://www.boxofficemojo.com/movies/?page=main&id=psiloveyou.htm   [Accessed 17 October 2014].

Bracken, C. and Radley, E. (eds) (2013) *Viewpoints: Theoretical Perspectives on Irish Visual Texts.* Cork: Cork University Press.

Bracken, C. and Radley, E. (2007) 'A Mirror up to Irishness: Hollywood Hard Men and Witty Women', in Balzano, W., Mulhall, A. and Sullivan, M. (eds) *Irish Postmodernism and Popular Culture.* Basingstoke: Palgrave, pp. 157–68.

Brereton, P. (2009) 'Hollywood Representations of Irish Journalism: A Case Study of Veronica Guerin'. *Irish Communications Review.* 11, pp. 104–14.

Brintnall, K. L. (2011) *Ecce Homo: The Male-Body-in-Pain as Redemptive Figure.* Chicago and London: The University of Chicago Press.

Bronfen, E. (2004) *Home in Hollywood.* New York: Columbia University Press.

Brown, J. A. (2002) 'The Tortures of Mel Gibson: Masochism and the Sexy Male Body'. *Men and Masculinities.* 5(2), pp. 123–43.

Bruzzi, S. (2011) 'Documentary, Performance and Questions of Authenticity. On British Filmmakers Molly Dineen and Nick Broomfield', [Online] Available at: http://www.zhdk.ch/fileadmin/data_subsites/data_zdok/Pub11_PDFs/A_Bruzzi_120311.pdf [Accessed 3 September 2014].

Butler, D. (1995) *The Trouble with Reporting Northern Ireland.* Aldershot: Avebury.

Campbell, K. L. (1995) *Ireland's History: Prehistory to Present.* London: Bloomsbury Publishing.

Carroll, L. (2008) *Alice's Adventures in Wonderland.* Mayo: Evertype.

Casey, N. (2006) ' "The Best Kept Secret in Retail": Selling Irishness in Contemporary America', in Negra, D. (ed) *The Irish in Us: Irishness, Performativity, and Popular Culture.* Durham/London: Duke University Press, pp. 84–109.

Chakravorty Spivak, G. (1988) 'Can the Subaltern Speak?', in Ashcroft, B., Griffiths, G. and Tiffin, H. (eds) *The Postcolonial Studies Reader.* London and New York: Routledge, pp. 24–28.

Chan, J. J. (2009) 'Exclusive: Steve McQueen Puts the Jigsaw Puzzle Together in Hunger', *Flavorwire,* [Online] Available at: http://flavorwire.com/15034/exclusive-steve-mcqueen-on-putting-the-jigsaw-puzzle-together-in-hunger [Accessed 24 October 2014].

Chandler, D. and Munday, R. (2011) *The Oxford Dictionary of Media and Communications*. Oxford: Oxford University Press.

Cleary, J. (2007) 'The Pogues and the Spirit of Capitalism', in Cleary, J. (ed) *Outrageous Fortune: Capital and Culture in Modern Ireland*. Dublin: Field Day Publications, pp. 261–94.

Coffey, E. (2011) 'This Winters Tale Springs a Surprise'. *Irish Independent*. 2 February, p. 20.

Corcoran, M. (2006) *Out of Order: The Political Imprisonment of Women in Northern Ireland, 1972–1999*. Devon: Willan Publishing.

Corner, J. (1996) *The Art of the Record: A Critical Introduction to Documentary*. Manchester: Manchester University Press.

Corrigan, C. (2015) 'The Worst Irish Accents in Hollywood Movies', *IrishCentral*, [Online] Available at: http://www.irishcentral.com/culture/entertainment/the-worst-irish-accents-in-hollywood-movies-125286393-237793271.html [Accessed 6 January 2015].

Coulter, C. (1991) *Web of Punishment*. Dublin: Attic Press.

Coupland, N. (2007) *Style: Language Variation and Identity*. Cambridge, UK: Cambridge University Press.

Coupland, N. (2009) 'Dialect Style, Social Class and Metacultural Performance: The Pantomime Dame', in Coupland, N. and Jaworski, A. (eds) *The New Sociolinguistics Reader*. Basingstoke: Palgrave Macmillan, pp. 311–25.

Cresswell, T. (1996) *In Place/out of Place: Geography, Ideology, and Transgression*. Minneapolis: University of Minnesota Press.

Cresswell, T. (2010) 'Towards a Politics of Mobility'. *Environment and Planning D: Society and Space*. 28(1), pp. 17–31.

Crosson, S. (2012) 'Horror, Hurling, and Bertie: Aspects of Contemporary Irish Horror Cinema'. *Kinema: Journal of Film and Audiovisual Media*. 37, pp. 65–83. Available at: http://www.kinema.uwaterloo.ca/article.php?id=513& feature [Accessed 5 November 2014].

Crowdus, G. (2009) 'The Human Body as Political Weapon: An Interview with Steve McQueen'. *Cineaste*. 34(2), pp. 22–25.

Cusack, T. (2001) 'A "Countryside Bright with Cosy Homesteads": Irish Nationalism and the Cottage Landscape'. *National Identities*. 3(3), pp. 221–38. [Online] Available at: http://www.tandfonline.com/doi/abs/10.1080/14608940120086885 [Accessed 7 May 2014].

Dargis, M. (21 December 2007) 'P.P.S. Take Tissues to This Weepy about Romance Tested by Death', *The New York Times*, [Online] Available at: http://www.nytimes.com [Accessed 17 October 2014].

Davidoff, L. and Hall, C. (1987) *Family Fortunes. Men and Women of the English Middle Class 1780–1850*. Chicago: University of Chicago Press.

Dawson, G. (2007) *Making Peace with the Past? Memory Trauma and the Irish Troubles*. Manchester: Manchester University Press.

Dowler, L. (1998) ' "And They Think I'm Just a Nice Old Lady": Women and War in Belfast, Northern Ireland'. *Gender, Place and Culture*. 5, pp. 159–76.

Doyle, R. (1996) *The Woman Who Walked into Doors*. London: Jonathan Cape.

Dudley, A. (2006) 'An Atlas of World Cinema', in Dennison, S. and Hwee Lim, S. (eds) *Remapping World Cinema: Identity, Culture and Politics in Film*. London: Wallflower Press, pp. 19–29.

Duffy, C. G., Sigerson, G. and Hyde, D. (1973) *The Revival of Irish Literary Addresses by Sir Charles Gavan Duffy, Dr. George Sigerson and Dr. Douglas Hyde*. New York: Lemma Publishing.

Dwyer, M. (21 December 2007) 'PS, I love You', *The Irish Times*, [Online] Available at: http://www.irishtimes.com [Accessed 13 November 2014].

Dyer, R. (1997) *White*. London and New York: Routledge.

Dyer, R. (1998) *Stars*. London: BFI Publishing.

Edwards, T. (2008) 'Spectacular Pain: Masculinity, Masochism and Men in the Movies', in Burr, V. and Hearn, J. (eds) *Sex, Violence and the Body: The Erotics of Wounding*. Houndmills, Basingstoke and Hampshire: Palgrave Macmillan, pp. 157–76.

Elder, S. (1995) 'Collaborative Filmmaking: An Open Space for Making Meaning. A Moral Ground for Ethnographic Film'. *Visual Anthropology Review*. 11(2), pp. 94–101.

Element Pictures (28 June 2010) 'Box-Office Success for Irish Documentary *His & Hers*', [Online] Available at: http://elementpictures.ie/news/film/box-office-success-for-irish-documentary-his-hers [Accessed 1 April 2013].

Ellman, M. (1993) *The Hunger Artists: Starving, Writing & Imprisonment*. London: Virago Press.

Elsaesser, T. (2005) *European Cinema: Face to Face with Hollywood*. Amsterdam: Amsterdam University Press.

Farley, F. (1999) 'Interrogating the Myths of Maternity in Irish Cinema: Margo Harkin's Hush-a-Bye Baby'. *Irish University Review*. 29(2), pp. 219–37.

Feldman, A. (1991) *Formations of Violence: The Narrative of the Body and Political Terror in Northern Ireland*. Chicago and London: The University of Chicago Press.

FilmIreland.net (27 May 2009) 'Ken Wardrop Winner of Directors Finders Series 2009', [Online] Available at: http://www.filmireland.net/2009/05/27/ken-wardrop-winner-of-directors-finders-series-2009/ [Accessed 15 January 2011].

Fischer, L. (1976) 'The Image of Woman as Image: The Optical Politics of "Dames"'. *Film Quarterly*. 30(1), pp. 2–11.

Fisher, M. (2009) *Capitalist Realism: Is There No Alternative?* Winchester: Zero Books.

Flynn, R. (2008) 'Altered States: Shrooms (2007) and Irish Cinema'. *Estudios Irlandeses*. 3, pp. 229–32.

François-Geiger, D. (1991) 'Panorama Des Argots Contemporains'. *Langue Française*. Larousse. 90, pp. 5–9.

Gans, H. J. (1979) 'Symbolic Ethnicity: The Future of Ethnic Groups and Cultures in America'. *Ethnic and Racial Studies*. 2(1), pp. 1–20.

Genette, G. (1980) *Narrative Discourse: An Essay in Method*. Ithaca and New York: Cornell University Press.

Genette, G. (1982) *Palimpsestes: La Literature Au Second Degree*. Paris: Editions du Serial, pp. 1–2.

Gibbons, L. (1988) 'Romanticism, Realism and Irish Cinema', in Rockett, K., Gibbons, L. and Hill, J. (eds) *Cinema and Ireland*. London: Routledge, pp. 194–257.

Gibbons, L. (2006) 'Foreword', in Barton, R. (ed) *Acting Irish in Hollywood: From Fitzgerald to Farrell*. Dublin: Irish Academic Press, pp. xv–xviii.

Ging, D. (2013) *Men and Masculinities in Irish Cinema*. Basingstoke: Palgrave Macmillan.

Gogarty, O. S. et al. (1930) 'Public Business – Censorship of Films (Amendment) Bill, 1930 – Second Stage', *Houses of the Oireachtas*, [Online] Available at: http://debates.oireachtas.ie/seanad/1930/05/07/00005.asp [Accessed 28 November 2014].

Graham, C. (2001) *Deconstructing Ireland: Identity, Theory, Culture*. Edinburgh: Edinburgh University Press.

Grosz, E. (1999) 'Bodies-Cities', in Price, J. and Shildrick, M. (eds) *Feminist Theory and the Body: A Reader*. New York: Routledge, pp. 381–7.

Guiney, E. (16 November 2013) Interview. National Media Conference Panel.

Hackett, C. and Rolston, B. (2009) 'The Burden of Memory: Victims, Storytelling and Resistance in Northern Ireland'. *Memory Studies*. 2(3), pp. 355–76.

Hake, S. (2008) *German National Cinema*. New York and London: Routledge.

Halter, M. (2000) *Shopping for Identity: The Marketing of Ethnicity*. New York: Schocken Books.

Hannam, K., Sheller, M. and Urry, J. (2006) 'Editorial: Mobilities, Immobilities and Moorings'. *Mobilities*. 1(1), pp. 1–22.

Harrington, R. (8 June 2005) ' "Elvis": No Mere Impersonation', *Washington Post*, [Online] Available at: http://www.washingtonpost.com/wp-dyn/content/article/2005/05/04/AR2005050400093.html [Accessed 3 October 2014].

Harvey, D. (2008) 'The Right to the City'. *New Left Review*. 53, pp. 23–40.

Hennebelle, G. (1974) 'Z-Movies, or What Hath Costa-Gavras Wrought'. *Cineaste*. 6(2), pp. 28–31.

Hickey, R. (2000) 'Dissociation as a Form of Language Change'. *European Journal of English Studies*. 4(3), pp. 303–15. [Online] Available at: https://www.uni-due.de/~lan300/27_Dissociation_as_a_Form_of_Language_Change_(Hickey).pdf [Accessed 19 February 2014].

Hickey, R. (2005) *Dublin English: Evolution and Change*. Amsterdam: J. Benjamins Pub. Co.

Hickey, R. (2007) *Irish English: History and Present-Day Forms*. Cambridge: Cambridge University Press.

Hickey, R. (2011) *The Dialects of Irish: Study of a Changing Landscape*. Berlin: De Gruyter Mouton.

Hill, J. (1987) 'Images of Violence', in Rockett, K., Gibbons, L. and Hill, J. (eds) *Cinema and Ireland*. London: Croom Helm, pp. 147–93.

Hill, J. (2006) *Cinema and Northern Ireland: Film, Culture and Politics*. London: BFI Publishing.

Hirst, M. (2007) *The Tudors: It's Good To Be King*. New York: Simon Spotlight Entertainment.

Hobsbawm, E. (2008) *Globalisation, Democracy and Terrorism*. London: Abacus.

Holfter, G. (2011) *Heinrich Böll and Ireland*. Newcastle: Cambridge Scholars.

Holland, K. (13 September 2001) 'Number of Ghost Estates Hits 2,881', in *The Irish Times*.

Holmes, H. K. (2005) 'A Relevance Approach to Irish–English Advertising: The Case of Brennan's Bread', in Barron, A. and Schneider, K. P. (eds) *The Pragmatics of Irish English*. Berlin: Mouton de Gruyter, pp. 367–89.

Holohan, C. and Tracy, T. (eds) (2014) *Masculinity and Irish Popular Culture: Tiger's Tales*. London: Palgrave Macmillan.

Howard, P. (2003) *Ross O'Carroll Kelly: The Teenage Dirtbag Years*. Dublin: O'Brien.

Hunt, L. (1993) *British Low Culture: From Safari Suits to Sexploitation*. London and New York: Routledge.

Huston, J. R. (31 March 2009) 'A Talk with Steve McQueen', *San Francisco Guardian Bay*, [Online] Available at: http://www.sfbg.com/pixel_vision/2009/03/31/talk-steve-mcqueen [Accessed 21 October 2014].

Hutcheon, L. (2006) *A Theory of Adaptation*. New York and London: Routledge.

Hyde, D. (1973) 'The Necessity for De-Anglicising Ireland', in Duffy, C. G., Sigerson, G. and Hyde, D. (eds) *The Revival of Irish Literature*. New York: Lemma Pub. Corp, pp. 115–61.

Ignatiev, N. (2008) *How the Irish Became White*. New York and London: Routledge.

Inglis, T. (1988) *Moral Monopoly*. Dublin: UCD Press.

Inglis, T. (2005) 'Origins and Legacies of Irish Prudery: Sexuality and Social Control in Modern Ireland'. *Eire-Ireland*. 40(3&4), pp. 9–37.

Innes, C. L. (1993) *Woman and Nation*. Hemel Hempstead: Harvester Wheatsheaf.

Irigaray, L. (1993/2007) *Je, Tu, Nous*. Abingdon: Routledge.

Irish Film and Television Network [Online] Available at: www.iftn.ie

Irishfilmboard.ie. (29 June 2010) 'Film Critics and Audiences Love Irish Documentary *His & Hers*', [Online] Available at: http://www.irishfilmboard.ie/irish_film_industry/news/Film_Critics_and_Audiences_Love_Irish_Documentary_His_amp_Hers/1326 [Accessed 1 April 2013].

Jones, K. W. (2001) ' "I've Called 'Em Tom-Ah-Toes All My Life and I'm Not Going to Change!'": Maintaining Linguistic Control Over English Identity in the US'. *Social Forces*. 79(3), 1061–94.

Joyce, J. (1986) *Ulysses*. New York: Vintage.

Kandiyoti, D. (1996a) 'Identity and Its Discontents: Women and the Nation', in Williams, P. and Chrisman, L. (eds) *Colonial Discourse and Post-Colonial Theory*. London: Harvester Wheatsheaf, pp. 376–91.

Kandiyoti, D. (1996b) 'Women, Ethnicity and Nationalism', in Hutchinson, L. and Smith, A. (eds) *Ethnicity*. Oxford: Oxford University Press, pp. 311–16.

Keane, J. B. (1966) *The Field*. Dublin, Ireland: Mercier Press.

Kelly, M. (2009) *The Irish Credit Bubble*, Dublin, [Online] Available at: https://www.ucd.ie/t4cms/WP09.32.pdf [Accessed 11 July 2014].

Kenny, C. (2009) 'Significant Television: Journalism, Sex Abuse and the Catholic Church', *Articles*, Paper 27, [Online] Available at: http://www.arrow.dit.ie/caschmedart/27 [Accessed 12 February 2013].

Kiberd, D. (2002) *Inventing Ireland*. London: Harvard University Press.

Kilpatrick, C. (28 December 2013) 'One Security Alert in Northern Ireland for Every Day of the Year', *Belfast Telegraph*, [Online] Available at: http://www.belfasttelegraph.co.uk/news/local-national/northern-ireland/one-security-alert-in-northern-ireland-for-every-day-of-the-year-29871264.html [Accessed 20 May 2014].

Le Corff, I. (2011) 'Le Cinéma Irlandais En France et la Légitimation Des œuvres', in Beylot, P., Le Corff, I. and Marie, M. (eds) *Les Images en Question*. Bordeaux: Presses Universitaires de Bordeaux, pp. 229–41.

Le Corff, I. and Épinoux, E. (eds) (2009) *Cinemas of Ireland*. Newcastle upon Tyne: Cambridge Scholars Press.

Le Corff, I. (2013) 'The Liminal Position of Irish Cinema: Is Using the English Language a Key to Success?' *Mise Au Point* n° 5, [Online] Available at: http://map.revues.org/1455 [Accessed 15 January 2015].

Lebeau, V. (2008) *Childhood and Cinema*. London: Reaktion Books.

Lee, A. (2013) 'Top 10 Dreadful Fake Irish Accents in Films', *Metro Top 10 Dreadful Fake Irish Accents Infilms Comments*, [Online] Available at: http://metro.co.uk/2013/03/17/top-10-dreadful-fake-irish-accents-in-films-3545809/ [Accessed 18 February 2014].

Lenehan, F. (2012) 'A Land and a People of Extremes – Ireland and the Irish in German Cinema'. *Irish Studies Review*. 20(1), pp. 25–46.

Lim, D. (2009) 'History through an Unblinking Lens', *The New York Times*, [Online] Available at: http://www.nytimes.com/2009/03/08/movies/08lim.html?pagewanted=all&_r=0 [Accessed 6 March 2009].

Linehan, H. (13 September 1996) 'There's No Such Thing as an Unbiased Film', *The Irish Times*, p. 11.

Linehan, H. (2000) 'Drama over Documentary', *The Irish Times*, p. B47.

Longley, E. and Kiberd, D. (2001) *Multi-Culturalism: The View from the Two Irelands*. Cork: Cork University Press.

Lumiere, Database on Admissions of Films Released in Europe, [Online] Available at: http://lumiere.obs.coe.int/web/search/ [Accessed 15 January 2015].

Lye, J. (1997/2008) 'Ideology: A Brief Guide', [Online] Available at: www.brocku.ca/english/jlyle/ideology/php date accessed 12/2/14 [Accessed 10 December 2013].

MacKeogh, C. and O'Connell, D. (2012) 'Introduction', in MacKeogh, C. and O'Connell, D. (eds) *Documentary in a Changing State. Ireland since the 1990s*. Cork: Cork University Press, pp. 1–11.

MacLaughlin, N. and McLoone, M. (2000) 'Hybridity and National Musics: The Case of Irish Rock Music'. *Popular Music*. 19(2), pp. 181–99.

MacLaughlin, N. and McLoone, M. (2012) *Rock and Popular Music in Ireland: Before and After U2*. Dublin and Portland: Irish Academic Press.

Maguire, J. (27 April 2011) 'Snap', *Confessions of a Film Critic*, [Online] Available at: http://maguiresmovies.blogspot.com/2011/04/snap.html [Accessed 5 November 2014].

Mairs, J. and McLaughlin, C. (2012) 'Unheard Voices: Recording Stories from the Troubles', in MacKeogh, C. and O'Connell, D. (eds) *Documentary in a Changing State: Ireland since the 1990s*. Cork: Cork University Press, pp. 29–41.

Mairs, J. (2013) *Audiovisual Storytelling in Post-Conflict Northern Ireland – Participant and Audience Responses to Filming, Editing and Exhibiting Memories of the Troubles via Two Practice-Led Collaborative Documentary Film Productions*. PhD Thesis. University of Ulster.

Massey, D. (1993) 'Power-Geometry and a Progressive Sense of Place', in Bird, J., Curtis, B., Putnam, T. and Tickner, L. (eds) *Mapping the Futures: Local Cultures, Global Change*. London: Routledge, pp. 59–69.

Massey, D. (1994) *Space, Place and Gender*. Minneapolis: University of Minnesota Press, [Online] Available at: http://scholar.google.com/scholar?hl=en&btnG=Search&q=intitle:Space,+Place+and+gender#0 [Accessed 8 May 2014].

Massey, D. (2005) *For Space*. London: Thousand Oaks.

McCafferty, N. (1981) *The Armagh Women*. Michigan: Co-Op Books.

McCafferty, O. (1998) *Mojo Mickybo*. London: Nick Hern Books.

McClintock, A. (1993) 'Family Feuds: Gender, Nationalism and the Family'. *Feminist Review*. 44, pp. 61–80.

McCourt, F. (1996) *Angela's Ashes*. New York: Scribner.

McDermott, R. (7 April 2011) 'Interview: Carmel Winters, Director of *Snap*', *Roe McDermott's Screen Lover: The Hot Press Film Blog*, [Online] Available at: http://wordpress.hotpress.com/screenlover/2011/04/07/interviewcarmel-winters-director-of-snap/ [Accessed 5 November 2014].

McDonald, H. (3 December 2013) 'Belfast "Peace Walls" Will Come down Only by Community Consent', *The Guardian*, [Online] Available at: http://www.theguardian.com/uk-news/2013/dec/03/belfast-peace-walls-dismantled-community-consent-minister [Accessed 20 January 2014].

McDonald, H. (31 December 2013) 'Northern Ireland Talks Collapse as Main Unionist Parties Reject Haass Proposals', *The Guardian*, [Online] Available at: http://www.theguardian.com/uk-news/2013/dec/31/northern-ireland-talks-collapse-as-main-unionist-parties-reject-haass-proposals [Accessed 20 January 2014].

McIlroy, B. (ed) (2007) *Genre and Cinema: Ireland and Transnationalism*. New York and London: Routledge.

McIvor, C. (2009) ' "I'm Black an' I'm Proud": Ruth Negga, *Breakfast on Pluto*, and Invisible Irelands'. *InVisible Culture*. Issue 13 (Spring 2009), pp. 22–36.

McKeown, L. (2001) *Out of Time: Irish Republican Prisoners Long Kesh 1972–2000*. Belfast: Beyond the Pale.

McKittrick, D. and McVea, D. (2001) *Making Sense of the Troubles: A History of the Northern Ireland Conflict*. London: Penguin.

McLaughlin, G and Baker, S. (2010) *The Propaganda of Peace: The Role of Culture and Media in the Northern Ireland Peace Process*. Bristol: Intellect Books.

McLaughlin, N. and McLoone, M. (2012) *Rock and Popular Music in Ireland: Before and After U2*. Dublin and Portland: Irish Academic Press.

McLoone, M. (1994) 'National Cinema and Cultural Identity: Ireland and Europe', in Hill, J., McLoone, M. and Hainsworth, P. (eds) *Border Crossing: Film in Ireland, Britain and Europe*. Belfast: Institute of Irish Studies/British Film Institute, pp. 146–73.

McLoone, M. (2000) *Irish Film: The Emergence of a Contemporary Cinema*. London: British Film Institute.

McLoone, M. (2008) *Film, Media and Popular Culture in Ireland*. Dublin: Irish Academic Press.

McLoone, M. (2009) 'National Cinema and Global Culture: The Case of Irish Cinema', in Le Corff, I. and Épinoux, E. (eds) *Cinemas of Ireland*. Newcastle upon Tyne: Cambridge Scholars Press, pp. 14–27.

McRobbie, A. (2009) *The Aftermath of Feminism: Gender, Culture and Social Change*. London, Thousand Oaks, New Delhi and Singapore: SAGE Publications.

Meaney, G. (1998) 'Landscapes of Desire: Women and Ireland on film'. *Women: A Cultural Review*. 9(3), pp. 237–51.

Meaney, G. (2007) 'Not Irish Enough?: Masculinity and Ethnicity in *The Wire* and *Rescue Me*', in Balzano, W., Mulhall, A. and Sullivan, M. (eds) *Irish Postmodernisms and Popular Culture*. Basingstoke: Palgrave Macmillan, pp. 3–14.

Merivirta, R. (2013) 'Gendered Conflicts in Northern Ireland: Motherhood, the Male Body and Borders in *Some Mother's Son* and *Hunger*', in Merivirta, R.,

Ahonen, K., Mulari, H. and Mähkä, R. (eds) *Frontiers of Screen History: Imagining European Borders in Cinema, 1945–2010*. Bristol: Intellect, pp. 235–60.

Miller, L., Luchs, M. and Jalea, G. D. (2011) 'Mapping Memories: Participatory Media, Place-Based Stories & Refugee Youth', *Centre for Oral History and Digital Storytelling Concordia University*, [Online] Available at: http://www. mappingmemories.ca/book [Accessed 6 May 2012].

Miller, L. and Michele S. (2012) 'Dissemination and Ownership of Knowledge', Milne, E. J., Mitchell, C. and de Lange, N. (eds) *Handbook of Participatory Video*. Lanham: AltaMira Press, pp. 331–48.

Moloney, M. (2014) *Reaching Out from the Archive: The Role of Community Oral History Archives in Conflict Transformation in Northern Ireland*. PhD Thesis. University of Ulster.

Monahan, B. (2009a) 'Defining Ourselves through the Irishness We Sell: The Comedy of Cultural Commodification in Mark Joffe's *The Matchmaker* (1997)', in Barton R. (ed) *Screening Irish America*. Dublin and Portland: Irish Academic Press, pp. 326–38.

Monahan, B. (2009b) *Ireland's Theatre on Film: Style, Stories and the National Stage on Screen*. Dublin, Ireland: Irish Academic Press.

Moore, R. (2011) ' "If I Actually Talked Like That, I'd Pull a Gun on Myself": Accent, Avoidance, and Moral Panic in Irish English'. *Anthropological Quarterly*. 84(1), pp. 41–64.

Muldoon, O., Schmid, K., Downes, C., Kremer, J. and Trew, K. (2005) 'The Legacy of the Troubles: Experience of the Troubles, Mental Health and Social Attitudes', *Queen's University Belfast*, [Online] Available at: http://www. legacyofthetroubles.qub.ac.uk/ [Accessed 5 November 2011].

Mulvey, L. (1975) 'Visual Pleasure and Narrative Cinema'. *Screen*. 16(3), pp. 6–18.

Murphy, N. (8 September 2010) '*His & Hers* Becomes Biggest Irish Documentary in Years', *Scannain*, [Online] Available at: http://www.scannain.com/movies-news/his-hers-becomes-biggest-irish-documentary-in-years [Accessed 6 January 2015].

Murray, R. (1998) *Hard Time: Armagh Gaol 1971–1986*. Dublin: Mercier Press.

Naremore, J. (2000) *Film Adaptation*. New Brunswick: Rutgers University Press.

Nash, C. (1993) 'Remapping and Renaming: New Cartographies of Identity, Gender and Landscape in Ireland'. *Feminist Review*. 44, pp. 39–57. [Online] Available at: http://www.jstor.org/stable/1395194 [Accessed 8 May 2014].

Neale, S. (1992) 'Masculinity as Spectacle', in Creed, B. and Merck, M. (eds) *The Sexual Subject: A Screen Reader in Sexuality*. London and New York: Routledge, pp. 277–90.

Negra, D. (2001a) 'Consuming Ireland: Lucky Charms Cereal, Irish Spring Soap, and 1-800-Shamrock'. *Cultural Studies*. 15(1), pp. 76–97.

Negra, D. (2001b) *Off-White Hollywood: American Culture and Ethnic Female Stardom*. London and New York: Routledge.

Negra, D. (2006) 'Irishness, Innocence, and American Identity Politics before and after September 11', in Negra, D. (ed) *The Irish in Us: Irishness, Performativity, and Popular Culture*. Durham and London: Duke University Press, pp. 354–72.

Negra, D. (2009) 'Irishness, Anger and Masculinity in Recent Film and Television', in Barton, R. (ed) *Screening Irish-America*. Dublin: Irish Academic Press, pp. 279–96.

Negra, D. (2010) 'Urban Space, Luxury Retailing and the New Irishness'. *Cultural Studies*. 24(6), pp. 836–53. [Online] Available at: http://www.tandfonline.com/doi/abs/10.1080/09502386.2010.502732 [Accessed 11 July 2014].

Nichols, B. (2001) *Introduction to Documentary*. Bloomington: Indiana University Press.

Northern Ireland Screen (2013) *Opening Doors: A Strategy to Transform the Screen Industries in Northern Ireland*. Belfast: NI Screen.

O'Brien, H. (2012) 'Speaking out. The Role of Documentary', in MacKeogh, C. and O'Connell, D. (eds) *Documentary in a Changing State. Ireland since the 1990s*. Cork: Cork University Press, pp. 15–18.

O'Connell, D. (2012) 'Interview with Ken Wardrop, Director of *His & Hers* (2010)', in MacKeogh, C. and O'Connell, D. (eds) *Documentary in a Changing State. Ireland since the 1990s*. Cork: Cork University Press, pp. 135–44.

O'Connor, F. (1982) 'Guests of the Nation', in *Frank O'Connor: Collected Stories*. New York: Vintage Books, pp. 3–12.

O'Hagan, S. (12 October 2008) 'McQueen and Country', *The Guardian*, [Online] Available at: http://www.theguardian.com/film/2008/oct/12/2 [Accessed 24 October 2014].

O'Regan, N. (21 September 2014) 'Artistic Licence: The Truth Always Hurts', 'Agenda', *Sunday Business Post*, p. 1.

O'Sullivan, K. (18 November 2011) 'Was It for This?', in *The Irish Times*.

O'Tuama, S. (1995) *Repossessions: Selected Essays on the Irish Literary Heritage*. Cork: Cork University Press.

Olaziregi, M. J., White, L. and Addis, K. (2004) *An Anthology of Basque Short Stories*. Reno: Center for Basque Studies, University of Nevada, Reno.

Parpart, L. (2011) 'Crying over the Mother: Reading (and Feeling) Ken Wardrop's Contradictory Construction of Maternal Femininity'. *Short Film Studies*. 1(1), pp. 77–81.

Pettitt, L. (2000) *Screening Ireland: Film and Television Representation*. Manchester and New York: Manchester University Press.

Phelan, A. (2014) 'Begorrah, Sure Is That for Real? Ten Worst Irish Accents in Film', *Independent.ie*, [Online] Available at: http://www.independent.ie/entertainment/movies/begorrah-sure-is-that-for-real-ten-worst-irish-accents-in-film-30037102.html [Accessed 18 November 2014].

Pine, E. (2011) *The Politics of Irish Memory: Performing Remembrance in Contemporary Irish Culture*. London and New York: Palgrave Macmillan.

Pink, S. (2007) *Doing Visual Ethnography*. London: Sage.

Potter, A. (2012) *Entertainmentwise*, [Online] Available at: http://www.entertainmentwise.com/photos/68488/1/Entertainmentwise-Chats-With-The-Tudors-Michael-Hirst [Accessed 3 October 2014].

Power, E. (24 March 2005) 'It's Just Like So the End of Irish Accents', *Irish Independent*, [Online] Available at: http://www.independent.ie/unsorted/features/its-just-like-so-the-end-of-irish-accents-25996450.html [Accessed 12 November 2013].

Puwar, N. (2004) *Space Invaders: Race, Gender and Bodies out of Place*. Oxford and New York: Berg.

Radley, E. (2013) 'Violent Transpositions: The Disturbing "Appearance" of the Irish Horror Film', in Bracken, C. and Radley, E. (eds) *Viewpoints: Theoretical Perspectives on Irish Visual Texts*. Cork: Cork University Press, pp. 109–23.

Rains, S. (2007) *The Irish-American in Popular Culture: 1945–2000.* Dublin: Irish Academic Press.

Renner, K. (ed.) (2013) *The 'Evil Child' in Literature, Film and Popular Culture.* New York: Routledge.

Riggs, T. (1998) 'Richard Hamilton. The Citizen 1981–3', [Online] Available at: http://www.tate.org.uk/http://www.tate.org.uk/art/artworks/hamilton-the-citizen-t03980/text-summary [Accessed 24 October 2014].

Rockett, K. (1991) 'Aspects of the Los Angelesation of Ireland'. *Irish Communications Review.* 01, pp. 18–23. [Online] Available at: http://dit.ie/icr/currentandpastissues/volume011991/ [Accessed 19 February 2015].

Rockett, K., Gibbons, L. and Hill, J. (1988) *Cinema and Ireland.* Syracuse, New York: Syracuse University Press.

Rogers, K. L., Leydesdorff, S. and Dawson, G. (eds) (2004) *Trauma: Life Stories of Survivors.* New Brunswick: Transaction Publishers.

Rotten Tomatoes (2014) '*P.S. I Love You*', [Online] Available at: http://www.rottentomatoes.com/m/ps_i_love_you/ [Accessed 17 October 2014].

Ruth Negga (on *BBC Breakfast*) (26 September 2011) *YouTube*, [Online] Available at: https://www.youtube.com/watch?v=Ggx0qSjnbME [Accessed 21 April 2014].

Ryan, L. (1998) 'Negotiating Modernity and Tradition: Newspaper Debates on the "Modern Girl" in the Irish Free State'. *Journal of Gender Studies.* 7(2), pp. 181–97.

Ryan, M and Kellner, D. (1990) *Camera Politica.* Bloomington, IN: Indiana University Press.

Ryder, C. (2000) *Inside the Maze: The Untold Story of the Northern Ireland Prison Service.* London: Methuen.

Sackett, S. J. (1979) 'Prestige Dialect and the Pop Singer'. *American Speech.* 54(3), pp. 234–7. [Online] Available at: http://www.jstor.org/stable/10.2307/454954?ref=no-x-route:4d69f37bd385b0cca3dd1d1f36b09936 [Accessed 1 December 2014].

Said, E. W. (1983) *The World, the Text and the Critic.* Cambridge: Harvard University Press.

Saoirse Ronan (on *Ellen*). *YouTube*, [Online] Available at: https://www.youtube.com/watch?v=Ggx0qSjnbME [Accessed 21 April 2014].

Schildt, A. and Siegfried, D. (2009) *Deutsche Kulturgeschichte: Die Bundesrepublik – 1945 bis zur Gegenwart.* Bonn: Bundeszentrale für politische Bildung.

Selby, J. (2014) 'St Patrick's Day 2014: The Worst Irish Accents in Film History', *The Independent*, [Online] Available at: http://www.independent.co.uk/arts-entertainment/films/news/st-patricks-day-2014-the-worst-irish-accents-in-film-history-9193269.html [Accessed 17 February 2015].

Shannon, C. (2009) 'The Bowery Cinderella', in Barton, R. (ed) *Screening Irish-America.* Dublin: Irish Academic Press, pp. 77–88.

Sheller, M. and Urry, J. (2000) 'The City and the Car'. *International Journal of Urban and Regional Research.* 24(4), pp. 737–57.

Sheller, M. and Urry, J. (2006) 'The New Mobilities Paradigm'. *Environment and Planning A.* 38(2), pp. 207–26.

Sheller, M. (2014) 'The New Mobilities Paradigm for a Live Sociology'. *Current Sociology.* 62(6), pp. 789–811.

Shirlow, P. and McEvoy, K. (2008) *Beyond the Wire: Former Prisoners and Conflict Transformation in Northern Ireland.* London: Pluto Press.

Skeggs, B. (2004) *Class, Self, Culture*. London: Routledge.

Slim, H., Thompson, P., Bennett, O. and Cross, N. (2006) 'Ways of Listening', in Perks, R. and Thomson, A. (eds) *The Oral History Reader*. London: Routledge, pp. 129–54.

Smith, J. M. (2007) *Ireland's Magdalen Laundries and the Nation's Architecture of Containment*. Notre Dame: University of Notre Dame.

Sollors, W. (1986) *Beyond Ethnicity: Consent and Descent in American Culture*. New York/Oxford: Oxford University Press.

Somerset Fry, P. and Somerset Fry, F. (1991) *A History of Ireland*. London: Routledge.

Spivak, G. C. (1998) 'Can the Subaltern Speak?', in Nelson, C. and Grossberg, L. (eds) *Marxism and the Interpretation of Culture*. Urbana and Chicago: University of Illinois Press, pp. 71–313.

Steffensen, K. N. (2012) 'BBC English with an Accent: "African" and "Asian" Accents and the Translation of Culture in British Broadcasting'. *Meta: Journal des traducteurs*. 57(2), pp. 510–27. [Online] Available at: http://www.erudit.org/revue/meta/2012/v57/n2/1013959ar.html [Accessed 19 January 2015].

Stoneman, R. (1996) 'Nine Notes on Film and Television', in Hill, J. and McLoone, M. (eds) *Big Picture, Small Screen: The Relations between Film and Television*. Luton: University of Luton Press/John Libbey Media, pp. 118–32.

Studlar, G. (2002) 'Oh, "Doll Divine": Mary Pickford, Masquerade and the Pedophilic Gaze', in Bean J. M. and Negra, D. (eds) *A Feminist Reader in Early Cinema*. Durham and London: Duke University Press, pp. 349–73.

Sullivan, M. (1999) *Women in Northern Ireland*. Florida: University Press of Florida.

Touchstone Pictures (2003) *Veronica Guerin Production Information*. [Online] Available at: http://ciaranhinds.eu/pdf/guerin.pdf [Accessed 6 October 2014].

Turner, T. (1992) 'Defiant Images: The Kayapo Appropriation of Video'. *Anthropology Today*. 8(6), pp. 5–16.

Waters, M. C. (1990) *Ethnic Options: Choosing Identities in America*. Berkeley, Los Angeles and London: University of California Press.

Ward, R. (2006) *Women Unionism and Loyalism in Northern Ireland: From 'Tea-Makers' to Political Actors*. Dublin: Irish Academy Press.

Wardrop, K and Freedman, A. (2009) *Film Ireland* – Issue 128 May/June 2009, [Online] Available at: http://filmireland.net/2009/05/01/film-ireland-mayjune-2009-issue-128/ [Accessed 3 March 2013].

Watson, K. (2011) 'Misfits Actress Ruth Negga Talks Robert Sheehan and the Irish Accent', [Online] Available at: http://metro.co.uk/2011/09/26/msifits-actress-ruth-negga-talks-robert-sheehan-and-the-irish-accent-163619/ [Accessed 26 September 2011].

Whitaker, R. (2009) 'Short Is Sweet, Feature Is Sweeter', *Film Ireland* – Issue 129 Tuesday 7 July 2009, [Online] Available at: http://www.filmireland.net/2009/07/07/issue-129-short-is-sweet-feature-is-sweeter [Accessed 15 January 2011].

Whitelock, C., Lamb, M. and Rentfrow, P. (2013) 'Overcoming Trauma: Psychological and Demographic Characteristics of Child Sexual Abuse Survivors in Adulthood'. *Clinical Psychological Science*. 1(4), pp. 351–62.

Wigon, Z. (27 March 2009) 'You Use Your Body to Die: An Interview with Steve McQueen', *Notebook*, [Online] Available at: https://mubi.com/notebook/posts/you-use-your-body-to-die-an-interview-with-steve-mcqueen [Accessed 24 October 2014].

Wilde, O. (1997) *The Picture of Dorian Gray and Other Writings*. Sydney: Simon & Schuster.

Wimmer L. (2009) *Cross-Channel Perspectives: The French Reception of British Cinema*. Bern: Peter Lang.

Winston, B. (2012) 'Foreward', in MacKeogh, C. and O'Connell, D. (eds) *Documentary in a Changing State. Ireland since the 1990s*. Cork: Cork University Press, pp. xvii–xviii.

Winters, C. (3 April 2011) Interview. '*Snap*: Carmel Winters Talks about the Highly Rated Irish Movie'. Interview by Brogen Hayes for *movies.ie*.

Winters, C. (29 March 2013) E-mail to K. Vejvoda.

Wise, J. (2000) 'Home, Territory and Identity'. *Cultural studies*. 4, pp. 295–310. [Online] Available at: http://www.tandfonline.com/doi/abs/10.1080/095023800334896 [Accessed 8 May 2014].

Zavarzadeh, M. (1991) *Seeing Films Politically*. New York: State University of New York Press.

Zembrzycki, S. (2009) 'Sharing Authority with Baba'. *Journal of Canadian Studies/Revue d'estudes canadiennes*. 43(1), winter, pp. 219–38.

Žižek, S. (2009) *First as Tragedy, Then as Farce*. London: Verso.

Filmography

12 Years a Slave (2013) Directed by Steve McQueen
A Dangerous Method (2011) Directed by David Cronenberg
About Adam (2001) Directed by Gerard Stembridge
Adam and Paul (2004) Directed by Lenny Abrahamson
Alexander (2005) Directed by Oliver Stone
An Everlasting Piece (2000) Directed by Barry Levinson
Atonement (2007) Directed by Joe Wright
Bamako (2006) Directed by Abderrahmane Sissako
Betrayed (1988) Directed by Costa-Gavras
Between the Canals (2011) Directed by Mark O'Connor
Blown Away (1994) Directed by Stephen Hopkins
Boogaloo and Graham (2015) Directed by Michael Lennox
Breakfast on Pluto (2005) Directed by Neil Jordan
Breaking Bad (2008–13) Created by Vince Gilligan
Butch Cassidy and the Sundance Kid (1969) Directed by George Roy Hill
Cal (1984) Directed by Pat O'Connor
Calvary (2014) Directed by John Michael McDonagh
Caoineadh Airt Uí Laoire (Lament for Art O'Leary) (1975) Directed by Bob Quinn
Challenge for Change (1960–80) Directed by Colin Low et al.
Cowboys and Angels (2003) Directed by David Gleeson
Damo & Ivor (2013–) Directed by Robert Quinn et al.
Danny Boy (1940) Directed by Oswald Mitchell
Darby O'Gill and the Little People (1959) Directed by Robert Stevenson
Dear Daughter (1996) Directed by Louis Lentin TV
December Bride (1990) Directed by Thaddeus O'Sullivan
Devil's Rock (1938) Directed by Germain Burger
Disco Pigs (2001) Directed by Kirsten Sheridan
Divorcing Jack (1998) Directed by David Caffery
Dollhouse (2012) Directed by Kirsten Sheridan
Doughboys in Ireland (1943) Directed by Lew Landers
East Is East (1999) Directed by Damien O'Donnell
Elvis: The Early Years (2005) Directed by James Steven Sadwith
Exposure (1978) Directed by Kieran Hickey
Fair City (1988–) Directed by Gary Agnew et al.
Finian's Rainbow (1968) Directed by Francis Ford Coppola
Frank (2014) Directed by Lenny Abrahamson
Fury (2012) Directed by David Weaver
Game of Thrones (2011–) Created by David Benioff and D. B. Weiss
Garage (2007) Directed by Lenny Abrahamson
Going My Way (1944) Directed by Leo McCarey
Goldfish Memory (2003) Directed by Liz Gill
Good Vibrations (2012) Directed by Lisa Barros D'Sa and Glenn Leyburn
Gormenghast (2000) Directed by Andy Wilson

H3 (2001) Directed by Les Blair
Hanna (2011) Directed by Joe Wright
Hidden Agenda (1990) Directed by Ken Loach
High Boot Benny (1993) Directed by Joe Comerford
His & Hers (2009) Directed by Ken Wardrop
Hunger (2008) Directed by Steve McQueen
Hush-a-Bye Baby (1992) Directed by Margo Harkin
I Went Down (1997) Directed by Paddy Breathnach
In Bruges (2008) Directed by Martin McDonagh
In the Name of the Father (1993) Directed by Jim Sheridan
Intermission (2003) Directed by John Crowley
Interview with the Vampire (1994) Directed by Neil Jordan
Into the West (1992) Directed by Mike Newell
Irish and Proud of It (1936) Directed by Donovan Pedelty
Irish Eyes Are Smiling (1944) Directed by Gregory Ratoff
Irish for Luck (1936) Directed by Arthur B. Woods
Isolation (2005) Directed by Billy O'Brien
Jimi: All Is by My Side (2013) Directed by John Ridley
Kathleen Mavourneen (1937) Directed by Norman Lee
Kisses (2010) Directed by Lance Daly
Leap Year (2010) Directed by Anand Tucker
Let's Be Famous (1939) Directed by Walter Forde
Life's a Breeze (2013) Directed by Lance Daly
Lillian Russell (1940) Directed by Irving Cummings
Lionheart (2003) Directed by Andrey Konchalovskiy
Little Nelly Kelly (1940) Directed by Norman Taurog
Love/Hate (2010–14) Directed by Stuart Carolan
Maeve (1982) Directed by Pat Murphy
Man of Steel (2013) Directed by Zack Snyder
Match Point (2005) Directed by Woody Allen
Michael Collins (1996) Directed by Neil Jordan
Mickybo and Me (2004) Directed by Terry Loane
Misfits (2009–13) Directed by Howard Overman
Missing (1982) Directed by Costa-Gavras
Mona Lisa (1986) Directed by Neil Jordan
My Left Foot (1989) Directed by Jim Sheridan
My Name Is Joe (1998) Directed by Ken Loach
My Wild Irish Rose (1947) Directed by David Butler
Nanook of the North (1922) Directed by Robert Flaherty
Noble (2014) Directed by Stephen Bradley
Non-Stop (2014) Directed by Collet-Serra
…nur der Wind (*Only the Wind*) (1961) Directed by Fritz Umgelter
Once (2006) Directed by John Carney
Ondine (2010) Directed by Neil Jordan
Ordinary Decent Criminal (2000) Directed by Thaddeus O'Sullivan
P.S. I Love You (2007) Directed by Richard LaGravenese
Park (1999) Directed by John Carney and Tom Hall
Parked (2013) Directed by Darragh Byrne
Patriot Games (1992) Directed by Phillip Noyce

Penny Dreadful (2014–) Created by John Logan
Perrier's Bounty (2010) Directed by Ian FitzGibbon
Philomena (2013) Directed by Stephen Frears
Pigs (1984) Directed by Cathal Black
Poitín (1978) Directed by Bob Quinn
Raining Stones (1993) Directed by Ken Loach
Reefer and the Model (1987) Directed by Joe Comerford
Rescue Me (2004–11) Directed by John Fortenberry et al.
Ride with the Devil (1999) Directed by Ang Lee
Ripper Street (2012–) Directed by Richard Warlow
Samson and Delilah (1996) Directed by Nicholas Roeg
Shame (2011) Directed by Steve McQueen
Shamrock Hill (1949) Directed by Arthur Dreifuss
Shirley (2011) Directed by Colin Teague
Shrooms (2007) Directed by Paddy Breathnach
Silent Grace (2001) Directed by Maeve Murphy
Smiling Irish Eyes (1929) Directed by William A. Seiter
Snap (2010) Directed by Carmel Winters
Some Mother's Son (1996) Directed by Terry George
Song for a Raggy Boy (2003) Directed by Aisling Walsh
Song o' My Heart (1930) Directed by Frank Borzage
Stalker (2012) Directed by Mark O'Connor
Stand by Me (1986) Directed by Rob Reiner
Standby (2014) Directed by Rob and Ronan Burke
Star Wars: Episode VII – The Force Awakens (2015) Directed by J. J. Abrams
State of Siege (1972) Directed by Costa-Gavras
States of Fear (1999) Produced by Mary Raftery
Sweet Rosie O'Grady (1943) Directed by Irving Cummings
Sweet Sixteen (2002) Directed by Ken Loach
The Babadook (2014) Directed by Jennifer Kent
The Boxer (1996) Directed by Jim Sheridan
The Butcher Boy (1997) Directed by Neil Jordan
The Butterfly Effect (2004) Directed by Eric Bress and J. Mackye Gruber
The Commitments (1991) Directed by Alan Parker
The Company of Wolves (1984) Directed by Neil Jordan
The Confession (1970) Directed by Costa-Gavras
The Courier (1988) Directed by Frank Deasy and Joe Lee
The Crying Game (1992) Directed by Neil Jordan
The Daisy Chain (2008) Directed by Aisling Walsh
The Devil's Own (1997) Directed by Alan J. Pakula
The Emperor's Wife (2003) Directed by Julien Vrebos
The Exorcist (1973) Directed by William Friedkin
The Field (1990) Directed by Jim Sheridan
The General (1997) Directed by John Boorman
The Good Thief (2002) Directed by Neil Jordan
The Governess (1998) Directed by Sandra Goldbacher
The Grand Budapest Hotel (2014) Directed by Wes Anderson
The Guard (201) Directed by John Michael McDonagh
The Hills of Donegal (1947) Directed by John Argyle

The Host (2013) Directed by Andrew Niccol
The Londonderry Air (1938) Directed by Alex Bryce
The Long Good Friday (1980) Directed by John Mackenzie
The Lovely Bones (2009) Directed by Peter Jackson
The Magdalene Sisters (2002) Directed by Peter Mullan
The Matchmaker (1997) Directed by Mark Joffe
The Mighty Celt (2005) Directed by Pearse Elliot
The Minstrel Boy (1937) Directed by Sydney Morgan
The Most Fertile Man in Ireland (1999) Directed by Dudi Appleton
The Music Box (1989) Directed by Costa-Gavras
The Passion of the Christ (2004) Directed by Mel Gibson
The Public Enemy (1931) Directed by William A. Wellman
The Quiet Man (1952) Directed by John Ford
The Shore (2011) Directed by Terry George
The Snapper (1993) Directed by Stephen Frears
The Sopranos (1999–2007) Created by David Chase
The Tudors (2007) Directed by Michael Hirst
The Van (1996) Directed by Stephen Frears
The Wind That Shakes the Barley (2006) Directed by Ken Loach
The Wire (2002–08) Created by David Simon
Titanic Town (1998) Directed by Roger Michell
Titus (1999) Directed by Julie Taymor
Top o' the Morning (1949) Directed by David Miller
Total Recall (2012) Directed by Len Wiseman
Trouble with Sex (2005) Directed by Fintan Connolly
Undressing My Mother (2004) Directed by Ken Wardrop
Vanity Fair (2004) Directed by Mira Nair
Vent d'Est (1970) Directed by Jean-Luc Godard
Veronica Guerin (2003) Directed by Joel Schumacher
Vicious Circle (1999) Directed by David Blair
Vikings (2013–) Created by Michael Hirst
Wake Wood (2010) Directed by David Keating
We Were There (2014) Directed by Laura Aguiar and Cahal McLaughlin
What Richard Did (2012) Directed by Lenny Abrahamson
When Brendan Met Trudy (2000) Directed by Kieron J. Walsh
When the Sky Falls (1999) Directed by John Mackenzie
Wings of the Morning (1937) Directed by Harold D. Schuster
With or Without You (2000) Directed by Michael Winterbottom
World War Z (2013) Directed by Marc Forster
X-Men: First Class (2011) Directed by Matthew Vaughan
Yankee Doodle Dandy (1942) Directed by Michael Curtiz
Z (1969) Directed by Costa-Gavras

Index